The Complete Instructional Baseball Manual

by
Fred Stanley
and
Lynn Stanley

ISBN 0-9619817-0-9

©1988 by
The Stanley Company, Inc.
8711 E. Pinnacle Peak Road
Scottsdale, Arizona 85255

THE COMPLETE INSTRUCTIONAL BASEBALL MANUAL *is a thorough and easily understood text which is sure to be a hit with players and coaches alike. I can't think of a single fundamental which isn't covered and carefully explained in this detailed instructional guide. It's complete, right down to graphic instructions for the execution of nearly every possible defensive situation. It's a learning tool as essential to amateur coaches and players as the right glove or the proper bat. It's unique, timeless and complete in every aspect of the game.* THE COMPLETE INSTRUCTIONAL BASEBALL MANUAL *covers all the basics of good, sound baseball.*

—*Billy Martin*
One of the most successful
Major League Managers of all
time; 4-time Manager of the Year.

For Florence and Blair Stanley

Without their encouragement and devotion, Fred's dream may have never become a reality.

And for Tracie and B. J.,

... who are the inspiration for everything we do.

"The difference between success and failure is doing a thing right and doing it exactly right."

—Edward Simmons

TABLE OF CONTENTS

THE BASEBALL MANAGER/COACH

A manager is more than just a "coach" to his players. At times, he will be forced to become a disciplinarian, a father, a teacher, a motivator and a friend.

As a coach, it is up to you to set an example for your kids to follow. In the lower classifications, this means that you must teach sportsmanship as well as mechanics. Keep your temper under control and conduct yourself in a sportsman-like manner both on and off the field. Avoid arguing with umpires—you only encourage your players to do the same thing. Be a coach that your kids can admire, a role model for them to follow.

The player's desire to win is directly related to his feeling for you as an individual. Earning the player's respect should be a primary concern of every dedicated manager. *Don't lie to your players;* they won't admire someone they cannot trust. Tell them the truth regarding their status on the team. If the player's ability is at issue, you only compound an already difficult situation by putting the player off. Further, your players deserve to know the truth; you would not tolerate a player who lies to you, so give your players the same consideration.

Make it clear from the beginning what you expect—and what you demand—from your players. Don't take anything for granted. Be consistent and fair with your players; once they know that you are *firm but fair,* they will respond in kind. *Always give your players the same respect that you want from them.*

In being fair, make sure that any rules you establish apply to *all* players. Though some of them may not agree with the rules you set down, they will admire your consistency in discipline.

Maintain your own health and physical appearance. You cannot credibly emphasize the importance of good physical conditioning if you yourself are overweight and out of shape.

Know all the rules of baseball.

COACHING 3RD BASE

There are no hard-and-fast rules for coaching 3rd base; a good 3rd base coach relies primarily on his instincts and must consider the following factors:

THE NUMBER OF OUTS
THE INNING
THE SPEED OF THE RUNNER
THE POSITION OF THE OUTFIELDERS
HOW HARD, AND WHERE THE BALL WAS HIT
THE STRENGTH OF THE OUTFIELDER'S ARM

With a runner in scoring position, most 3rd base coaches will try and pick up the baserunner's jump.* *Don't* look right away to see what jump he gets. Stay with the ball. *Concentrate on the ball, not the runner.*

As a rule—and again, this will vary depending on the game situation, if the runner reaches the bag before the outfielder has the ball, send him. If there is a runner at 2nd and no outs, hold the runner if you have any doubts at all. With one out, you have an option. With two outs, you send the runner.

With a runner at 2nd and the ball hit hard to the outfield, think "stop", but don't signal *"stop"*. Get way down the 3rd base line and *watch the ball.* What the outfielder does with the ball will aid you in making the right decision. Don't get too close to 3rd base. *Keep your distance from the bag and off the line.*

With a runner at 3rd with one or no outs, have the runner shorten his lead; the runner cannot be doubled off in this situation.

When giving the signals, get up in front of the box so all runners can see your signs. If there is any doubt at all, *stop, get the hitter out of the box and start over.* If a player misses a sign, it is the 3rd base coaches fault! It is your responsibility to make sure that he has the sign; if that means jumping onto the field and yelling at the player, then do it!

*Leading off is not permitted in Little League.

2

Any hand signal should also be given verbally. Make sure the runner at 2nd understands what you want him to watch for. Make him give the number of outs back to you.

A very difficult play for a 3rd base coach is with a runner at 1st and 3rd and one or no outs. This is purely a judgement decision. If the ball is hit hard, you send the runner home. If the ball is merely topped, keep the runners at 3rd. It's better to have runners at 2nd and 3rd than at 1st and 2nd." One way to help the runner in this situation is to tell him *not to break hard his first two steps.* This will help him judge the speed of the ball and the direction that it is going.

Here are some things a good 3rd base coach should know:

1. Get in front of the box to give the sign.

2. After the hitter reaches 1st base and becomes a baserunner, you should get his attention *and* the attention of the hitter. Give your signs, *up in front of the coach's box.* After you give the sign, you should:

Alert the baserunner to locate the outfielders. If a soft line drive is hit, he can judge it better and get a good jump.

Tell the runner at 1st to watch a line drive; you don't want him to get picked off and ruin the inning.

Tell the runner not to let the 2nd baseman tag him on a slow roller to second base. Have him stop or slide into the 2nd baseman so he can't complete the double play.

Tell the runner to concentrate on making a good turn at 2nd base and to pick you up if he needs help.

Try to stay about 6' from the 3rd base bag in either direction so if the runner looks for you, he can pick you up easily.

3. With runners at 1st and 2nd:

Give the signs in front of the box. *Make sure everyone can see your sign!*

Runners should be aware of where the outfielders are playing. This will enable them to get a good jump on a soft liner or a ball in the gap.

Again, alert the baserunners to a line drive.

Tell the runner at 1st to watch the runner in front of him so he won't over-run him. On a double steal, it is his responsibility to go when the runner at 2nd goes.

Alert the runner at 1st that he should not allow the 2nd baseman to tag him.

Tell the runner at 2nd to make a good turn at 3rd. (You do this vocally, and by pointing at the 3rd base bag.)

With no outs and a long fly ball, have both runners tag up. This is a judgement play on the part of both runners, but *especially* at 1st. You *cannot* have your runner at 1st thrown out at 2nd for a double play! *He must watch the flight of the ball!*

Position yourself *at least* 15' from the bag towards home. This will help you make the decision to send the runner home or stop him. The farther you are down the line, the longer you have to either send the runner or hold him up. *Remember:* Don't watch the runner! *Stay with the ball!* You should already know who's running, what inning it is, what the score is, the number of outs and the strength of the outfielder's arms. All of these factors will aid you in your decision to send or hold a runner.

If you decide to send the runner, use your arms in a big circular motion, and yell at him; *you have to score!* BE VOCAL! You *must* be certain that he understands you. Once you've sent the runner home, hurry back to 3rd to help the runner rounding 2nd.

4. With 1 out:

If the ball is hit very high and deep and you're 100% sure that the ball will be caught, have the runner tag up. Otherwise, the runner will go as far down the line as he can and still get back safely if the ball is caught. The term most widely used is: "Go half way!" I would rather see a baserunner go as far as he thinks he can. In some cases, the runner at 1st can go right to the bag at 2nd.

5. With a runner at 2nd:

Give the sign in front of the box so both the hitter and the runner can see it clearly.

Let the runner know how many outs there are.

Alert him to where the outfielders are playing.

Tell him to watch for the line drive.

With one or no out, the runner must be sure that any ground ball hit to his right goes through the infield before he comes over to 3rd.

If the ball is hit to his left, he should advance to 3rd.

The runner should watch the pitcher. You will let him know if any of the middle infielders are moving toward him.

Be consistent with your verbal warnings. For example: "You're all right", "He's right behind you", "Get back!", etc. By being consistent, the runner will know how close the SS or 2nd baseman is to him.

On a long fly ball to the outfield, tell the runner to tag.

Tell the runner to make a good turn at 3rd.

Be will up the line towards home. Remember: The farther up the line you are, the easier it is to stop or advance the runner.

STAY WITH THE BALL, don't watch the runner! The status of the ball in the outfield or during the relay will help you make your decision regarding the runner.

THE MANAGER/COACH RELATIONSHIP

Your coaches should be indispensable. Delegate responsibility to them, they are qualified to handle it.

Be specific with your coaches regarding their duties. Make it clear what you expect from them and then have the confidence in them to let them do their jobs.

Your coaches should know that you demand their loyalty. Under no circumstances should your coaches second-guess you. Coaches must *never* discuss confidential matters with players or anyone else.

Loyalty and unity are foremost in the manager-coach relationship.

TIPS FOR HANDLING PITCHERS

It is important for managers and coaches to know their pitchers individually. What specific problems do they have? What are their strengths and weaknesses? What does it take to motivate them as individuals?

Just as there are no two hitting styles alike, there are no two pitching styles alike. Every pitcher has a "natural" way of throwing. By placing your pitchers in the outfield and hitting balls to them, you can easily determine the pitcher's natural throwing motion by studying him as he returns the ball to you.

Good strategy and a winning pitcher go hand-in-hand. Make sure your pitchers *know the hitters*. Discuss mistakes and work hard with your pitchers. Stress the mental preparation necessary before going to the mound. (See "Mental Preparation for Pitchers")

Teach your pitchers to field their position. They must know where to go on defensive situations. They must know how to hit, bunt, and run the bases effectively. It's not enough just to get the ball over the plate; pitchers should be *complete players,* educated in *every aspect* of the game of baseball.

Be careful not to overuse young pitchers with good arms. If you use such a pitcher too often, you run the risk of ruining his arm. In higher classifications, if you use relievers two nights in a row, it's a good idea to rest them for a couple of days.

The pitcher runs the ball game and should be alert to all game situations. He must always know the inning, the number of outs, the runners on base and the hitter at the plate.

Teach your pitchers to think *"low and hard"* and to pitch *in and hard.*

A good pitcher must:

MASTER THE FUNDAMENTALS

SACRIFICE

RUN HARD

BE DETERMINED

BE ABLE TO RECOVER FROM A LOSS

If a pitcher begins to lose control, it is your job to calm him down without destroying his confidence. If you notice him "tensing up", help him to relax and regain control. (See "Controlled Breathing Techniques")

The mound and the rubber are the pitcher's advantages. *Use them to their fullest.* The mound and the rubber are aids to the pitcher—the mound for height and the rubber for pushing toward the plate.

TIMING YOUR PITCHERS

When your pitcher is in the stretch position, take a stop watch and start it on his first movement. You stop the watch when the ball hits the catcher's glove. This constitutes the pitcher's time to the plate.

For example, in the Major Leagues, a good time to the plate for a righthanded pitcher is 1.30 seconds or less with a runner on 1st. With runners on 1st and 2nd, a good time is 1.35 seconds or less. Since there is less threat of a stolen base in this situation, the pitcher can take a little more time. More often than not, lefthanded pitchers are slower to the plate. They will try and hold, or fool the baserunner. A good time for a lefthanded pitcher in the Major Leagues is 1.40 with a runner on 1st; he should be quicker with a runner on 2nd—1.35 or better.

With a runner on 3rd, make sure your pitchers do the following:

CHECK THE RUNNER
GET THE SIGN
RE-CHECK THE RUNNER
MAKE THE PITCH

This method will help stop the forced balk. If the pitcher does not want to pitch out of the stretch, make sure he keeps his weight on the *pivot* foot. For example, righthanded pitchers should keep their weight on the left foot. Lefthanded pitchers should keep their weight on their right foot.

An important rule for every manager to know is this: *If you get your best reliever up, put him in the ball game.* If you warm him up and don't use him, you'll only tire him out and maybe decrease his effectiveness if you should need him later in the game.

SELECTING YOUR DEFENSE

THE CATCHER:

The catcher should be alert and aggressive. He should be able to "take charge", and should be able to run the game correctly. He should be gutsy and smart and have a strong, accurate throwing arm.

THE 1ST BASEMAN:

Every 1st baseman must have good hands. He must be able to handle low throws and short hops. He should have good control of his body and be able to coordinate movement of his feet.

THE 2ND BASEMAN:

He should have a good pair of hands and a strong throwing arm. He must be quick, alert and sure on his feet in all directions.

THE SHORTSTOP:

Shortstop is the most important position in the infield. The SS usually makes more plays than anyone else; he is the key to the defense on most teams. He must be alert and quick on his feet. He must have sure hands and a strong throwing arm and he *must know the hitters.*

THE 3RD BASEMAN:

The man at the "hot corner" must be quick to react to all game situations. He must have good hands, and a strong arm. He has to be able to charge in either direction and must be able to manage an off-balance throw with something on it to 1st base.

THE OUTFIELDERS:

All outfielders must be alert for all plays and have a strong, accurate throwing arm. They must be able to think quickly and must be aware of the game situation at all times. A good outfielder hustles 100% of the time. He should *back up every throw and base hit,* always assuming that the infielder will misplay the ball. He must be able to *throw the ball to the right place at the right time.*

THE LEFT FIELDER:

He usually has the weakest arm of all the outfielders. If possible, he should be lefthanded. This allows him to go into the left field foul area and catch the ball without having to back-hand it.*

CENTER FIELDER:

The center fielder should be one of your best athletes. He will probably cover the most ground. he must have a good arm. *Remember: You must be strong up the middle—shortstop, 2nd baseman and center fielder.*

RIGHT FIELDER:

He must have a good, strong arm and be righthanded if possible.*
This allows him to go into the right field foul line and catch the ball
without having to back-hand it.

*I know that some coaches will say that by having a lefthanded left
fielder or a righthanded right fielder the fielders will have to turn all
the way around to throw to 2nd base. Though that may be true in
some cases, it really depends on how fast the fielders are and how
hard the ball was hit. If the ball was hit hard enough for them to
turn all the way around, you can almost bet that the runner would
have been safe at 2nd anyway. By not having to back-hand the ball,
the outfielder may save a step and be able to eliminate the possible
triple or inside-the-park homerun.

ESTABLISHING A BATTING ORDER

The batters placed in front of the lineup will bat more often so,
naturally, you want your strongest hitters to bat first.

> #1 BATTER: This batter is the "lead off man". He isn't
> necessarily a "long ball" or homerun hitter, but should be a
> player who gets on base consistently. He needs a good
> knowledge of the strike zone and should not strike out often.

> #2 BATTER: He will often be called upon to sacrifice. He
> should be a good bunter and should be able to hit to right field
> for a hit and run play. Hitting lefthanded would be a big asset;
> he would block the catcher's view of 1st base, giving the run-
> ner an extra step. A lefthanded hitter can pull the ball in the
> hole between 1st and 2nd and, if he has good speed, he can
> reduce the chance of a double play.

> #3 BATTER: He should be your most dependable hitter. As
> he may often come to the plate in a double play situation, he
> should have good speed, be a smart baserunner, and have fair
> power.

> #4 BATTER: The #4 batter is your "clean up man". He
> should be a power hitter, able to clear the bases.

> #5 BATTER: He will often come to the plate with runners in
> scoring position. He should be a consistent hitter with some
> power.

#6 BATTER: As the batting order progresses, the #6 batter may become your "lead off man" in later innings. He should be able to get on base. As he will often come to the plate with runners on, he should be able to hit for power.

#7 BATTER: He will frequently be in a position to advance runners into scoring position. He should be a good bunter, and should have occasional power.

#8 BATTER: As this hitter bats in front of the pitcher, who is usually your weakest hitter, he should have some speed so the pitcher can advance him with a bunt if he should get on base.

#9 BATTER: Your weakest hitter should bat in the #9 spot. However, this depends on whether or not you use the Designated Hitter Rule. If you do, insert the DH in the spot you feel he is best suited for. Otherwise, the pitcher generally hits in this spot.

In higher classifications, you may want to use right and lefthanded hitters, alternating in the order so that the opposing team is forced to use their entire bullpen.

TAKING INFIELD PRACTICE

The infield practice method described below is used by about 90% of all Major League teams:

OUTFIELD:

1. Hit 2 ground balls to left. The left fielder throws a one-hopper to the SS, who covers 2nd. The 2nd baseman backs up the SS.

2. Hit 1 ground ball and 1 fly ball to left. The left fielder throws home, a one or two-hopper to the catcher. Make sure he throws low enough so the 3rd baseman can cut it off. The SS covers 3rd, the 2nd baseman covers 2nd, etc.

3. Hit 2 grounders to the center fielder. He throws the ball low enough for the SS to cut it off. The SS should have his hands in the air and in a direct line to 3rd.

4. Hit 1 ground ball and 1 fly ball to center. The center fielder throws the ball at the cut off man's *chest.* Do not allow him to throw the ball all the way in the air. The ball should hit on the

home plate side of the pitcher's mound, *just past the dirt.*

5. Hit 2 ground balls to right field. The SS should be on the infield grass about 20-30' from 2nd, in *direct line* from right fielder and 3rd baseman, with hands in air. Right fielder hits SS in the *chest* with the ball. (Throw LOW)

6. Hit 1 ground ball, 1 fly ball. Right fielder throws a strike to 1st baseman (cut-off man—who is even with the pitcher).

INFIELD—GET ONE:

1. Hit 1 ground ball at each position. After they throw to 1st, they go to the bag and receive a throw from the catcher.

2. Hit a ground ball directly at the 3rd baseman. He throws to 1st. The 1st baseman throws home and the catcher throws to 3rd. Have the 3rd baseman make a *tag,* then throw to 2nd, where the 2nd baseman turns a double play.

3. Hit a ground ball to the SS. He throws to 1st. The 1st baseman throws to the catcher, who throws to 2nd. The SS makes a *tag* and then throws to 3rd. The 3rd baseman throws home.

4. Do the same drill for the 2nd baseman.

5. Hit a grounder to the 1st baseman. He fields the ball and throws to the SS who touches the bag as if he were turning a double play. The SS throws back to 1st, the 1st baseman covers the bag and then throws home.

6. Toss the ball away from the catcher as if it were a bunt. He races for the ball and throws to 1st. The 1st baseman throws to the SS at 2nd base. The SS throws *home,* not to 3rd. Repeat the same procedure, only hit the ball to right this time.

INFIELD—GET TWO:

1. Hit one ball up the middle and one to the right, following the same procedure as before. This time, the catcher throws to 2nd for a double play.

2. After two double play rounds, hit the last round forcing each player to go far to his right. Example: The 3rd baseman should field the ball almost on the line, and the 2nd baseman almost behind 2nd base.

3. No throw from the catcher. For the last ground ball, you can either have the infield charge slow rollers and throw to 1st, or you can have the infield in with the throw going home. If you can, hit the catcher a pop fly.

SELECTING THE PROPER EQUIPMENT

OUTFIELD:

The outfielder usually uses a glove with longer fingers. This gives him an extra inch or two on ground balls and a little added reach on balls hit over his head. The fingers are normally pulled fairly tight, which helps him hold on to the ball.

INFIELD:

3rd BASEMAN: He usually uses the biggest glove in the infield. His glove can be longer and deeper than either the SS or the 2nd baseman. The fingers are pulled tightly, helping him snag line drives. Tight fingers also aids the fielder in back-handing ground balls.

SHORTSTOP: His glove is usually just a little shorter and not as deep in the pocket as the 3rd baseman's. The SS must be sure handed; he doesn't have the luxury of being able to knock the ball down before throwing the runner out.

2ND BASEMAN: The 2nd baseman uses the smallest glove in the infield. It not only has the shortest fingers, it has the flattest pocket. The flat or shallow pocket enables the 2nd baseman to get the ball out of his glove quickly and throw to 1st base with one fluid motion.

WHEN TO TAKE A PITCH

When to have a player take a pitch is an individual decision which changes with every hitter. Basically, if you have your best base-stealer on 1st and he breaks for 2nd, the batter should swing through the ball. By swinging through, or bunting, the catcher must stay back; this will give your baserunner an added step.

If it's late in the game, you're behind by a run or two, and you have your 7th, 8th or 9th batter up, I would say that you might want to have them take a strike—the pitcher may just walk one or two of them! The best way for a player to get a walk is to get right on top of the plate and crouch down; this reduces the strike zone. Many pitchers will start aiming the ball because they are afraid they will hit the batter.

About 90% of the time, if the first batter in the inning hits the first pitch for an out, the second batter should take a pitch. You don't want two pitches and two outs; you want to give your own pitcher a chance to catch his breath. This is especially true if the opposing pitcher is in a groove and yours is struggling.

When a hitter has three balls and no strikes, it's usually a good idea to have him take a pitch, (unless you have a homerun hitter at the plate). In this situation, most batters get over anxious and instead of waiting for a good pitch to hit, they swing at something they can't hit hard anyway.

PRACTICE SESSIONS

The manager sets the tone during practice sessions. If you are full of enthusiasm and encouragement for your players, it will rub off on them. If I had to offer one piece of advice for a successful practice session, it would be this: *Be organized!* Don't let your players stand around. Let the pitchers hit ground balls to the infielders and fly balls to your outfielders. All infielders should take at least 50 ground balls per session; they should field ground balls to their right and left and with the infield in. The SS and 2nd baseman should work on double plays, the 1st and 3rd basemen should work on charging for a bunts and slow rollers. The catcher should work on blocking balls in the dirt, throwing to 2nd, catching pop-flys. Outfielders work on charging ground ball *hard* and fielding them cleanly.

If you are organized, a one-hour practice session three times a week is plenty for Little Leaguers; anything longer than that and your team will show it on the field. In higher classifications, coaches must determine what is reasonable. However, on all levels, I encourage coaches to be consistent; if you tell players and parents that a session will end at six o'clock, *end it* at six o'clock.

Encourage your players to hustle 100% if the time. Never allow players to walk on or off the playing field. Players who don't hustle during practice should be disciplined. And, in the case of Little Leaguers, stress the importance of keeping with the flow of the game and knowing play situations. Encourage young ballplayers to use their time on the bench to study the game and the hitters.

Coaches should have a routine set-up for conducting batting practice. Here is an example:

1. Bunt—one down 1st, one down 3rd.

2. Hit and run.

3. Now the batter must hit the ball to the right side of the diamond to advance the runner from 2nd to 3rd.

4. Fly ball—hit a sacrifice fly.

5. Squeeze bunt.

6. Batter takes 5 swings.

This routine makes the batter think about game situations and makes the baserunner concentrate on what he should do on the basepath.

Don't allow your team to just go through the motions during practice sessions. *How you practice is how you'll play.*

"Perfect practice makes perfect play."

CONDITIONING

Too often, players put strenuous demands on their bodies without the proper preparation. In the minor leagues especially, the travel schedule (usually on busses), did not allow us enough time to really loosen up before a game. *Poor pre-game warm up is the cause of most baseball injuries.* Good physical conditioning will minimize strains, muscle pulls and shin-splints. A twenty to thirty minute warm up period is recommended prior to each game and work out. The stretching exercises described on the following pages are designed to condition the muscles most frequently used in baseball.

It is imperative that these stretching exercises are done carefully, "eased into". *Do not bounce or overstretch. Do not start or stop quickly. Go at your own pace.* Eight-counts are recommended for these exercises as follows:

1-2 begin the stretch,
3-4 *ease* into the stretch,
5-6-7 Reach your maximum position and hold to 8.

STRETCHING EXERCISES

STRETCHING THE CALF MUSCLES:

Done religiously, this exercise nearly eliminates the possibility of shin splints (tightness of the calf muscle which causes pain to the front of the leg.)

1. Stand with feet hip-width apart, toes slightly "pigeon toed", weight on the outsides of the feet.

2. Lean against a wall with feet apart, (about 18" from the base of the wall), and with a slight stretch on the calf muscle.

3. Lean forward, bending elbows just enough to slightly increase the stretch in the calf muscle. *Keep heels on the ground and do not strain.* Hold for 10 seconds. Repeat 10 times.

The calf muscle stretch takes only about 3 minutes and should be done three times a day during the playing season. As the muscle becomes more flexible, move the feet farther out from the wall. Used frequently, this exercise will eliminate any tightness in the calf.

From a squat position, stretch the right leg straight out to the side. Lean toward your right foot. Hold 8 seconds and repeat with the opposite leg.

Repeat as above, toes pointing up this time.

SHOULDER EXERCISES:

The Roll: Arms outstretched, start with small circular motions forward, gradually increasing the size of the circles. Reverse. Do 8 reps.

Circles: With arms at your sides, make large circular motions, first forward and then reverse. Do 8 reps.

Hugs: Arms outstretched, "Hug" yourself, slapping your shoulder blades. Return your arms to the outstretched position. Do 8 reps.

Shoulder Stretch:

1. With arm overhead, hold your elbow with your opposite hand, pulling gently. Hold 8 seconds.

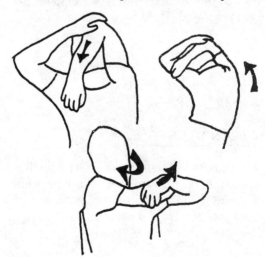

2. Gently pull to the opposite side while bending at the waist. Hold 8 seconds.

3. Gently pull your elbow across your chest, toward the

opposite shoulder. Hold 8 seconds.

TRUNK ROTATIONS:

With hands stretched in front of your chest, rotate upper body right and left. Do not move your hips. 8 reps.

BACK FLEXION:

Lying prone, lift legs and chest off the ground at the same time. Return to a flat position. Do 12 reps.

BENT KNEE SIT UPS:

Lay on the ground, knees slightly bent and hands behind your head. Pull up, *keeping your elbows back.* Use your stomach muscles *not your arms,* to pull yourself up. Go back half way, and don't let your head touch the ground. 25 reps.

LEG LIFTS:

Lay down, legs straight. Lift legs up to a 90 degree angle and lower them to about 3" off the ground with your elbows flat on the ground. Hold 8 seconds.

GROIN STRETCH

Sit with the soles of your feet together. Gently bend forward from the hips while pushing your knees to the ground with your elbows. Hold 8 seconds.

HIP STRETCH:

With left leg out in front, grab the right ankle with your left hand and pull up to the left shoulder. Right hand and forearm should be supporting the right knee. Hold 8 seconds; repeat to opposite side.

ACHILLES TENDON STRETCH:

In a semi-kneeling position, the toes of your right foot should be even with your left knee. The heel of the bent leg can come off the ground about 1". Lower your heel to the ground, *keeping it flat* while you push forward on your thigh with your chest and shoulder. Repeat, changing legs.

FOREARM STRETCH:

Arms straight out in front of you, grasp right hand with left and flex your wrist. Hold for 8 seconds and repeat with the opposite arm.

HAMSTRING STRETCH:

Put left foot slightly in front of the right and bend forward at the waist while keeping your right leg straight. Hold 8 seconds. Repeat, with your left foot forward this time.

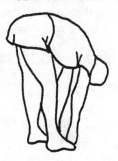

BACK STRETCHES:

Sit with your left leg straight. Place right foot outside of left knee, and left elbow outside of right knee. Rotate lower trunk to the right while looking back as far as possible. Hold 8 seconds and repeat to the opposite side.

Laying on your back with right leg straight, place left foot outside of right knee. Drop right knee to the ground *while keeping both shoulders on the ground.* Repeat to opposite side.

Lay down, arms outstretched. Raise right leg, bringing right foot to your left hand. Alternate. 12 reps.

Lying down, pull left knee to chest. Hold 8 seconds and repeat with right knee.

Raise legs slowly over your head until your toes touch the ground. Point your toes and stretch. Hold 10 seconds. Relax, maintaining your position. Now, rest the balls of your feet on the ground and flex. Hold 10 seconds. Come down slowly, one vertebrae at a time.

QUADRICEP STRETCH:

Left leg extended out in front, sit with right leg bent, heel touching right hip. Bend backward, forcing your knee flat on the ground. Hold for 8 seconds, switch and repeat.

ABDOMINAL STRETCH:

Lying prone, grasp your ankles and pull up, lifting your chest and legs off the ground. Hold 8 seconds, repeat.

HIP FLEXOR STRETCH:

In a semi-squat position, force your hip downward. Hold 8 seconds. Switch legs and repeat.

SKY REACHES:

Stand with feet together. Keeping your legs straight, bend at the waist and touch the ground. Coming up on your tip-toes, reach to the sky, stretching from the waist. 15 reps.

Utility players are more susceptible to pulled and strained muscles because they do not play every day. They should run daily with the pitchers in addition to their stretching exercises. Remind these players of their importance; if there is an injury to one of your starters, the utility men must be ready at a moment's notice.

WEIGHT TRAINING

I feel this book would not be complete without a section on weight training. When I first signed in 1966, weight training was used primarily for football players, or for players who had been injured and were placed on rehab programs. If one did any weight lifting at all, it was done for the purpose of building endurance—lots of reps and very little weight.

When I first signed, I was 5'10" and weighed 150 lbs. By the time I had been playing six years of pro ball, I was 5'11" and weighed 160 lbs. If I had it to do over again, I assure you that I would lift weights to make myself stronger. I really feel that my career was cut short because I did not keep up with the times. Athletes today are bigger, stronger, faster and smarter. They are better in every aspect of the game than they were ten or twelve years ago. Had I lifted weights and become stronger, I'm sure that I could have driven the ball with more consistency. I honestly do not know a good hitter in the Major Leagues who does not have very strong hands, wrists, forearms, shoulders and legs. To create bat speed, you must have a strong upper body.

I have cited some weight programs which may aid you in becoming a better athlete. Though I strongly encourage the use of these programs, I cannot over stress the importance of professional supervision before undertaking *any* weight program. Professional strength coaches are trained to know the individual needs of each body type. The programs listed are merely suggestions for strengthening the specific portions of the body used in baseball.

The programs cited do not specify the amount of weight for each set. This was done purposely because everyone is not the same strength—what might be fine for you may be too heavy for your friend. Let a professional test you; he can tell what is a safe weight for you. *Remember: You can seriously injure yourself lifting weights if you don't know what you're doing. Don't be foolish and jeopardize your career.*

BEGINNER WEIGHT PROGRAM
AGES 10-14

Do this program twice a week, preferably on Monday and Thursday. Always do major lifts first.

1. Leg press—5 sets of 6 reps.

2. Knee extensions—5 sets of 8 reps.

3. Knee flexions—4 sets of 5 reps.

4 Incline dumbell press—5 sets of 5 reps.

5. Toe raises—3 sets of 5 reps.

6. Bent arm pullovers—5 sets of 5 reps.

7. Curls (dumbbells, bar or cables)—5 sets of 5 reps.

8. Tricep extensions (dumbbells, bar or universal latt pull bar)—5 sets of 5 reps.

9. Dips—3 sets of 15 reps.

10. Crunchies—3 sets of 15 reps.

11. Situps, twisting—one set of 50 twists each way.

INTERMEDIATE WEIGHT PROGRAM
AGES 15-16

Do this program three times a week, Monday, Wednesday and Friday. Always do major lifts first.

1. Leg press—6 sets of 8 reps.

2. Leg extensions—5 sets of 10 reps.

3. Leg flexions—4 sets of 5 reps.

4. Bench press—5 sets of 5 reps.

5. Military press (dumbbells)—5 sets of 5 reps.

6. Dumbbell or barbell curls—5 sets of 6 reps.

7. Tricep extensions (dumbbells, bar or universal latt pull bar)—5 sets of 5 reps.

8. Toe raises—3 sets of 20 reps.

9. Wrist rolls, forward and reverse—2 sets each way.

10. Finger squeezes and hand squeezes—Using a tennis or racquet ball, squeeze until the hands and forearms feel fatique.

11. Bent leg sit ups, twisting—1 set of 50 twists each way.

12. Side bends—50 each way.

13. Twisters—50 each way.

ADVANCED WEIGHT PROGRAM
AGES 17 AND UP

Do this program 3 times a week, Monday, Wednesday and Friday.

1. Squats—5 sets of 5 reps.

2. Incline press—5 sets of 6 reps.

3. Bent arm pullovers—5 sets of 6 reps.

4. Toe raises—3 sets of 25 reps.

5. Upright rows—5 sets of 5 reps.

6. Stiff leg deadlifts—3 sets of 25, 15, and 10 reps each.

7. Curls—(dumbbells or barbells)—5 sets of 8 reps.

8. Tricep extensions (dumbbells, bar or universal latt pull bar)—5 sets of 6 reps.

9. Wrist rolls, forward and reverse—3 sets each way.

10. Bent leg situps—3 sets of 25 reps.

11. Side bends (dumbbells)—75 each way.

AT-HOME WORKOUT

If you don't have easy access to a gym, here is a good workout you can do at home:

1. Toe raises: Bend your body in a 45 degree angle while resting your hands on a bench. Have someone sit on your lower back-buttock area. Raise your heels up with your toes in, out, and straight ahead.

2. Finger and hand squeezes: Squeeze a racquet or tennis ball until you can't squeeze anymore. Do 3 reps.

3. Finger pushups: Do as many pushups on your fingertips as you can.

4. Twisters: With a broomstick behind your neck, keep your body stationary from the waist down while twisting the upper body from right to left. Do 3 sets of 50.

5. Side bends: With a broomstick behind your neck, bend from side to side without moving your lower body. Do 3 sets of 25 to each side, alternating after each 25.

6 Hanging obliques: Hang from a chin-up bar so that your legs lift while your body twists.

7. Crunchies: Lay on the floor and bend your legs over a bench at your knees. Do 3 sets of 20 situps from this position.

8. Wrist rolls: Drill a hole in a rounded stick. (A broken bat works well if you saw off the handle. It should be about 12-15" long.) Run a cord through it and tie a knot in one end so the string will not come out. Tie the other end of the string to a barbell plate. Roll the cord up and then down, keeping your arms and elbows straight out in front of you. Roll *slowly.* Do 3 reps.

NUTRITION

The athlete's body is to him what a finely tuned race car is to a professional driver—it is impossible to operate at peak performance without a properly fueled body. A professional driver would never consider putting anything but the highest quality fuel into his car. The serious athlete must fuel his body with only the most nutritious foods. Twenty years ago, it was believed that a pre-game diet of high-protein, low carbohydrate foods was essential for optimum physical performance. However, all of the information available today proves contrary to that belief. Almost without exception, medical experts and athletes alike agree that carbohydrates should be the primary ingredient in the athlete's diet. Carbohydrates, or "glycogen", are stored in the muscle tissue. From there, they "feed" the muscle cells during physical activity. *It is a medical fact that, when glycogen runs out, physical exhaustion results.* Unfortunately, the body stores carbohydrates in only limited quantities. An inactive person carries about a six-hour supply of glycogen. Active persons must "refuel" by eating carbohydrates several times throughout the day. Nutritious carbohydrate foods include: White, and preferably whole-grain breads and cereals, potatoes and rice, pasta and fresh fruit.

WATER

Every bit as important as what we eat is what we drink. *Large amounts of water are essential for a healthy body.* Water regulates the body temperature and aids in eliminating toxic wastes; it supplies muscles and vital organs with oxygen and nutrients and helps to maintain proper volume and pressure of the blood. *Inadequate water supply is one of the primary causes of poor perfor-*

mance in any physical activity. Every athlete should make a conscious effort to think about his consumption of liquids. At least *1 quart* of water should be consumed for every 1,000 calories of food eaten.

As a general rule, three or more glasses of water should be consumed about three hours before a game. Another two glasses should be drunk from 15-30 minutes before. During a game, two glasses of water *per hour* are recommended.

Beverages such as iced tea and colas should be avoided before a game. These drinks are high in caffeine, which increases nervous tension and forces the heart to work harder. In addition, caffeine depletes water and salt from the body through increased urination. I am personally opposed to the use of colas or other carbonated sodas as beverage before a game. Besides being exceptionally high in sugar content, these drinks tend to cause gas and a bloated feeling.

Serious athletes should avoid the use of alcohol. Alcohol dehydrates cells and impairs muscle efficiency, coordination and mental judgment. *Alcohol should never be consumed before competition.*

REMEMBER: Water loss occurs constantly, and at an increased rate during physical activity. Water supply should be continually replenished throughout prolonged physical activity. *Don't wait until you're thirsty to drink!*

SALT

As we sweat, we lose salt from our bodies. Many athletes believe that salt tablets are necessary to replenish this loss. The truth is: *Salt tablets are dangerous.* They increase the level of salt at too fast a rate and distort the natural salt-to-water ratio in the body. The easiest, and safest way to replenish salt loss is by drinking water.

If athletes use caution in selecting the foods they eat, there should be no need for vitamin supplements. Basically, this means eating a well-balanced variety of food from the four basic food groups. However, most athletes require higher amounts of certain micronutrients than non athletes. Specifically, these are Potassium, Magnesium, and Thiamin.

Below are some suggested foods which are high in these nutrients:

POTASSIUM-RICH FOODS: Orange juice, bananas, dried fruits and unsalted nuts.

MAGNESIUM-RICH FOODS: Almond and cashew nuts, other unsalted nuts, meat, fish, whole-grain breads and cereals, milk and leafy green vegetables.

THIAMIN-RICH FOODS: Whole-grain breads and cereals, milk, eggs, organ meats and pork.

WEIGHT CONTROL

It should be obvious to everyone that an overweight athlete becomes fatigued more easily than one who is not. Excess weight effects speed and agility—elements essential to the game of baseball. Since the average athlete burns up at least 3,000 calories per day, a 2,000 calorie diet is recommended when weight loss is desired. At this rate, a loss of two pounds per week will result. It is inadvisable for an active athlete to lose weight at a faster rate than this.

For athletes who wish to gain weight, foods such as peanut-butter, whole-grain breads and cereals, raisins, bananas, and yoghurt are suggested as healthy snack foods.

PRE GAME MEALS

In considering what to eat before a game, keep in mind that the foods you eat must do the following things: 1) Provide energy and keep you from getting hungry during a game, 2) prevent gastrointestinal upset during the game and 3) be combined with the proper amounts of water to prevent dehydration. Avoid raw fruits which may cause gas and bulk foods such as raw vegetables (except lettuce), nuts, popcorn, seeds and other whole-grain foods before competition. It is best to eat 3-4 hours before the game; this allows time for your food to digest and aids in preventing gastrointestinal upset. As fats and proteins take a long time to digest, your pre-game meal should be low in fatty foods and high in carbohydrates. *Avoid sugar* before a game; it often causes acute hunger pangs hours after it is digested. Here is an example of a recommended pre-game meal:

2 oz. poultry or fish (not fried)
8 oz. skim milk
pasta or baked potato
banana
plain lettuce salad or cooked carrots
2 cups clear bouillon
oatmeal cookie or yoghurt

In summary, your pre-game meal should consist of 60% carbohydrate, 20% protein, 20% fat, and be less than 500 calories. At least one serving per day should be eaten from each of the following food groups:

Milk
Protein
Bread/Cereal
Vitamin C
Dark-Green Vegetables
Other Vegetables
Fresh Fruit

1. Limit your intake of fats.

2. Increase your intake of whole-grain products.

3. Eat only fresh fruits and vegetables whenever possible. If you can't get fresh, frozen are preferable to canned products, which are high in salt and preservatives.

4. Eat generous quantities of dark green vegetables—these are excessively high in folic acid, a compound necessary for production of red blood cells. Some of these vegetables are: Broccoli, Spinach, Romain and Red-Leaf Lettuce, and Fresh Green Beans.

5. Limit your use of fats such as butter, margarine, mayonaise, whole milk and ice cream.

The chart on the following page can be removed from this book and placed in your kitchen. It provides an excellent guide to the calories in foods and should be used when planning your menus.

"FREE FOODS"

Alfalfa Sprouts
Asparagus
Broccoli
Cabbage
Cucumbers
Green Beans
Green Peppers
Lettuce
Radishes
Tomatoes
Plain Popcorn
Vegetable Juice
Lemon

Artichokes
Bean Sprouts
Brussel Sprouts
Celery
Eggplant
Green Onions
Greens
Mushrooms
Spinach
Zucchini
Mineral Water
Spices
Vinegar

"LIGHT FOODS"

Non-Fat Milk
Low-Fat Milk
Buttermilk
Plain Yoghurt
Wheat Bread
Fish
Skinless Chicken
Turkey
Beans
Peas
Apples
Bananas
Peaches
Grapes
Strawberries

Pineapple
Oranges
Carrots
Potatoes
Cottage Cheese
Puffed Wheat
Shredded Wheat
Corn Tortillas
Whole Grain Crackers
Oat Meal
Whole Grain Pasta
Barley
Brown Rice
Grapefruit

(See over for *"Heavy Foods"*)

"HEAVY FOODS"

Whole Milk
Flavored Yoghurt
Cheese
Beef, Pork, Lamb
Ham, Bacon
Luncheon Meats
Sausage
Waffles
Pancakes
Hot Dogs
Hamburgers
T.V. Dinners
Tacos
Fried Rice
Snack Crackers

Avacados
Peanut Butter
Raisins
Canned Fruit
Biscuits
Sweet Muffins
Salami
Fish Sticks
French Toast
Coffee Cake
Doughnuts
Sweetened Cereals
Burritos
Pizza
Creamed Soups

This list of *"Heavy Foods"* includes all foods high in sugar content.

RUNNING

Running is probably the single most important phase of good conditioning. It not only maintains physical fitness overall, it improves the functions of the circulatory and respiratory systems, thus increasing the stamina and endurance so necessary for athletes. Running strengthens the leg muscles and increases the flexibility of the body. I cannot overemphasize the importance of a daily running program for ballplayers.

If the desire is there, anyone can learn to run faster. In addition to the power running program outlined herein, I have listed some tips to aid players in running *correctly* in order to increase their speed.

1. Relax. In order to perform at optimum level, the body must be flexible and yielding.

2. *Run only on the balls of your feet.*

3. The toes should be pointed *straight ahead.* This can mean a difference of as much as ½ step on each stride.

4. Run in a *straight line.*

5. *Don't overstride.* Proper stride is about equal to the height of your body. It takes time to develop the proper stride. *Running must be practiced.*

6. The body should lean slightly forward, head up. Ankles, hips, shoulders and head should be in a straight line. *Don't lean backwards.*

7. *Use your arms.* Opposite arm and leg should move in unison.

Do short sprints to develop speed, distance running to develop endurance and running in circles to strengthen ankles, hips and back.

THE POWER RUNNING PROGRAM

This program was designed by Olympic Gold Medalist Herman Frazier. The basic principle behind the PRP is for the runner to generate a strong arm drive and a high knee lift. This program combines this technique with controlled breathing and muscle relaxation. It is an excellent running program and will aid in improving the athlete's agility and power. Players who run the 40 yard dash in 4.6 should improve to 4.3 or 4.4 with any effort at all. You will see the results of the PRP if you time your players twice a month in the 40 yard dash.

Do these drills twice weekly throughout the season.

ARM DRIVE:

Do two 1-minute exercises.

1. Standing in place, keep elbows locked at a 90 degree angle.

2. Relax the hands. Thumb and index finger should be lightly touching.

3. Relax the facial muscles.

4. Arm motion:
Back Stroke—hands even with back pockets. Up Stroke—hands in front of nose.

SITTING DRILL:

1. Sit with legs fully extended in front of you. Have a partner hold your ankles.

2. Using *full range of motion and a good arm drive, go hard!* If done properly, you should bounce off your buttocks. Keep your facial muscles relaxed.

3. Do this exercise twice for 15 seconds, then twice for 20 seconds. Alternate with your partner.

RUNNING IN PLACE:

Do two 1-minute exercises, *emphasizing the arm drive and knee lift.*

CONTROLLED BREATHING—"POPS":

1. Inhale to start and hold your breath.

2. Exhale at 25 yards.

3. Inhale at 30 yards and hold until the finish (40 yards).

4. On 30 yards, inhale and quicken the arm drive; this is the "pop".

CARIOCA—SIDE RUN, CROSS OVER:

Start easy and smooth, with knees high. Do 4 times at 25 yards and walk back.

RUNNING BACKWARDS:

Go at 80-90%—do 3 times at 25 yards.

BOUNDING UP AND OUT:
Bound up into the air with exaggerated strides. Do 3 times at 25 yards.

Players should be timed twice a month in the 40 yard dash. In addition to the PRP, players should be able to run the mile in under 6 minutes. The long distance helps maintain the endurance necessary for a long and strenuous season.

CONTROLLED BREATHING TECHNIQUES

Disorganized thinking, anxiety or nervousness, can lead to shortness of breath, or "hyperventilation". This increases muscular tension throughout the body. As muscles tense, they become hard and contract. For example, the tighter a hitter grasps his bat, the stiffer his arms become.

The ability to control one's breathing is instrumental in easing the tension which accumulates in stress situations. Our breathing affects our coordination, timing, balance, and range of motion, as well as our tension level, accuracy and power. Every athlete who wishes to be successful must learn to control his pattern of breathing. This takes time and must be practiced. Below are a couple of exercises which may prove helpful in lowering the tension level. Ideally, these exercises should be done in a quiet atmosphere before too much tension accumulates. Again, these exercises *must be practiced.* Once they have been mastered, players will find it easy to relax and control their breathing at will.

FILLING THE LUNGS WITH CLEAN AIR:

Lay on your back in a relaxed position. Stretch out your arms and legs, close your eyes and take a deep breath, allowing your chest to fill with clean air. Imagine your chest is a balloon, "inflating" with air until it feels as if it will burst. Now, hold your breath until you begin to feel slight discomfort. Let the air out S L O W L Y and relax. Repeat.

MUSCLE TENSING:

In the same position, tense every muscle in your body, starting with your toes and feet. Tighten your shin and clave muscles, your knees, thighs and buttocks...tighten every muscle up to and including your jaw. Now, squeeze your eyes shut tightly and hold for several seconds. Release the tension slowly, feeling all of the tightness leave your body until every muscle is completely free and relaxed. Let out all of your breath and lay quietly, feeling the tingling sensation throughout your muscles. *Concentrate on slow, even breathing.* If done properly, once is enough for this exercise. However, if you still feel tension in your muscles, repeat it.

QUICKNESS AND AGILITY DRILLS

AGILITY SIDE STEP: In a period of 10 seconds, see how many side steps you can take: Alternate moving to the right and then to the left in a "shuffle", without crossing your feet. Weight should be on the balls of the feet, arms should hang losely at the sides. Repeat 5 times to each side.

QUICK STARTS: The runner *explodes* from a stand-still position. Run forward 25 yards, accelerating as you go. Return the same way. Repeat, only this time *explode* again for another 25 yards. Return the same way. 5 reps.

"GO STARTS": The runner should be in a starting position, ready to "go" when the ball is hit. Feet should be hip width apart, weight on the balls of the feet, arms lose, body relaxed and glove open.

    1. Cross the right foot over the left and go 4 steps, reaching for the ball with the glove hand, arm extended. *Drop the right foot behind the left* and come up throwing to 1st base with a

sidearm or ¾ action. Repeat 10 times.

2. Cross the left foot over the right, "sliding" into a plant position, left foot slightly in front of the right, about shoulder width apart. With your glove open, bring your hands toward your chest in a "fielding" motion. Shift your weight to your back foot, drop your arm back and throw the ball hard to 1st or 2nd base, being as quick and accurate as possible. Repeat 10 times.

3. "Bust" on a ground ball. Stay low, field the ball and take a quick shuffle step to regain your balance. Now, throw to 1st from close to the ground. Repeat this drill, throwing from about half way up the second time. *Your main objective here is to regain your balance quickly and get rid of the ball as fast as you can.* Repeat 10 times.

4. Imagine a pop fly is hit behind you. Drop the left foot back and move to your left. Run to a spot slightly further than where you think the ball is. Using your glove to shield the sun, try to catch the ball. Repeat to the right, dropping the right foot back. Repeat 10 times.

5. Skip rope, alternate speeds and turn left and right.

6. Throw balls against a wall and field them. Your glove should be open and in front of you, forming a triangle to each shoulder. Bring the glove back to your chest, regaining your balance with quick shuffle steps. Do this exercise for 15 minutes per day.

3

HITTING—BASIC FUNDAMENTALS

There are no two hitters who hit alike, just as there are no two golf or tennis swings exactly alike. Hitting is an individual thing, and hitting style must be developed by each individual batter. There are, however, some basic fundamentals and methods of training which can be taught and will aid young ballplayers in becoming better hitters.

BE COMFORTABLE

USE YOUR HANDS

DON'T USE TOO MUCH BODY

KEEP YOUR EYES ON THE BALL

PICK UP THE BALL FROM THE RELEASE POINT

As each player is physically and mentally different, it is difficult to say what hitting style is best for you. You must ask yourself:

1. Am I big and strong? Could I become a home run hitter?

2. Should I be a contact hitter—make the pitcher work? Should I try to hit the ball to all fields?

3. Should I attempt to become a good bunter to compensate for my lack of power? (Draw the infield in and try to hit ground balls past them?)

Once you have answered these questions, you can then select a bat and stance which will help you to become the type of hitter you want to be.

SELECTING THE PROPER BAT:

1. Select a bat that you can control throughout the entire swing.

2. Your strength and the amount of speed you can generate with the bat (through the strike zone) will determine the length and weight of the bat you should use.

3. Generally speaking, if you have small hands, you will be better off with a small-handled bat.

4. It is better to have a bat which is too light than one which is too heavy. A heavy bat can cause mechanical breakdown, which is hard to eliminate once it becomes habit—this is especially true for younger ballplayers. Also, a heavy bat must be started earlier in the swing; this does not give the hitter the luxury of being able to wait on the pitch. Heavy bats do not drive the ball any further than light ones—bat *speed* determines distance.

GRIP ON THE BAT:

The bat should be placed at the base of the fingers. If it is placed

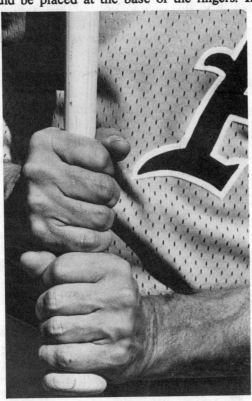

too far back in the palm of the hand, it will restrict good hand actions. A hitter who has the bat placed deep in the palm of his hand will have a tendency to "sweep" the bat, which retards bat speed.

Here is one method used to help a hitter get the bat into the base of of his fingers: Stand, placing the bat against your left leg. Bend down and put your left hand on the bat, placing it at the base of your fingers. Take your right hand and place it on top of your left. Now, pick up the bat. It should be placed exactly at the base of your fingers, with the middle knuckles somewhat aligned.

Physical strength cannot be overstressed. It takes strong hands, wrists, shoulders and legs to drive the ball consistently. Weaker hitters may want to flatten the bat; this will aid in shortening the stroke, thus making the bat quicker.

THE HANDS:

It's better to have your hands held at the top of the strike zone; this allows the hitter to move in only one direction with his hands—on a downward plain with the ball. If you consider yourself a homerun hitter, you will want to move your hands a little lower so you can get the ball in the air. *To achieve the maximum bat speed, the hitter's hands must go back before they come forward.*

THE STRIDE:

The stride should be made directly toward the pitcher just *after* he releases the ball. Your stride should be a soft "glide" on to your big toe. By touching your big toe to the ground, the soft glide will help you stay back on your *back* leg and will aid in eliminating the lunge. (Lunging makes the hitter susceptible to off-speed pitches.) Your hands, body weight and head should all remain *back* during the stride.

THE HIPS:

The hips should not start to open until the batter has seen the pitch. Your swing will automatically bring your hips through.

FRONT SHOULDER:

The front shoulder is the guide to the ball; it should always point to the ball until the swing actually occurs. *Keeping the front shoulder in is essential on breaking pitches.* If your front shoulder flies out too soon, you will pull off of the breaking pitch.

Anything off speed, or a ball breaking away from you will give you problems. You will also lose bat speed. When your shoulder flies out too soon, so does your head.

HEAD AND EYES:

The hitter should train his eyes to pick up the ball as soon as possible. The hitter should have a feeling of his head remaining *over* the ball during the swing. His head should be turned toward the pitcher so the hitter can see the pitcher with *both* eyes. (Head comes back and down with the pitch—the eyes alone cannot track the flight of the ball.)

WEIGHT DISTRIBUTION:

The hitter must keep his body weight on the balls of his feet. About 70% of the weight should be on his back foot. *Power and stability come from hitting off of the back foot.* The weight will transfer from the back to the front foot through the hips (not the shoulders), as the bat comes forward through the ball.

STANCE:

Your position in the batter's box will aid you in achieving optimum plate coverage and is important in determining the type of hitter you will become. The further back in the box you stand, the more time you will have to "read" the pitch. When facing a power pitcher, you might want to stand deeper in the box; this will allow you a longer look at the ball. If you are facing a breaking-ball or sinker-ball pitcher, you might want to move up in the box; you will have a better chance to hit the pitch before it breaks. But remember: If you move up, you are closer to the pitcher and that gives you less time to react to a fast ball.

If you consider yourself a pull hitter, you will move closer to the plate. Hitters with slow bat speed might be more successful further back in the box. You alone must determine where to stand, considering that your position can be adjusted according to the type of pitcher throwing.

Your feet should be a little more than shoulder-width apart. (Driving the ball becomes difficult if the feet are *too* far apart.) In addition, too wide a stance will restrict the hips and slow you down when you are leaving the box. If your feet are too close together, it could result in lunging at the ball; an ideal stance is one which is somewhere in between and is comfortable for you. Your weight should be on the front halves of your feet.

Many young hitters tend to have the back shoulder lower than the front. This forces the hitter to upper-cut the ball and makes the swing long and slow. *The front shoulder should be level with, or slightly lower than the back shoulder.* This will help you swing down on the ball. A *slight* bend at the waist and knees will help you relax as you wait for the pitch. Your hands should be about chest-high and about 6" away from the point of your back shoulder (directly out from the back arm pit). *The further away from the body your hands are, the more you will sweep the bat— sweeping will result in loss of speed and control of the bat.* If you have your hands too close to your body, you will drag the bat (or "inside-out" your swing), and will probably hit a lot of balls to the opposite field. In addition, dragging the bat reduces bat speed.

These are the three basic bat stances:

1. OPEN STANCE: Your front foot should be further from home-plate than your back foot. This stance is helpful to players who are having trouble picking up the breaking ball. If you use this stance, it is important that you *step toward the pitcher,* otherwise you may have some trouble with the outside pitch.

2. THE STRAIGHTAWAY STANCE: Both feet are about the same distance away from the plate. You *must step toward the pitcher.*

3. THE CLOSED STANCE: The front foot is closer to the plate than the back foot. This is probably used more often than any other stance. The closed stance helps you to keep your head and shoulders in and enables you to stay with the breaking ball a little longer. When you use this stance, you might want to get off the plate a little more and stride toward the pitcher, (being careful not to lock your hips.) This stance aids in driving the ball to the opposite field.

HITTING SUMMARY

As you have learned, there is a lot more to hitting than just swinging the bat. Each batter must take advantage of his individual abilities, must find a style of hitting which is suited for him, and must develop a positive mental attitude which will enable him to handle the pressure of hitting in various game situations. Once he has done this, he will be a successful hitter, and will have the confidence it takes to do his job right. *Remember:* "Success breeds confidence and confidence breeds success."

Courage and Concentration are two elements which, more than anything else, can determine the success or failure of a hitter. Without courage, there is no way a hitter can achieve concentration. With the ball traveling at speeds in excess of 80 MPH, it takes courage for a hitter to concentrate on hitting the ball while disregarding the possibility that he may strike out, or he may not get the sacrifice his team so badly needs or—worst of all—that he may be hit by the pitch. *It takes courage to concentrate.* Further, as a player advances in classification, he is exposed to more and more outside interference. There are more fans, bigger ballparks, and a lot more distractions. Without *total* concentration, the hitter will not be able to perform at his optimum level. *A successful hitter can block out everything except the ball as it leaves the pitcher's hand.*

HITTING TIPS

1. *Select a bat you can handle.*

2. *Keep your head still—back and down with the pitch (following the ball into the catcher's mitt).*

3. *Direct your entire attention to the ball.*

4. *Hit strikes.*

5. *Keep front shoulder and chin tucked in.*

6. *Swing fungo for bat speed.*

7. *Don't commit too soon.*

8. *Hit the ball where it's pitched. Learn to hit to all fields.*

9. *Turn your head so both eyes are on the pitcher—don't look around your nose.*

10 *Lay the bat on your shoulder while waiting for the pitcher to get ready.*

11. *If you hold the bat up for any length of time—this will cause tension in your hands and arms and detracts from a free and fluid swing. In addition, you may "loop" the bat.*

12. *Hit your strength. Every hitter has a strength, just as every pitcher has a weakness. Wait for your pitch.*

13. *Stay on the balls of your feet.*

14. *Keep off your heels.*

15. *Be ready to hit. Get the bat off your shoulder before the pitcher delivers the ball.*

16. *When stepping in to hit, make sure you have maximum plate coverage.*

17. *Get a comfortable stance in the batter's box.*

18. *Look to see where the fat part of the bat is in covering home plate. Don't have your handle over the plate.*

19. *Start the bat to create hand action and bat speed; if you like the pitch, hit it—if you don't, hold up your swing.*

20. *Stride into the pitch.*

21. *Swing down on all pitches to create a level swing.*

22. *Keep your stride short.*

23. *Don't overswing.*

24. *Look for the fast ball. Adjust to the off-speed pitch.*

25. *Make the pitcher come to you—don't go out after him.*

26. *Keep your hands back and hit with your hands, not your head.*

27. *Keep your hands relaxed; as contact is made, your hands will tighten.*

28. *When hitting to the opposite field, hit the ball on the ground. You do this by hitting down on the ball.*

29. *Faster ballplayers should take advantage of their speed— concentrate on hitting the ball on the ground and making contact.*

30. *Choke up if you are having trouble controlling the bat. With two strikes, choking up will give you better bat control.*

31. Don't fall away at home plate—keep your buttocks in.

32. Be aggressive with the bat.

33. Follow through with your swing after contact is made— don't quit your swing.

34. Hit with your top hand and roll your wrist after contact.

35. Don't let the barrel of the bat get ahead of your hands too soon.

HITTING PROBLEMS AND SOLUTIONS

PROBLEM: Overstriding

SOLUTIONS:

1. You can shorten your stride by widening your stance.

2. Put exaggerated weight on your back leg.

3. Bend your knees and crouch, shifting your weight to the ball of your back foot.

PROBLEM: Sweeping the bat

SOLUTIONS:
1. The bat should be in the fingers, not far back in the hand.

2. Relax your arms and roll your wrist after contact.

3. Try to achieve a sensation of hitting only with your wrist.

4. "Feel" the bat in your hands. Start hands forward *toward the pitcher* (not out and forward).

PROBLEM: Hand Hitches (The hitter constantly gets hit on the fist or has trouble getting the bat back up and through in time to hit the pitch.)

SOLUTIONS:
1. Move your hands back instead of dropping them down.

2. Put your bat on your shoulder. Bring your hands up until they are parallel with the shoulders and hit from there. *Do not pick the bat up. Just hit from the shoulder.*

PROBLEM: Head Pulling

SOLUTIONS:

1. Don't look where the ball will go.

2. Watch the ball hit the bat and hit the ball up the middle.

3. Don't try to pull the ball.

4. Swing down. In taking a longer look to swing down, your head will automatically have to look at the ball longer.

5. Don't try to hit the ball in the air.

6. Keep your chin and shoulders tucked in and keep your head steady.

PROBLEM: Uppercutting

SOLUTIONS:

1. Carry your bat flat, not vertical.

2. Lay your bat on your shoulder and don't pick it up until the pitcher is ready to throw.

3. *Concentrate* on swinging down on the ball. Though you can't actually swing down, the down arc will force you to swing level.

4. Practice hitting the ball on the ground.

5. Keep your shoulders and hips level and *don't drop your back shoulder to hit.*

HITTING EXERCISES

WRISTS AND FOREARMS:

Do wrist curls, using a 5 lb. dumbbell. Hold the dumbbell with your palm up. Using only the wrist, raise and lower the weight until you feel a burning sensation. Now, turn the palm down and repeat.

Do the same exercise again, rotating the wrist from side to side this time. Do this every other day. When you can do 100 reps without burning, increase the weight to 10 lbs.

BAT SPEED:

Using a batting tee, swing a bat at least 100 times. If no batting tee is available, a small homemade "ball" (use rags, as paper will tear) hanging from a string works just as well. A broom handle can be used in place of a bat. This is an excellent drill for improving hand-eye coordination. Swinging a weighted bat is also an excellent way to increase your bat speed.

SLUMPS

No book on baseball would be complete without a section on "slumps". Slumps are to a ballplayer what bunyons are to a mailman—they're painful, they're irritating, and every ballplayer is going to have one sooner or later. What most ballplayers don't realize is that slumps usually begin when the hitter is doing *well* at the plate. A hitter builds a "hot streak" over a period of time. Likewise, he "cools off" over a period of time. All some players need is *one* bad game or *one* poor at-bat and they begin to doubt their hitting ability. They begin to ask themselves what they're doing wrong. They often begin to overswing in an effort to compensate; they may change their stance or adjust their hands. Maybe they'll "tighten up" or wear the same sox they wore the last time they had a base hit. In short, a player who feels he's in a slump will do virtually *anything* to get on base. Though he may only be 0-for-10, he feels like he's 0-for-100; thus is born "The Slump".

Though slumps are sometimes the result of doing something mechanically wrong, they are more often caused by the hitter's mental attitude. he begins to doubt his ability, and instead of approaching the plate with a positive mental attitude and a feeling of confidence, he goes up to bat subconsciously thinking that he *won't* hit the ball. Slumps which result from a poor mental attitude are much harder to deal with. The most common complaint from hitters who feel they are in a slump is that they "just aren't seeing the ball". If the hitter isn't seeing the ball, he's not *concentrating on the ball.* He's probably thinking about his mechanics, his statistics, or perhaps a defensive misque he committed in the previous inning. Oftentimes, the player approaches the plate thinking "I've *got* to get a hit", when he should be thinking *"watch the ball".*

Visualization is a useful tool in dealing with the problem of not seeing the ball. Visualization is a mental technique whereby one *imagines* himself in a certain hitting (or, in the case of pitchers, a pitching) situation. Visualization enables the player to mentally "replay" a situation where he struck out, or chased a bad pitch. For example: When a player swings at, and misses a pitch he usually hits, he can remove himself from the batter's box and quickly replay the pitch again, this time *visualizing the results he wants.*

Great hitters like Carl Yazstremski and Willie Stargell admit to taking "mental BP" before every game; they consider it an important part of their pre-game preparation. Like good hitting, visualization is a *skill,* and must be *practiced.* The more realistic the visualization, the more beneficial it will be. Developing strong mental images may require standing in the proper stance, with a bat in your hand. If this is what it takes for you to get a *clear mental image,* then by all means, do it. In a good visualization, the hitter will *see* the ball as it leaves the pitcher's hand. (You should go so far as to know exactly who the pitcher is...) He will *feel* the ball hit the bat and he will *hear* how it sounds. Imagine what happens *after* a hit—see yourself rounding the bases; hear the cheers of the crowd...

This type of *positive visualization* can and should be practiced daily. The more the player carries positive mental images in his mind, the more successful he will be. It takes practice. It requires concentration. *It works!*

TO SUMMARIZE

1. *Concentrate on "seeing" the ball.*

2. *Don't rush yourself.*

3. *Be mentally ready before you step into the batter's box.*

4. *Check your mechanics.*

5. *Be emotionally in control before you enter the batter's box. Learn to control your breathing and relax. Concentrate on positive visualizations.*

6. *Consider only two things while you are in the box: 1) Are you comfortable? and 2) Do you see the ball?*

7. *Don't experiment in batting practice in an effort to find a solution for your problem at the plate. This can be harmful;*

you may develop bad habits which will carry over to actual game situations. Use BP to stay lose and keep your fundamentals sharp. If you concentrate and relax, your "problem" will take care of itself.

5

BUNTING

Bunting is one of the most important plays in baseball. Unfortunately, it is also one of the most poorly executed. Failure to advance a baserunner is probably the primary reason for losing ballgames. A hitter who can lay down a bunt when necessary increases his value a thousandfold. *Practice bunting on a regular basis.*

There are three basic types of bunts: 1) The sacrifice bunt, 2) the drag, or push bunt, and 3) the suicide squeeze.

THE SACRIFICE BUNT:

When attempting a sacrifice bunt, the batter must "sacrifice" his turn at bat to advance the runner. He does this by placing the ball on the *ground, in a good location.* He is *not trying to get a base hit.* If the batter tries to be too perfect, waits too long to show the bunt, or runs before the ball is on the ground, he often indicates that he is trying to reach base safely.

SQUARING TO BUNT:

There are two methods used when squaring to bunt.

1. Squaring Around: The back foot is moved forward so the toes are parallel to each other.

2. Heel-Toe Pivot: The hitter pivots on the heel of his front foot and the toe of his back foot. This type of pivot can be used in all three bunting situations. It allows the hitter to wait a little longer and does not tip off the opposing team that you are bunting.

With either method, it is important that the hips and shoulders be square to the pitcher. *Do not try to be too perfect in the placement of the bunted ball.* You should be thinking. "If I bunt the ball, it will be close to the line (usually toward 1st), not too hard. If

I miss it, it will go foul and I'll have another chance..." *Never hit the ball back to the pitcher.*

BUNTING WITH RUNNERS AT 1ST AND 2ND:

The best place to sacrifice in this situation is down the 3rd base line. You want the 3rd baseman to field the ball. The bunt should be close to the line so the pitcher can't get it, and *hard* enough so the 3rd baseman must charge. (Usually, the 1st baseman will be charging hard; this is the reason for bunting toward 3rd.)

Once the bunt sign has been given, the hitter should move up in the batter's box, toward the pitcher. This gives him a better chance of keeping the ball in fair territory after it is bunted. The further back the hitter stands in the box, the greater chance he has of hitting the ball foul. Obviously, too drastic a change in the batter's position will alert the opposition that a bunt play is on. Once the hitter has squared his hips and shoulders toward the pitcher, he should:

1. Bend slightly at the knees.

2. Shift most of his weight to his front foot. This will keep him from lunging at the ball.

3. *Slide* his top hand up the barrel of the bat, approximately to the trademark area. The bat should be held with the fingers in a pinch-type grasp—this will keep the fingers from being hit by the ball.

4. Extending both arms forward, keep the top hand at the top of your strike zone. The bottom hand should be about 1" lower. The bat should stay at this level. If you flatten it, any ball in the air will probably be caught. With the bat held at the proper angle, most balls hit in the air will go foul.

5. The hitter should bend at the knees, *keeping his eyes on the same plain as the ball.*

6. *Don't "jab" at the ball.* Try to "catch" it on the barrel of the bat. Be careful not to grip the bat too tightly.

7. *Bunt the ball on the bottom half of the bat.* Keeping the bat at the proper angle will help you do this.

8. The bottom hand guides the angle of the bat. For example, a righthanded hitter, sacrificing to 1st, would point the nob of his bat toward 3rd. If he was buntining to 3rd, he would point

the barrel toward 1st.

9. Arms should be slightly bent and out away from the body.

10. *Bunt strikes when possible.* Don't try to bunt the high fastball; it is the most difficult pitch to bunt. *Think down*—the ball must be belt-high or lower.

BUNTING FOR A BASE HIT:

Learn to recognize the defense: Which men are playing "in" and which are playing "back"? When the 3rd baseman is even with the bag, he is playing in. The righthanded hitter can assume that anytime the 3rd baseman is even with the bag or deeper, he is back far enough for a successful bunt. For lefthanded hitters, if you learn to bunt properly, you can beat the ball even if the 3rd baseman is on the edge of the grass. *You must practice!*

Practice until you can bunt 5 out of 10 times successfully. A good bunter becomes a real threat because he forces the 1st, 2nd and 3rd basemen to play in—this increases his chance of putting a ball through the infield hole for a base hit.

In addition, a consistently good bunter intimidates pitchers.

THE DRAG BUNT:

A good drag bunter can increase his batting average by as much as 20 points. *Proper execution* and *Deception* are the keys to a successful drag bunt. It is not necessary for a drag bunter to be exceptionally fast; *when and where* the ball is bunted will determine how successful he is.

Most drag bunt attempts occur on the first pitch. If no attempt is made, many coaches have the corner men drop back. If you are a confident bunter, the best time to bunt is after the first pitch.

RIGHTHANDED DRAG BUNT:

1. Cheat *up* in the batter's box slightly.

2. Move the right foot back slightly away from the plate as the ball is released.

3. *Slide* the right hand up to the trademark area, gripping the bat the same way you would for a sacrifice bunt. The left hand pulls the knob down to a position approximately six inches in

front of the right hip. *Keep the barrel of the bat slightly up.*

4. *Always look for the perfect bunt.* You want to bunt the ball just fair, or in foul territory but *never back to the pitcher.*

5. *Bunt strikes*—look for a ball *down.*

6. Don't run too soon.

7. Hands and arms should be out in front. Don't let the ball penetrate the strike zone too far. This will cause you to bunt the ball back to the pitcher.

LEFTHANDED DRAG BUNT:

1. Cheat *up* in the box.

2. Open your front foot slightly.

3. Shift your weight to the right foot as the ball leaves the pitcher's hand. The left foot comes forward (cross-over step) *directly toward the pitcher.*

4. *Never attempt to run before the ball has made contact with the bat.*

5. The right hand is the guide; you can drag down the 1st or 3rd base line.

6. The left hand should slide up the barrel in the same manner as for a sacrifice bunt.

7. *Bunt Strikes.*

8. Don't attempt to bunt the high fast ball.

9. The ball should be just fair, or foul giving you another chance.

10. The barrel of the bat should be slightly up.

11. Bunt the ball on the bottom half of the bat and keep it out of the air.

12. Don't grip the bat too tightly; you want to deaden the ball.

THE PUSH BUNT:

The push bunt is used when the 1st baseman is playing back. The ideal time to attempt a push bunt is when you have a lefthanded pitcher who falls off the side of the mound, is a poor fielder, or is slow covering 1st base.

The ball is "pushed" on the ground somewhere between the pitcher and the 1st baseman. The ball must be hit softly enough so that the 2nd baseman can't handle it; the ideal spot is on the grass, just before the dirt.

The perfect time for a push bunt is when you have a weak hitter at the plate, the tying or winning run at 2nd and *no outs*. You *must advance the runner to 3rd* in this situation. You may have already failed a sacrifice bunt attempt and you cannot afford a ground ball to the left side of the infield, stranding the runner at 2nd.

The push bunt is used primarily by righthanded hitters because placement of the ball is so important. A lefthanded hitter can pull the ball on the ground using the same techniques as on the drag bunt, but the ball must be hit a little harder. *The ball must get past the pitcher in order for the bunt to be successful.*

RIGHTHANDED HITTER PUSH BUNT:

1. The ball should be up, preferably a fast ball, and out over the plate.

2. After the ball is released, the hitter should move his right hand up toward the trademark, just as he would in the other bunts. He will hold the bat a little firmer with his right hand. He is not trying to deaden the ball, just push it past the pitcher.

3. The barrel of the bat should be slightly up.

4. *Don't* extend your arms.

5. Bring the nob of the bat close to the left side of your chest. Your right hand should be at the top of your strike zone.

6. Weight should shift to the left side, exactly as in the heel-toe pivot in the sacrifice bunt. This is done as the ball is

released; the right foot starts forward on contact.

7. Hands and arms should push the bat to the ball, pushing the ball *on the ground between the pitcher and 1st baseman.*

8. Hit strikes up in the strike zone.

9. *Practice! Practice! Practice!*

SUICIDE SQUEEZE:

The suicide squeeze is an offensive weapon usually used late in the game. The batter attempts to bunt in the tying or winning run, which is on 3rd base.

Billy Martin used the squeeze very effectively. By having a reputation for using the squeeze, many managers would try to outsmart Billy by pitching out. If they guessed wrong, the pitcher would be in the hole and eventually, would have to throw a strike.

The squeeze is usually used when the batter is ahead of the pitcher on the count.

TIPS FOR EXECUTING THE SQUEEZE:

1. As soon as the "squeeze" sign is given, the batter *must bunt the next pitch,* no matter where the ball is thrown.

2. The ball must be hit *on the ground.*

3. It doesn't have to be a perfect bunt.

4. Don't reveal your strategy by squaring too soon. In higher classifications of baseball, the pitcher is instructed to knock the hitter down if he squares too soon.

5. Don't run before the ball has made contact with the bat. *You are not bunting for a base hit.*

6. Use whatever bunting method you have the most success with.

7. *The runner at 3rd must not break too soon.** If he does, the pitcher can throw a pitch which the batter has no chance to bunt. For example, in the Major Leagues, if the runner breaks too soon and the pitcher has time to adjust, he'll throw the ball at the batter's neck. I can tell you from experience: "That's a tough ball to bunt!"

*Leading off is not permitted in Little League.

The runner at 3rd should take his normal lead. When the pitcher starts his wind up, the baserunner should start *walking* toward home. When the pitcher's front foot hits the ground, the runner should *break hard* for home. If the batter misses the ball, try and keep from being tagged out until the other baserunners advance to scoring position.

6

BASERUNNING

Numerous games are won or lost on the basepaths. The importance of good baserunning cannot be overstressed. Baserunning should be diligently practiced.

Below is a list of things a good baserunner should know:

The signs.

The game situation: outs, score, inning, etc.

Always force the fielders to hurry—this can cause a situation for an error.

Always challenge an outfielder on balls hit to his glove hand.

Be daring and aggressive, but never foolish.

All baserunning is controlled by the game situation.

Know the pitcher's weaknesses.

Run through the 1st bag.

Know your own speed and the condition of the infield.

Know the strength of the outfielder's arm. You can be more aggressive with a righthanded right fielder, as his momentum will carry him away from any possible throw to the infield. Likewise with the lefthanded left fielder.

Good judgment is the key to good baserunning.

TAKING LEADS* AND STEALING BASES:

Always take your lead anticipating the catcher's best throw. After the pitch makes contact with the catcher's glove, the baserunner's first few steps should be hard back to the bag.

THE PRIMARY LEAD:

The runner takes a primary lead when the pitcher is in the set position. His *main concern is his ability to get back to 1st base.* The length of his lead is determined by:

1. His ability to get back to 1st.

2. The game situation.

3. The condition of the infield.

If the steal sign is on, the runner will use one of the following primary leads:

1. The Two-Way Lead: The runner wants to be as far away from 1st as possible, but must be close enough to get back safely if the pitcher attempts to pick him off. The runner's right foot should be a little behind the left and slightly open toward 2nd. This will give him quicker acceleration toward 2nd base. Baserunners should remain relaxed while in their stealing stance; if the pitcher holds the ball too long, it's up to the hitter to protect the runner by calling for a time-out. If the runner remains too long in his stealing stance he will stiffen up, making it difficult for him to get his best jump toward 2nd base. The runner begins his acceleration toward 2nd as soon as he knows that the pitcher is going to deliver to the plate.

2. The One-Way Lead: The primary objective of the one-way lead is for the baserunner to force the pitcher to try and pick him off. With a one-way lead, you are *not attempting to steal,* you are just helping the 1st base coach and the rest of the team pick up a "key" in the pitcher's move which will aid other runners in getting a better jump. Take a larger lead than normal. On the pitcher's first movement, you must break back to the 1st base bag. If he throws home, you must recover and get into your secondary lead.

THE SECONDARY LEAD:

The runner moves from the primary into the secondary lead by taking 3 short shuffle steps toward 2nd base *after the pitcher releases the ball.* The runner should watch the ball leave the pitcher's hand.

*Leading off is not permitted in Little League.

Again, his lead should be as large as possible while still enabling him to return safely to 1st in the event of a pick-off attempt. This distance varies with each runner and must be perfected during practice sessions. The 1st base coach will watch the pitcher and advise the runner if the pitcher makes a move toward 1st. The length of the secondary lead is determined by:

1. The length of the primary lead the runner has taken.

2. The runner's speed.

3. The catcher's arm.

4. The condition of the infield.

5. The position of the 1st baseman.

6. The pitcher—right or lefthanded?

7. Does the score of the game allow the runner to take a chance?

THE WALKING LEAD:

After the pitcher begins to go into his set position, the runner takes short, controlled side steps toward 2nd base. This allows him to be in motion when he takes off for 2nd. All good pitchers will force the baserunner to stop; use caution so you can get back to the bag. This lead is usually used by baserunners who don't normally steal.

THE FALSE BREAK:

The runner takes several quick steps toward 2nd, stops and checks to see where the ball is. This breaks up the infield as it causes the SS or 2nd baseman to shift their positions,* depending upon who is covering the bag on a steal. The baserunner puts pressure on the defense and often on the pitcher as he hurrys his throw to homeplate.

*If done properly, the 1st baseman will yell "There he goes!"

THE DELAYED STEAL:

If the baserunner feels that the SS, 2nd baseman and catcher are not alert, he will take his normal lead, making his usual move toward 2nd base. He will use three side steps; at the end of the third step, he will break hard for 2nd base. The baserunner who utilizes this technique is normally not a basestealing threat.

THE DOUBLE STEAL—1ST AND 3RD SITUATION:

The runner going into 2nd lays back as the infielder attempts to tag him, putting himself in a run-down situation so the runner at 3rd can score. If the infielder throws to home, the runner continues on to 2nd base.

Knowing that the double steal is in order, the runner on 3rd walks directly on the 3rd base foul line. If he stays in front of the bag, the catcher will not be able to determine the length of his lead. When the runner has an extended, safe lead, he will stop and watch the pitcher's delivery to home plate. At this point, the runner on 1st breaks for 2nd. When the runner at 3rd sees the catcher's throw go over the pitcher's head to 2nd base, he breaks for home.

Watch for a fake throw to 2nd. Be sure you see the throw go over the pitcher's head!

The runner at 1st must watch the runner at 2nd. The runner at 2nd must use a sign to alert the runner at 1st that he is going. *The runner at 1st must break with the runner at 2nd, thus eliminating a 1st and 3rd situation and a possible double play.* If the runner at 1st does not break and the runner at 2nd gets thrown out at 3rd, you won't have a runner in scoring position.

THE STRAIGHT STEAL:

With the steal sign on, the runner wants to get as big a lead as possible (see "Leads"). Once the lead has been established, the baserunner will look for some flaw in the pitcher's delivery that will help him to get the maximum jump. Remember: Bases are stolen as a result of the pitcher's weakness. Below are some "keys" to look for that will aid you in finding these weaknesses.

RIGHTHANDED PITCHERS:

Look for:

1. Opening of the front shoulder.

2. Cracking of the front knee.

3. Does he lean away from home plate?

4. Is there movement of his back right heel?

5. Is his movement exaggerated, either quick or slow?

LEFTHANDED PITCHERS:

Look for:

1. Is he leaning back?

2. Does he lean toward, or away from home plate?

3. Where does he look on his first movement?

4. Is his leg straight?

5. Is his movement exaggerated, either quick or slow?

*When stealing 3rd, remember that most lefties break or bend the back leg before throwing home.

Once a potential basestealer has picked up a "key" and gotten the maximum lead, I suggest that the right foot be a little behind the left and opened slightly toward 2nd base. Weight should be on the balls of your feet, hands should *not* be on your knees.

Your first move is to pivot on the ball of your right foot, dropping the right arm and shoulder toward 2nd base as you cross over with your left foot. Stay low, driving off toward 2nd.

There are two different theories regarding position of the head when stealing a base. One is that the baserunner should take a quick peek into the home plate area to pick up the action; the other is that the runner should lower his head and concentrate on only one thing—beating the ball to the bag. The method you choose is purely a matter of personal preference.

THE THREE MOST COMMON BASERUNNING SITUATIONS:

1. Runner on 1st—no outs: Do not get thrown out at 3rd on a base hit. You are in a much better situation with runners at 1st and 2nd and no outs than you are with one out and a runner on 1st.

2. Runner on 1st—1 out: This is a good time to take a chance and try to go from 1st to 3rd if you think you can make it. With runners at both corners, you can get a run on a squeeze, a sacrifice fly or a missed double play.

3. Runner on 1st—2 outs: Don't get thrown out at 3rd on a base

hit. Any runner who can get from 1st to 3rd on a sharp base hit can score from 2nd on the same. The squeeze, sacrifice fly, or a missed double play do not exist with two outs; the passed ball or error are often few and far between.

HIT AND RUN SITUATION:

Remember, in a hit and run situation, *you are not attempting to steal a base* so you might want to shorten your lead. *make sure the pitcher is throwing to home plate before you break.*

Break on the pitch, with a quick peek into the home plate area to pick up the action. If you can't find the ball, look for help from the 3rd base coach.

Don't be fooled by the infielder's reactions.

If a line drive is hit, just keep going; you couldn't get back anyway.

ROUNDING THE BASES:

Ideally, the baserunner wants to take as short a turn as possible without losing speed on his approach to the bag. As speed and running style vary with each individual runner, each should be encouraged and coached in developing a base-rounding technique which is most suitable for him. Once the runner or the 1st base coach has established that a turn at 1st base is necessary, the runner's concentration should be devoted to that *one* thing: *Rounding the bases.*

GENERAL INSTRUCTIONS FOR ROUNDING BASES:

Concentrate

Touch Every Base

Push Off The Front Inside Corner Of The Bag*

Dip Left Shoulder And Don't Break Your Stride

*It is preferable to use the left foot; this helps the runer get a good lean and enables him to push toward 2nd with his right foot.

ROUNDING 1st:

1. Begin to veer out (approximately 3') as soon as you leave the

batter's box. The key is for each individual to find the perfect spot on the basepath to begin his turn.

2. Approach the bag just outside of the foul line (about 7') and further out if necessary.

3. Glance quickly at the bag as you touch it. Your body should lean toward the infield side of 1st base on contact with the bag; this makes it easier to push off toward 2nd. As soon as you have touched the bag...

4. Locate the ball.

5. Round the bag aggressively, generating speed toward 2nd base. Make the outfielder hurry—this may cause him to misplay the ball. *Make the outfielder stop you.* (Sometimes, this maneuver can cause an inexperienced outfielder to throw to 1st—if this happens, you should be on your way to 2nd base.)

ROUNDING 2ND:

When the runner is about 30' from the bag he should pick up the 3rd base coach on balls hit behind him.

ROUNDING 3RD:

The runner is guided by hand signs from the 3rd base coach. Run *hard* and *do only what the 3rd base coach tells you;* the outfielder or relay man may misplay the ball.

SIGNS FROM THE 3RD BASE COACH:

SIGN	MEANS
Waves one or both arms in the air in a circular motion:	Score on the play.
Holds both arms high in the air:	Do not attempt to score.
On one knee, bringing both arms down toward the ground:	A play will be made at 3rd base and the runner must *slide* into the bag.

As soon as the runner rounds the bag, he should locate the ball. If the ball has been mishandled, valuable time would be lost if the runner relied on the coach for this information.

RUNNING TO 1ST BASE:

A good follow through enables the hitter to get out of the batter's box quickly. The lefthanded hitter has an obvious advantage when leaving the box; his follow through automatically carries him toward 1st base. By contrast, the righthanded hitter carries his body away from 1st base on his follow through; he is forced to push off with his left foot and shift his weight in the direction of the base. He may lose as many as two or three steps in doing this.

THINGS TO REMEMBER WHEN RUNNING TO 1ST:

Don't look to where the ball was hit.

Concentrate only on building up your speed toward 1st base.

Stay low the first few steps, then get into proper running form: Propel yourself with your arms and upper body. (See: "Power Running")

Pick up the ball through the corner of your eye.

Run slightly to the outside of the 1st base foul line—this is done so that if the pitcher or catcher throws to 1st and hits you, you won't be called out for obstruction.

Run in a straight line, keeping eyes focused on the front of the bag.

Run full speed through the bag.

Never jump or leap into the bag.

Lean across the bag on contact—don't lunge or break your stride.

Run full speed to 1st on every play.

After touching the bag, look to foul territory for a wild throw.

Watch the 1st baseman's feet.* If he moves down the 1st base line, you may have to slide into 1st to avoid a tag. This is the only time you slide into 1st base!!

*This is a very difficult maneuver and is a purely instinctive play. Very seldom do you have time to think about sliding. If this play is not properly executed, injury may occur.

AFTER YOU REACH 1ST BASE:

1. Review the game situation: Number of outs, score, inning, hitter at the plate, etc.

2. Keep your left foot on the bag.

3. Check the position of the outfielders and know the strength of their arms.

4. Check the 3rd base coach for a sign.

5. Take your lead toward 2nd. From 2½ to 4½ steps (this represents the full length of your body). *Never cross over when taking your lead.* Steps should be short, sliding side-steps. Keep your hands off your knees.

6. After you have taken your lead, weight should be on the balls of your feet, knees bent, heels off the ground, arms relaxed in front of your body, eyes focused on the pitcher.

7. When going *back* to 1st, touch the far corner of the bag with the left foot, swinging the body to the right and planting your right foot in foul territory somewhere in the direction of right field. *Always check the 1st base coach as you return to the bag.* Or, slide in head-first, touching the outside corner of the bag with your right hand. This is *not a leap;* stay low to the ground and drive with your legs. By touching the outside of the bag, you lengthen the tag for the 1st baseman. Always turn your head away from the ball.

8. Never take your eyes off the ball.

9. Know the pitcher and his weakness.

THE RUNNER AT 2ND BASE:

1. Always approach 2nd with the intention of going to 3rd, but *watch the 3rd base coach*—he'll tell you whether or not to continue on to 3rd.

2. Be prepared to slide if there is a chance for a force play.

3. The runner at 2nd can usually take a bigger lead than the runner at 1st *if* he feels it's necessary. The ideal lead from 2nd base is 5 or 6 steps. As the pitcher commits to home plate, the runner may slide into a 20-25' lead.

4. Take your lead slightly behind the straight line from 2nd to 3rd. This allows a good turning radius around 3rd.

5. Be conscious of the SS—he may step in behind the runner for a pickoff.

THE RUNNER AT 3RD BASE:

1. With 1 or no outs, shorten your lead so you can't get picked off on a line drive.

2. Always take your lead in foul territory; this will eliminate the possibility of you getting called out if you are hit by the ball.

3. The length of your lead is determined by: The distance the 3rd baseman has from the bag, whether or not the 3rd base coach wants you to go on any ground ball, and the strength of the catcher's arm.

4. As soon as the ball crosses the plate you want to get on the infield side of the line in order to obstruct the throw from the catcher to the 3rd baseman.

5. Never commit to home plate until you are certain that the pitcher is going to deliver to the hitter.

6. With a righthanded hitter at the plate, the runner at 3rd can add a step to his secondary lead. This is possible because the hitter obstructs the catcher's view of the runner.

7. Be alert for wild pitches and passed balls. The coach cannot help you here—it's up to you whether to go or not.

8. Hips and shoulders should be pointed toward home plate. Right foot in the air and heading toward the ground as the ball reaches the hitting zone. If the batter does not swing at the pitch, the baserunner immediately pivots on the balls of his feet, drives off his right foot and breaks hard back to the bag *in fair territory*.

SLIDING:

Sliding is probably the most difficult fundamental that a ballplayer must learn. If not done properly, serious injury may result. The younger player's anxiety over getting hurt sometimes makes sliding a difficult thing to teach. The coach's patience and understanding are vitally important.

The baserunner usually slides for three reasons: 1) to get to the bag, 2) to avoid a tag, or 3) to break up a double play.

THE BENT-LEG OR "STRAIGHT" SLIDE:

1. Begin the slide approximately 10' from the bag.

2. Don't slide too close to the bag.

3. Take off from either leg and bend it under.

4. Keep the weight on the outside of the bent leg. The calf should break the slide, followed by the thigh and then the rear-end.

5. *Don't leap or jump into the slide.*

6. Stay low to the ground.

7. As both legs bend, throw your head slightly backward. This prevents the knees from hitting the ground.

8. Always touch the base with the toe of the foot that is extended.

9. Keep the leg relaxed, knee slightly bent and the *heel off the ground.*

THE HOOK SLIDE:

The hook slide can be made to either side of the bag and is used to avoid a tag. The runner slides to the side *opposite* where the infielder has indicated he will catch the ball. The hook slide is used when the baserunner feels that the ball will beat him to the bag.

The hook slide is slower than the straight slide because the runner is forced to tag the base with the leg farthest back. For example, if the runner is sliding to the right side of the bag he will tag the base with his left foot.

When sliding to the right side (most common), the runner will push off the left foot just before starting his slide.

1. Feet and legs should be extended in front of the body. Legs *should not* be tucked.

2. The runner slides more on the upper thigh than on the calf

and leg.

3. The runner should not bend the left knee any more than necessary to touch the base. The more the knee bends, the longer it will take to touch the base.

BREAKING UP THE DOUBLE PLAY:*

This type of slide increases the chance of injury as the baserunner attempts to make contact with the pivot man at 2nd base. Either the bent-leg or the hook slide may be used.

The purpose of this slide is to disrupt the infielder's pivot and his throw to another base. In addition, the anticipation of a hard slide threatens an infielder and may keep him from trying the same movement if a similar situation arises.

Remember: you are *not* trying to hurt the pivot man. You're only attempting to disrupt his concentration and his throw to 1st base.

1. During infield, watch which side of the bag the SS and 2nd baseman make their pivot and throw. This will enable you to slide to that point before the pivot man gets there.

2. You should attempt to disrupt the infielder by driving into his lower legs, knocking his legs out from under him. Use the upper part of your foot (shoe-string area) *not your cleats*, to make the contact with the pivot man's leg.

3. When you slide, you must be able to make contact with the base with some part of your body. If you can't, you will be called out and so will the runner going to 1st.

4. *Don't use a rolling block.* Not only is this dangerous for the slider and the infielder, it is *illegal* and you will be called out. The slider must be on the ground when he makes contact with the infielder.

SLIDING HEAD-FIRST:

Avoid sliding head-first whenever possible. Many injuries are

*This information is included for the benefit of higher classifications of baseball. Please be advised that Little League Baseball does not encourage a specific type of play intended to break up a double play.

caused as a result of head-first sliding. A runner can break a finger, jam a shoulder, suffer neck injuries. With his fingers exposed on the bag, it is easy for an infielder to step on them, causing serious problems.

Never slide head-first into home plate!! The catcher can drop his shin guards in your face. The area around home plate is very hard and often has holes where the hitters have dug in; a baserunner can jam a finger, or suffer serious injury to his neck or shoulders.

SUMMARY

1. *When in doubt, slide!*

2. *Concentrate on the base you are sliding into.*

3. *Keep your hands and arms above your head.*

4. *Don't run over the catcher if you can avoid it; you run over the catcher only if he completely takes the line and home plate away from you. If you can see any sign of home plate, slide for it! If a collision with the catcher is unavoidable, hit him on his glove side; you may knock the ball out of his hand. Stay low!*

PLAYING THE POSITIONS

PITCHING

Obviously, pitching is the best defense a team can have. As with hitting, pitching is an individual thing and depends upon several factors, physical strength and mental composition foremost among them. There are no hard and fast rules when it comes to pitching but there are some specifics which all young pitchers should be aware of.

First of all, the pitcher must recognize his capabilities. In the case of Little Leaguers, this is the responsibility of the parents and the coach. In my opinion, many young pitchers make a mistake by trying to throw a curve ball before they are ready. Their arms aren't strong enough at an early age and further, there are very few amateur coaches qualified to instruct a young athlete in the proper way to throw a breaking pitch. My advice to all beginning pitchers is: *Learn how to throw a fast ball. Throw it hard and throw it for strikes.*

Ideally, every pitcher should have three good pitches. He should strive to perfect these three pitches before he even thinks about trying to develop a fourth. *Young pitchers should strive for control.* Find a target and throw to it! Catfish Hunter once told me that he used to spend hours just throwing baseballs through an old tire which swung from a tree in his back yard. *It doesn't matter how hard a pitcher throws if he can't put the ball where he wants it.*

I would guess that 100% of the successful pitchers in the Major Leagues would tell you that their preparation for a game begins days before they actually step onto the mound. Tom Seaver once said that "Pitching effects everything I do. It determines what I eat, where I go and what time I go to sleep at night." Most experts agree that pitching is 85% of the game. It would be ridiculous to assume that a pitcher comes out of the bullpen and begins to throw with no mental preparation. Yet this is an aspect of pitching which is largely ignored and must be taught, just as the physical mechanics of pitching are taught. *Good pitching begins on the bench. Know your hitters and use your time on the bench to study their strengths and weaknesses.*

ASSETS OF A WINNING PITCHER

A pitcher who wants to win consistently must:

1. Have good control.

2. Know how to field his position.

3. Analyze the hitters and know their strengths and weaknesses.

4. Have confidence in his ability.

5. Keep his body—especially his legs—in top physical condition.

6. Form good pitching habits.

7. Concentrate. Pick out a spot and throw to it.

8. Communicate with his catcher.

9. Think pitching and pitch thinking.

10. Practice and use "mental pictures".

11. Change speeds on the hitter.

12. Pitch *"in"*.

13. Work *fast.* *

*The game should be won or lost in two hours. The longer you hold the ball, the harder it is for the infielders to keep their concentration. Catfish Hunter, Tommy John, Ron Guidry, Steve Carlton, Don Sutton—the list goes on and on—all work *fast.*

THINGS A GOOD PITCHER SHOULD KNOW:

1. Stay ahead of the hitter.

2. Make the hitter hit your pitch.

3. Know your best pitch and use it when you're in trouble.

4. Have confidence.

5. Know your weakness and work hard to overcome it.

6. Know the game situation.

7. Know the importance of the outs and the runners on base.

8. Know who is covering what base.

9. Field all ground balls unless you're called off.

10. Control your temper, never argue with an umpire.

11. Keep control of yourself when errors are made behind you.

12. Pick up your target before making the pitch.

13. Be in control—be mean and aggressive.

14. Develop *one* style of pitching.

15. Follow through on all deliveries. This is a natural motion and will ease the strain on the pitching arm.

16. Back up plays from the outfield to 3rd and home.

18. Throw all pitches with the same motion.

19. Break for 1st on balls hit to the right side of the infield; be ready to take a toss at 1st if the 1st baseman is pulled away from the bag.

20. Throw curve balls around the knees; don't try to throw them high.

21. Know your hitters and watch for "keys"; some hitters will tip you off as to what they're looking for.

22. Throw high and hard in possible bunt situations.

23. Have an idea of what you're going to do on every pitch. Know the inning, score and count on every hitter *all the time.*

MENTAL PREPARATION FOR PITCHERS

Know your strengths and weaknesses. The number one rule in pitching is: "Never get beat with your second or third best pitch." This means that if you are in a situation where you can lose the game, don't let a hitter beat you on anything less than your best pitch. Of course, there will be days when you will not be effective with your "best" pitch, so you must feel confident with your second and third pitches as well. *Remember:* Situations vary. On a given day, your second or third best pitch may become your *best* pitch! A successful pitcher will recognize this.

A successful hitter in the Major Leagues will get a hit only 3 out of 10 times. With these odds, the pitcher already has a great advantage. Don't give the advantage back to the hitter by throwing him a pitch that you don't have complete confidence in.

Learn to control your emotions and actions. If an umpire misses a pitch, get the ball back and *don't dwell on the mistake.* Think *only* about the next pitch. The worst thing a pitcher can do in this situation is become upset with the umpire. Pitchers who consistently argue with umpires over called strikes develop reputations which encourage umpires to be hard on them. If the pitcher continually attempts to "show up" the umpire, he may take his frustration out on your team as a whole.

Pitchers who train themselves to regain their composure after a bad call (and this *does* take training), will gain the respect of the umpires. More often than not, this pitcher will "get" the close calls.

Catfish Hunter was one of the best pitchers I've ever seen in a situation where an umpire made a bad call. He would get the ball, get back on the mound and go after the hitter with a vengeance. By not showing up the umpire, he received more favorable calls than most. By keeping his emotions under control, Catfish did not allow the hitter at the plate to take advantage of the umpire's mistake by anticipating that an angry pitcher would throw anything less than his best pitch.

Learn to handle pressure. Many pitchers find that the pre-game warm up is the perfect time to prepare mentally for their job on the mound. They use this time to develop "mental pictures", in which they imagine themselves facing a particular hitter. Some even imagine the count and the game situation. In doing this, the pitcher is mentally prepared when the hitter comes to the plate. Many times, the pitcher actually finds himself in the very situation that he imagined in his visualization. Since he wisely used his warm up to anticipate the game situation, and actually "saw" the results he wanted to achieve, he is now ready to deal with it effectively.

The relief pitcher's approach to getting ready is different from a starter's because relievers must be ready every day. The reliever usually begins his mental preparation after infield practice. Early in the game, he begins to study the opposing hitters, anticipating which of them he may be brought in to face. He is *always* aware of the flow of the game. When he is called upon to "get loose", he is *mentally ready*.

Pitchers who feel good about their pre-game warm up can handle the pressure of a real game situation. They enter the game with a *positive mental attitude;* they feel confident because they know they are prepared.

If a pitcher loses his effectiveness on the mound, he is doing one of two things wrong: He has lost his concentration, or he has allowed himself to tense up. One usually leads to the other. *This is the time for him to get the ball, take a few deep breaths and concentrate only on the next pitch!* If this requires him calling a time-out, then he should do it.

Be aware of your mistakes, but don't dwell on them. Many pitchers try to be too smart; they're not content with just getting the hitter out—they try and embarrass him by making him look bad. In doing this, they often over-throw the ball. The result is that they may hang a curveball or throw the fastball over the heart of the plate, allowing the hitter to drive the ball. Another example is when the catcher may call for a pitch which isn't the one you wanted to throw. You throw it without having *total concentration*—you're thinking "I should be throwing a fastball, not a curve", when you should be thinking: "I'm going to throw my best curve and get this guy out." If the hitter hits your curveball, it's easy to lose your concentration and dwell on the catcher's mistake instead of bearing down on the next pitch so that you don't get yourself in a bigger jam. *A good pitcher will take control in this situation—he will shake off the catcher and take charge.*

The success of any pitcher is dependent upon the defense behind him. Avoid embarrassing your teammates by becoming angry when an error is committed behind you.

Like any infielder, I committed errors. When a pitcher stared me down, kicked the dirt, or otherwise tried to show me up, I became upset with him. Instead of concentrating on the next play, I would find myself dwelling on the fact that he had purposely gone out of his way to embarrass me. No one in the ballpark was more aware than I that I had made an error; I didn't need a pitcher to rub salt in my wound! By contrast, some pitchers will leave the mound and offer encouragement to the infielder who has misqued—as a result, the infielder recovers quickly and can give his full attention to the next play. By regaining your composure, you will win the respect of your teammates; they will compensate for the error by bearing down.

It is in the best interest of every pitcher to gain the respect of his defense. This will encourage them to make an extra effort when you pitch.

While you must be aware of these mistakes, you must not allow them to effect your pitching. The time to think about your mistakes is *after* the game. Put yourself back into the problem situation and think about what you *should have done, what you will do the next time, and what the positive results will be when you do the thing right.*

When a catcher calls a pitch you don't feel comfortable with, step off the rubber or shake him off—do whatever it takes to regain total composure. You may even want to call time out and talk with him.

Good pitchers are never satisfied—They are continually striving for improvement.

Mental practice can be the most effective tool a pitcher has. A pitcher's imagination can mean the difference between success and failure. It's a fact that mental practice can have the same results as physical practice. Form mental pictures of various game situations and visualize what you will do and what the positive results will be. "See" the hitter. "Hear" the cheers from the crowd as you strike him out. Be as specific as you can in your mental pictures and make them as real as possible.

PITCHING FORM

STANCE:

Pitchers should have a *balanced starting position,* either from the wind-up or the set; this is vitally important and effects the delivery and release of any pitcher. Relax on the mound, using as little energy as possible—avoid unnecessary pacing. *Take slow, easy breaths.*

WIND-UP POSITION—RIGHTHANDED PITCHER (RHP):

The first thing to remember is that the wind-up should be *simple.* Don't get too fancy, just stick to the basic mechanics outlined here. Don't exert undue energy in your wind-up which could be better spent in your delivery. Keep your head up, eyes focused on your target.

The RHP places the front half of his right foot on the rubber, with the left foot slightly behind it and to the side. His pivot foot should be near the RH corner of the rubber. This gives him the best angle to the right side of the plate and enables his breaking ball to hit the middle of the plate (hence, the outside corner) more often. In addition, it is more difficult for the hitter to see the pitch from this angle. Likewise, the lefthanded pitcher (LHP) should place his pivot foot near the lefthand corner of the rubber.

With his right arm relaxed at his side, the RHP has the ball deep in his glove as he takes the sign from the catcher. After receiving the sign, he puts his right hand over his glove-hand wrist and grips the ball palm-to-palm. From here, he brings both hands just above the bill of his cap, being careful not to bring them too far over his head (which would allow the hitter to see the ball). As both arms swing downward, he begins to pivot on his right foot, bringing his left foot and knee back to a position that is about even, or slightly behind, the pitching rubber. Now, he puts the ball and hand out of the glove, swings his right arm down and back, shifts his weight, comes forward, plants the ball of his left foot and heel in a direction straight at home plate and, with a quick arm action forward (a ¾ to overhand delivery), he releases the ball to the plate. *Keep the ball well hidden; the hitter shouldn't see it until the point of release.* At this point, he brings his right foot forward, and plants it beside his left, at least shoulder width apart. He is now in a crouched position and is prepared to field the ball.

SET POSITION—RHP:

In the set position, the RHP straddles the rubber, his back to the runner(s) on base. He moves into a set position with his foot in contact with the rubber, takes his sign and straightens up, bringing both arms into a set position. Now, he checks the runner(s) and begins a quick left-leg pivot. Keep the foot close to the ground and use the same motion as in the wind-up position. The right knee should be slightly bent while in the set position; your legs should never be stiff in the stretch.

Use the rubber as an aid to help you drive toward the plate in all positions.

THE GRIP:

The grip is individual to each pitcher and must be made comfortable through trial and error. There are some basic tips on the grip used in specific pitches which will be discussed later. *Caution: Your grip will sometimes reveal the type of pitch you are going to throw.* For example, some pitchers will turn their wrist in before throwing a curve ball, or their wrist will be facing the hitter before throwing a fastball. Smart hitters are quick to pick up these weaknesses and most certainly will take advantage of them. *Keep the ball well hidden until the time of delivery!*

THE NO WIND-UP DELIVERY:

In the no wind-up delivery, pitchers do not bring their hands over their heads before they pivot on the rubber. The no wind-up delivery is good for pitchers who have trouble keeping their balance when using the conventional wind-up technique. It is also useful to pitchers who have difficulty hiding the ball before delivery.

THE DOUBLE-PUMP WIND-UP:

Considered to be a useful tool when trying to break a hitter's concentration, the double-pump wind-up is basically the same as the conventional wind-up except that once the pitcher has his hands over his head, he drops them down and begins the wind-up again, rocking back on his back foot. This sometimes throws off a hitter's timing as well.

DELIVERY:

Pitching is not all arm strength. *It is a total body action.* Concentrate on keeping your shoulder tucked (left shoulder for RHP, right shoulder for LHP). Drive with your legs, *low and hard. Use the rubber* as a tool to aid you in driving toward the plate. Think *"low and hard"* as you release the ball. If you make a mistake up, it can mean a home run. A mistake low may only result in a ground ball.

THE FOLLOW THROUGH:

Once the weight has been transferred to the left leg, the right (back) leg should follow through and finish up almost in a direct line, and squared off to the plate. The upper body should be bent forward at the waist, helping to pull the arm down and across the body. The elbow should end up touching the area of the left thigh and the hand and wrist should be outside the left knee. The complete follow through will find the glove hand somewhere out in front of the body; the body should be squared off, preparing the pitcher to field his position.

CONTROL:

Unquestionably, the most important element in pitching is control. Foremost in achieving control is the pitcher's mental approach to the game. Once he has mastered a positive mental attitude and feels confident on the mound, he must then consider the physical aspects of control which he has learned.

Good control is the result of consistent use of pitching mechanics and techniques. A pitcher with good control is consistent in his rhythm and style of delivery.

PROBLEM: Lack of concentration.

SOLUTIONS:

1. Study carefully the "Mental Preparation for Pitchers" in this book.

2. Pick up your target before beginning your wind-up. Keep your eye on the target until you release the ball.

3. Think *only* about the pitch you are *getting ready to throw.*

PROBLEM: Rushing the pitch.

SOLUTIONS:

1. *Relax.* Make sure you have good balance when taking the sign.

2. Don't move your body toward the plate too soon. There should be a slight bend of the knee on the pivot foot leg.

3. Don't step back too far with your non-pivot foot as you begin your motion into the wind-up.

4. Take a good, full pivot so the hitter can see your back pocket. For a RHP, the hitter should see your left pocket.

5. Concentrate on keeping your weight on your back leg.

PROBLEM: Throwing across the body.

SOLUTIONS:

1. The RHP should have the pivot foot near the RH corner of the rubber. The LHP should have his pivot foot near the LH corner of the rubber.

2. Draw a line from the pivot foot to and through the middle of home plate, making sure that the lead foot lands slightly to the left of that line.

PROBLEM: Improper arm action.

SOLUTIONS:

1. When removing the ball from your glove, make sure the palm of your hand is *down.*

2. Move your arms toward home plate, not toward 1st or 3rd base.

PROBLEM: Short arming (not using full arm action when throwing).

SOLUTIONS:

1. You may be rushing, or may not be getting a full back swing with your arm.

2. Are you recovering from an injury, or do you have a sore arm?

3. Have you been taught to use a *full* follow through?

PROBLEM: Control.

SOLUTIONS:

1. Check for rushing.

2. Are your basic pitching mechanics sound?

3. Do you have *total concentration?* Make sure you are *mentally prepared* before going to the mound.

PROBLEM: Loss of power on delivery.

SOLUTIONS:

1. Check your stride foot. Make sure you aren't opening up too much. The upper body should be closed until the arm has reached the top of the backswing and is moving toward the plate.

2. Drive *low and hard* toward the plate.

PROBLEM: Poor body balance.

SOLUTIONS:

1. Don't rock too far back on your wind-up or from the set position.

2. Are you rotating your hips far enough before delivery?

HOLDING RUNNERS ON:

The most important thing for a pitcher to remember with runners on base is: *never allow any baserunner to take a walking lead—it is up to you to stop him.* You do not want to appear "predictable" with runners on base. Remember to vary your moves and the number of times you pump. Vary the release point of your throw to 1st, and be aggressive in your efforts to hold the runner on. Know the game situation and the ability of the baserunner(s) at all times.

TAKING SIGNS:

1. Take signs from the rubber.

2. Relax.

3. Use your head and your glove to deceive the opposition.

4. Shake the catcher off if you are not comfortable with the sign.

5. Vary the number of times you pump; avoid forming patterns which will enable the hitter to predict what you are going to do.

6. After you have taken the sign, use your glove and body to hide the ball. The hitter shouldn't see the ball until delivery.

THE PITCHER AS A FIELDER:

A pitcher's job is just beginning when he delivers the ball. The importance of a pitcher as a good fielder cannot be overstressed. Frequently, a pitcher gets himself into trouble by his inability to field a ground ball. *A well pitched game can be lost by the pitcher's inability to field his position correctly.*

1. Field everything unless you are called off.

2. On balls hit to your left, break for 1st base. If necessary, cover the bag. Otherwise, stay out of the play.

3. Take all possible bunts. Break hard and "look" the ball into the glove before you try to throw it. Listen to the catcher—he'll tell you what base to throw to.

4. When a play is going to be made at 3rd or home, and runners are advancing, run half-way between the bases in *foul* territory before you decide which base to back up as the throw comes in.

THROWING TO 2ND FOR A DOUBLE PLAY:

1. Always know who is covering the base so that you can lead correctly. Usually it will be the SS, as it is an easier play for him to handle.

2. After you catch the ground ball, take a short shuffle step toward 2nd base. This will allow you to get your balance while giving the SS time to get to the bag.

3. Make a good, *chest high* throw to the infielder. *Don't overthrow the ball.*

THROWING THE BASIC PITCHES

THE FASTBALL:

There are two types of grips used in throwing the fastball:

1. Across the seams: The across the seams grip is primarily used by pitchers who want their fast ball to go at it's maximum velocity without much movement. Example: If you want to pitch a hitter up and in, you would want the ball to stay up and in. This pitch is used by power pitchers like Nolan Ryan and Rich Gossage. The ball is held across the seams, at the widest part, in order to achieve the four-seam rotation.

2. With the Seams: If a pitcher has problems getting his fastball to move, he can grip the ball with the seams. This grip is used by pitchers who want to sink the ball as well as make it move in and out.* Tommy John is a good example: He doesn't have an over-powering fastball, so he was forced to develop another pitch. He mastered the "sinker" and probably throws it at about 78 or 80 MPH. So you see, movement

is sometimes more important than speed when throwing a fastball.

* Though gripping the ball at the seams will cause it to move more, it can also cause loss of velocity and control problems. Each pitcher should experiment with the grips to see which is best for him.

When throwing the fastball, the index and middle fingers should not be too far apart. If they are, the wrist will lock. This prevents the pitcher from getting the maximum velocity. If the fingers are too close together, severe control problems will result as the ball can easily slide off the fingers as it is released. The ball should be gripped firmly, but not too tight, and as far toward the fingertips as possible. If you hold the ball too far back in your hand you will re-strict your fingers and wrist from their full range of motion; this will result in loss of velocity. *You should see light between your palm and the ball.*

THE SINKING FASTBALL:

If thrown properly, this is an ideal pitch to use in a DP situation, as it usually produces a ground ball. The sinker should be thrown with the fingers on the seams and a ¾ to side-arm motion. This will allow your wrist to turn over slightly as the ball is released. *Apply pressure with the index finger as the ball is released. Drive low and hard and stay on top of the ball.* The sinker is

a difficult pitch to master because of the arm motion needed.

However, if it is thrown properly, it is one of the most effective pitches a pitcher can throw.

THE CURVE BALL:

The curve ball can make or break a pitcher. If a pitcher doesn't have an effective breaking pitch the hitter will ignore his breaking ball and sit on his fastball. I don't care how hard a pitcher can throw, good hitters can eventually time your fastball and hit it hard. A curve is used to fool the batter, to disrupt his timing and keep him off balance. If thrown correctly, the curve should not put a strain on the pitcher's arm. Young pitchers should use caution when throwing these pitches before they are physically mature enough. I think age fourteen is about the right time for young pitchers to begin experimenting.

When throwing the curveball, the grip should be firm, but not too tight. Only the thumb and first two fingers should be used in throwing the curve. The ring and little finger should be bent into the palm. Any pressure by the ring or little finger will reduce both speed and rotation of the ball. The elbow should *always* be above the shoulder. The throwing shoulder must be above the lead shoulder. By doing this, you will  be releasing the ball down-hill. If the lead shoulder is higher than the back shoulder, the pitcher will have a difficult time getting on top; this results in the pitcher throwing a flat curve instead of a sharp curve.

The stride is shorter when throwing a curve than it is with a fastball; this enables the pitcher to get on top of the pitch. He must follow through completely so he can maintain the arm velocity necessary to "snap off" a good curve. In addition, a good follow through, with the arm coming across the body, helps the pitcher get into a good fielding position.

TIPS FOR THROWING A GOOD CURVE:

1. Don't try to throw it too hard.

2. Pull *down* on release, as if you are lowering a window shade.

3. Put pressure on the middle finger and thumb.

4. Use your index finger as a guide.

5. Keep your elbow *up* and parallel with your shoulder.

6. Cock your wrist. Poor wrist action will cause the ball to lose proper rotation.

7. Don't grip the ball too tightly or have it too far back in your palm. This will effect the spin. The loser the grip, the slower the curve.

8. Follow through, slapping yourself in the back.

9. Bring your hand and arm down on the opposite side of your throwing arm.

10. "Snap" your wrist.

11. Warm up slowly to get the proper spin.

12. Stay on top of the ball.

13. Keep your non-throwing shoulder in.

THE CHANGE-UP:

It requires a great deal of timing to hit a change-up. A properly thrown change-up makes a fastball appear to be traveling faster than it is, so it disrupts the hitter's timing. That is why the change-up is so effective. Throwing it is easily taught—the difficult part is getting the confidence to use it.

As the ball tends to travel high in the strike zone, a low release point is essential. Though a change-up does not have to be thrown at the knees to be effective, a ball low within the strike zone is less likely to be hit out of the ballpark. There are three commonly used grips:

1. The palm Ball: The ball is held back in the palm of your hand. Fingertips are raised slightly as you release the ball. Most of the pressure should be on the second row of knuckles on the first two fingers. On release, the hand is *behind the ball,* not on top.

2. Three Fingers: Some pitchers feel they get better control if they grip the ball with three fingers instead of two. By using three, you create a greater drag, which causes the ball to slow down.

3. Off Center: With the off center grip, you hold the ball with the middle and ring fingers on top. The thumb and index finger are held on the inside of the ball, touching slightly and forming a small circle. The little finger is held on the outside of the ball.

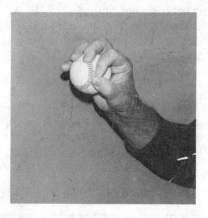

On all three grips, when the ball leaves your hand, the hitter should not be able to detect that a change-up will be thrown.

All of your actions—hand, wrist and arm—should indicate to the hitter that you are going to throw a fast ball. The grip and release of the change-up help to slow the velocity. Your wrist must be "dead"; there should be no "snap" as there is when you throw a fastball. The elbow on your throwing arm must be kept higher than your shoulder. This is to keep your change-up from getting too high in the strike zone. Try and hit home plate with the ball.

THE SLIDER:

When properly thrown, the slider will break faster and flatter than a curve ball. It should look like a fastball coming at the hitter and then break at the last second. As the slider doesn't break as hard as a curve, it is an easier pitch to throw for strikes. However, if not thrown correctly, the slider becomes a pitch that can hurt you because it is thrown with less velocity than a fastball. Instead of breaking, it can stay right where you throw it.

The slider has earned a reputation as a pitch which frequently causes arm problems for pitchers who use it. Sparky Lyle, one of the greatest relief pitchers of all times—and a master at the slider—feels that this reputation grew because most pitchers don't throw the slider correctly. They throw it across the body instead of staying on top of the ball and behind it. When Sparky finished, he tried to follow through so his left arm would finish under his right.

Sparky gripped the slider with no seams. This way, when he entered a game, he didn't have to worry about finding a ball with "good seams"; he could devote his entire concentration to his delivery and the rotation of the ball.

Some pitchers grip the slider the same way as the fastball except that they hold it *slightly* off center with the middle and index fingers placed to the *outside* of the ball. The index finger should be next to a seam with your thumb on a seam underneath the ball. The fingers and thumb should not grip the ball too tightly until the second of release. *Maximum pressure is placed on the ball with your middle finger.* To achieve tight spin on the slider, grip tightly with the index and middle fingers on release and "snap" the wrist just as you would when throwing a fastball.

The middle finger generates the spin which makes the ball slide. *Fingers must remain on top of the ball and slightly off center as the hand moves to the release point.* If your fingers move too far down on the side of the ball your slider will be slow and flat. *Don't turn your wrist inward as you release the ball.* This action will flatten out your slider and put *extreme pressure* on your elbow. Concentrate on a *full follow through* in order to get the maximum velocity.

CATCHING

The catcher is the pulse of a good defense. The other eight players will take their cues from you. You must be energetic and enthusiastic; you must *take charge of the defense and hustle 100% of the time.* You must *know the hitters:* First-ball hitters, good curveball hitters, etc. You have to know what each hitter is looking for when he comes to the plate. You must *know the pitcher.* What pitches are working for him? If he's not effective with his number one pitch, you have to be aware of that. Don't let him be too fine; you can't catch a walk!

1. Wear protective cup and helmet during BP, while in the bullpen, and during the game.

2. *Always* wear a catcher's mask when warming up pitchers.

3. During BP, protect your bare hand behind your back or knee. If you want to throw through to 2nd base, tell the batter to swing and miss. That way, you can receive the pitch and throw it properly without fear of a foul tip. Don't throw to 2nd more than 3 or 4 times in succession.

4. Don't catch BP on one knee; a foul tip on the thigh is painful and you won't be 100% for the game.

5. Catch as close to the hitter as you can. Foul tips will hit your glove more often.

6. Never use a new glove in a game.

7. Catch *every pitch.*

8. When giving signs, have your toes pointed straight ahead before crouching; this will keep your knees in and block your signs from

the opposing coaches.

9. Use your glove to hide signs even more; check with your 1st and 3rd basemen—if they can see your signs, so can the coaches.

10. Go from the sign to the receiving position in the same way on every pitch. Some catchers will move the right foot first on breaking pitches and the left foot first on fastballs; the opposition will pick this up.

11. Hold the bare hand loosely in a fist with the thumb inside the cup formed by the fingers.

12. Be ready to receive when the pitcher begins his wind-up. Don't give the sign, then stand up and go back into the receiving position. The pitcher will be half way through with his delivery and still won't have a target to aim at.

13. Anticipate a stolen base on every pitch. *Don't wait until you catch the ball to get your body into throwing position.*

14. *Don't jump up* as you catch, or you'll lose a lot of strikes for your pitcher.

15. Your glove should always move *toward* your body as you catch the pitch. Don't push low balls toward the ground or corner pitches away from the plate.

16. Check the defense before giving signs. You are the only player who can see the entire defense—know where you want every player to be. Don't hesitate to move players if they are out of position.

SHIFTING:

Shifting helps you get your body in front of the pitch and gets weight to your right foot for a throw. It's hard to get velocity on a throw without pushing off with your right foot. Shifting should be forward as well as lateral in order to get your body moving in the direction of the throw. It isn't necessary to shift on pitches you can catch between your shoulders; just keep your right foot planted and step toward your target with your left foot.

You should be in the process of shifting, or almost finished, *by the time you catch the ball.* On an outside pitch (righthanded hitter), step with the right foot to the right and forward as you catch the ball. Step toward your target with the left foot as you throw. With a lefthanded hitter, move your left foot first, to the left and forward as you catch. Plant the right foot behind the left as you step toward your target with your left foot.

THROWING:

1. Keep wrist and fingers upright. This will give you riding fastball rotation and helps eliminate throws which sink, tail or slide.

2. Try to grip the ball across the seams to obtain *four-seam* rotation. This will give your throw more carry and greater accuracy.

3. Always throw to the bag on stolen bases; it's the infielder's responsibility to get there.

4. When throwing to 3rd on a stolen base, throw *over* a right-handed hitter when possible. Otherwise, clear yourself from the hitter.

5. To throw to 3rd in front of a RH hitter, (pitch outside, or outside corner), step to the right and forward with the right foot.

6. To throw in back of a RH hitter, (most strikes and inside pitches) step behind him with the left foot. Bring the right foot behind the left, plant and throw.

BUNTS:

1. Call the fielder and the base to throw to on *all* bunts. *Call with authority!*

2. Field bunts with **both hands.** Use your glove to push the ball into the open, bare hand.

3. Get your body in position to throw before you field the ball.

4. On bunts to 3rd, circle to your left to get your body moving toward 1st as you field the ball. If the ball is stopped or moving slowly, you can bare-hand it and pivot away from the infield to make the throw.

5. With a runner on 1st and the 3rd baseman fielding the ball, it's the catcher's responsibility to cover 3rd.

POP-UPS:

1. *Go after every pop-up!*

2. All pop-ups curve toward 2nd base.

3. Try to have both feet planted and still before catching the ball. This will keep your head still and the ball won't seem to "bounce" so much.

4. Hold on to your mask until you are positive where the catch will be made. Then, *toss it in the other direction.*

TAG PLAYS:

Most tag plays at home are missed because the catcher doesn't catch the throw. During infield practice, wear your mask and shinguards while taking throws from the outfield; stay in there and catch every throw.

1. Avoid collisions whenever possible. Give the runner part of the plate to aim for.

2. If the runner isn't sliding, go meet him up the line if possible. "Give" with the tag as you spin toward home plate.

3. If a collision is unavoidable, *be ready.* Have your body low and make certain that your weight is *forward.*

4. When tagging a sliding runner, *point your left toe directly at him.* If your toe is pointing left, the inside of your knee is exposed and injury may occur. If it's pointing to the right, the outside of the knee is vulnerable.

BLOCKING BALLS:

With a pitch in the dirt and the runner stealing, you must try to catch the ball in order to have any chance at the would-be stealer. However, if there is a runner at 3rd, you must block the ball to keep the run from scoring.

The blocking position is on both knees, arms at your side (this makes you wider), chest squared to the pitch and your upper body curved forward to keep the ball in front of you. Blocking balls is a learned reaction, mastered only through a lot of practice. You can't become proficient at it merely by thinking about it—you have to get dirty!

Most low balls get past the catcher between his knees. *You must drop both knees at the same time and use your glove to cover the space between them.* Keep your glove on the ground and don't try to catch the ball. On balls in the dirt to your right or left, move forward as well as laterally. This will keep your chest squared to the pitch and the ball won't carom off to the side. *Be sure that you land on your knee.* If you shift on your foot first, the ball will be past you.

Because of the rotation, a RHP's breaking ball will kick toward your glove hand; the LHP's will kick toward your bare hand.

THE 1ST BASEMAN

STANCE AND FOOTWORK:

You should have movement toward the hitter as the pitcher releases the ball. As the ball passes the hitting zone, weight should be on the balls of your feet. Your legs should be shoulder-width apart, hands relaxed belt-high in front of you. Your eyes should be clearly focused on the hitting zone.

Break hard on all ground balls. *Don't watch the ball—find the bag.* Your body should face in the direction of the ground ball. Always set the same way with the same foot on the bag; preferably, corner-to-corner with your right foot on the right corner of the bag and your left foot on the left corner.

When a fielder releases the ball, stretch out as far as possible with the lead foot to catch the ball. *Don't stretch too early.* Use the crossover step to stretch on a ball opposite the glove-hand side. Keep your feet off the top of the bag; use the front corners as guideposts. Use either the right or left corner when you stretch, or use the middle on a good throw. Come off the bag on errant throws.

Make sure all runners tag the base.

POSITIONING AND CUT-OFFS:

The 1st baseman has three positions to take, depending on the game situation:

1. Back Position: With a lefthanded hitter and no chance of a bunt, make sure to get off the line so a step and a dive will cover it.

2. Half-way: Possible bunt situation, with a good bunter and fast runner. With a righthanded hitter get half-way, then move 3 or 4 steps to the right.

3. In Position: A definite bunt situation and a possible play at home with a runner on 3rd base.

Trail runners to 2nd base on extra base hits. *You are the cut-off man on extra base hits* if there is a runner on 1st. On a cut-off from CF, take the throw on top of the mound to prevent a bad hop off the rubber or mound. On a cut-off from RF, get deep toward the catcher and come back toward the throw.

Make a decision on all throws, considering the runner, the game situation and the type of throw. Use your best judgement, make your own decisions, and don't depend on the catcher for instructions.

Signal that you are the cut-off man by raising your arms high above your head and waving.

HOLDING RUNNERS ON:

1. Stay in fair territory.

2. When breaking off the bag, take a crossover step, then two shuffles with your knees bent. Take your glove to the ground with your eyes focused on the hitting zone.

3. Give a low target when holding runners on base.

4. Make a *firm tag* on your runner on *every* throw to the bag.

5. Alert the catcher when a runner goes.

CATCHING THE BALL:

1. Field from the ground up, low to high.

2. Catch the ball in the web.

3. Use *one* hand, except when blocking the ball.

4. On a throw into the runner, make the tag while "giving" with your arm to avoid injury. Let the runner tag himself out.

5. Always anticipate a bad throw.

6. On balls in the dirt, use soft hands and "give" with the glove toward your body. Start with your glove on the ground; make adjustments up.

7. On balls in the dirt with a runner at 2nd, *block the ball.* Come *off* the base on a wild throw.

8. Block ground balls to 1st with your body if necessary; you can still throw the runner out.

9. You may have to slide to the back part of the base on some

long hops and high throws.

10. *Don't overcharge.* Stay back and get a big hop, especially with runners in scoring position.

11. On foul balls, go to the fence and then work back.

12. Call off the catcher on pop-ups.

13. When the ball gets away from the catcher on the 3rd strike, give a good target, either inside or outside, depending on where the ball goes.

THROWING:

1. Give the pitcher the ball early.

2. *Get one out in all DP situations* where you throw to 2nd base. *Don't rush the throw;* let the SS turn the double play.

3. In a DP situation, *Don't throw across the runner.* Stay inside or out and throw for the SS's head. Don't watch the play, get back to the bag.

COMMUNICATION:

1. Tell the pitcher to get over with a lefthanded hitter.

2. Tell the 2nd baseman when you move and where you are playing.

3. On balls to your right, go as far as possible, then yield to the 2nd baseman. *Know your 2nd baseman's range!*

4. Have the 2nd baseman alert you to curve balls and change-ups.

5. Keep infielders alert by reminding them of the number of outs and the situation.

6. Remind the 3rd baseman of who is the cut-off man.

PLAYING THE INFIELD

JUMPS AND STANCE:

A phrase often applied to a well-fielded ball is that the infielder "got a great jump on it". The best infielders get better jumps because they know how to get ready (stance). Not all infielders are built alike. If you're 6'2" tall, you won't be able to get as low, or "bent" at the knees as a player who is 5'6"; you'll have to have a more upright stance. Your physical makeup and the position you play will determine which stance is best for you.

In the *proper stance*, feet should be shoulder-width apart. Weight is on the balls of the feet, hands are relaxed, about belt-high. Knees are slightly bent, back should be straight and head toward the hitter.

Infielders who get consistent good jumps have good lateral movement. If a player has poor lateral movement, he should check the following things:

1. Are his feet too close together?

2. Is he leaning too far forward? On his toes?

3. Is his weight on his heels?

4. Is he standing too upright?

5. Is he bent too much at the knees or at the waist?

SLOW ROLLERS:

If an infielder is having trouble handling slowly hit balls, he may be catching the ball off of the wrong foot. The correct way to field a slow roller is off of the *right* side. The fielder *breaks hard* for the ball. Just before he gets to the ball, he should slow down enough to get his balance and shift his body so he can field the ball off of his right side. His right foot should be back. Fielding the ball on the right side enables the fielder to throw the ball with one step and allows a quicker release because the ball is already on his right side. *If the ball is rolling with any speed at all, catch it with your glove. If it's setting down in the grass, bare-hand it in exactly the same way—off of your right side.*

A good drill for a 3rd baseman who's having trouble fielding slowly hit grounders is to get him back and hit him some slow rollers. *He should charge hard.* A common mistake among 3rd basemen is that they don't break hard in the beginning; they play too cautiously and then try to force the play. *Charge hard at first and then slow down to get control of your body.*

THE BACK-HAND:

When teaching infielders to back-hand the ball, stress the importance of keeping the left foot in front when catching the ball. This enables them to field the ball cleanly, take one step with their right foot, plant and throw. Catching the ball off of the right foot forces the fielder to take a step with his left foot and then his right. The result is that the fielder takes one, and sometimes two too many steps. (For 3rd basemen, this technique isn't always possible due to the velocity of the ball.)

STIFF HANDS:

A player who has "stiff hands" usually isn't relaxed and may not be as confident as he should be regarding his fielding ability. Here again, mental practice can prove invaluable. *Visualize* yourself in various fielding situations and *imagine positive results.*

If a player has stiff hands, he should check for the following things:

1. He may be "stabbing" at the ball instead of catching it. He should take some ground balls without his glove on; this will help him develop soft hands. Imagine that the ball is an egg—it should be caught with the hands out in front and very relaxed.

2. Is he overcharging?

HANDCUFFING:

"Handcuffing" is a term used when a player lets the ball get too close to his body before it makes contact with his glove. A player who is consistently handcuffed is probably doing one of the following things wrong:

1. He's letting the ball "play him". He should work on charging the ball while keeping his body under control. By charging the ball, he can choose the best possible hop.

2. He may be pounding his glove just before he attempts to catch the ball. This is a bad habit for a young player to get into. More often than not, he will pound his glove late; this will cause him to "stab" at the ball. Stabbing causes stiff hands, which causes handcuffing.

3. He may have his hands too close to his body. This causes him to be played by the ball. *He must keep his hands out in front and close to the ground. It's easier to come up for the ball than to go down after it.*

PIVOT AT 2ND BASE:

Successful execution of the double play is one of the most valuable defenses in the game. In order to execute the pivot at 2nd accurately, a 2nd baseman must do the following things:

1. Get to the bag early.

2. Get your body under control.

3. Bend at the knees and lower your center of gravity—this one thing alone will help keep your body under control.

4. Keep your hands soft and relaxed. *Let the ball come to you— don't reach out and get it.*

5. Always face the person you are receiving the ball from.

6. *Pivot:* Unless you are straddling the bag, you should always try to put your *left foot* on the bag. This enables you to come across the bag, plant your right foot and throw. On a ball up the middle, take the throw from the SS, plant your right foot and throw.

A good 2nd baseman knows *Different ways to turn a double play:*

1. Straddle: Self-explanatory.

2. Across the Bag: This method is usually used on a ball hit toward 2nd base where the SS can under-hand the ball to the 2nd baseman. This type of pivot helps the 2nd baseman get more on his throw.

The 2nd baseman places his left foot on the bag, just as he is receiving the ball. His right foot crosses over the bag and plants about 10" from it. He pivots on the right foot and throws to 1st base. *The 2nd baseman should not commit too soon; not all throws will be perfect.*

3. Step Back: Left foot on the bag. After receiving the throw, step back with your right foot, plant and throw.

4. Left Foot on the Bag: Follow the ball up the middle, facing the SS. Take the throw, almost like a 1st baseman, plant your right foot and throw.

THE SS AND THE DOUBLE PLAY:

The pivot for the shortstop is as follows:

1. Face the person you are receiving the throw from.

2. Have your body under control. Bend at the knees and lower your center of gravity; this will help you slow down.

3. Have your arms and hands relaxed and away from your body.

4. Let the ball come to you—*don't* reach out and grab it.

5. Give a target with your glove and right hand.

6. Stay behind the bag; you can adjust more easily if the throw is bad.

7. Touch the bag with your *right* foot. The only time you might tag it with your left is when you are taking the throw from the 1st baseman on the *inside* of the baseline.

8. *Use two hands.*

COVERING THE BASES ON A STEAL:

Depending on who's covering the bag, the 2nd baseman or the SS must cheat in his position by coming in and over on the pitch. Taking two short steps toward the baseline before breaking for the bag will allow him to cover his ground.

THE TAG PLAY:

The tag play at 2nd for a 2nd baseman is simple: You merely strad-dle the bag.

The SS has two options on a tag play: He can straddle the bag, or he can place his left foot up against the home plate side of the bag. In this method, he *must* let the ball come to him; if he gets in the habit of reaching for it, and the baserunner gets under his tag, *he should straddle the bag.* The advantage in placing your left foot inside the bag is that it allows you to move up the line and out of the way of the sliding baserunner while still enabling you to take the throw from the catcher and make the tag.

SUMMARY

A GOOD INFIELDER KNOWS:

1. The stretch of his arm and how deep he can play.

2. The SS and the 2nd baseman must cheat toward 2nd to turn the DP effectively.

3. The speed of the runner.

4. The atmospheric conditions: Wind, sun, type of playing surface.

5. A good infielder knows where the outfielders are playing and how far to go out for a relay play. He knows the strength of the out-fielder's arms.

6. Who is batting and how will he be pitched?

7. Who covers the bag on a steal?

8. Who covers the bag on balls hit back to the pitcher?

9. What bag do you cover in the following situations: Bunt? Relay? Pick off?

10. Know the infield fly rule: An infield fly is a fair fly ball (not including a line drive or a bunt) which can be caught by an infielder with ordinary effort. The ball is alive and runners may advance at the risk of the ball being caught, or retouch and advance after the ball is touched. *If a declared infield fly is allowed to fall untouched to the ground, and bounces foul before passing 1st*

or 3rd base, it is a foul ball. The infield fly rule is in effect with runners at 1st and 2nd, or bases loaded and one or no outs. If the ball goes into the air and, in the umpire's judgment, the infielder can catch the ball, he will signal the infield fly rule. After the fielder makes contact with the ball, the runners may advance at their own risk.

11. Exchanging runners: In case of a run down, always try to get the runner out of scoring position; get the fastest runner off base.

12. The obstruction rule: Obstruction occurs when a runner interferes with an infielder while he's in the process of fielding the ball. If no play is being made on an obstructed runner, the play will proceed until no further action is possible. The umpire will call time and impose such penalties as, in his judgment, will nullify the act of obstruction.

13. The interference rule: Offensive interference is an act by the team at bat which interferes with, obstructs, hinders or confuses a fielder attempting to make a play. If the umpire declares the batter, batter-runner or a runner out for interference, all other runners shall return to the last base that was, in the judgment of the umpire, legally touched at the time of interference.

PLAYING THE OUTFIELD

A good outfielder is smart, alert to all game situations, and hustles every minute. He backs up every throw and base hit possible, always assuming the infielder will miss the ball. He hustles 100% of the time and always knows when and where to throw the ball.

A good outfielder knows the following things:

1. The score.

2. The importance of the tying and winning run.

3. The count.

4. The type of hitter at the plate.

5. The speed of the infielders when going back on fly balls.

6. The infielder's weaknesses in moving right and left.

7. The strengths and weaknesses of the other outfielders in his unit.

8. The type of pitcher.

9. The speed of the runner.

10. How the ball rebounds from the fence and screen.

11. Atmospheric conditions and condition of the playing surface.

12. Which outfielder is in the best position to take the ball, pivot and throw?

13. The sun field.

14. The outfielder is in charge when it comes to running an infielder off the ball.

15. Back up the bases when bunts, pick-off plays, stolen bases and rundowns are in order.

16. A good outfielder knows when to catch a foul ball and when to let one go.

17. Know the warning track and the ground rules.

A good outfielder should *never:*

1. Chase ground balls on his heels.

2. Flip his sunglasses down before he locates the ball.

3. Catch the ball on the side when throwing.

4. Catch fly balls flat-footed when throwing to get the runner out.

5. Overcharge the ball when throwing.

6. Catch low line drives with his glove facing down.

7. Throw behind the runner.

8. Play all hitters the same depth.

9. Lift his head and watch the runner before fielding the ball. (You should "watch" the ball into your glove before you pick up your target.)

10 Run with the glove arm extended until the last step or two prior to the catch.

11. Miss the cut-off man.

12. Give up too soon on a fly ball.

13. Catch a ball one-handed when it's possible to catch it with two.

BASIC OUTFIELD DRILLS

CHARGE DRILL:

Begin by hitting five easy ground balls. Gradually hit them harder. After fifteen to each player, move them back 15-20 feet. Now, one at a time, each player charges the ball and attempts to catch it in front of the original 45' marker. This drill is particularly effective for players who hesitate when charging the ball.

THROW FROM THE MOUND:

Have the outfielder throw from the mound with particular emphasis on the break point. Keep his front shoulder down and turned in. Also emphasize a long throw and make sure he is throwing over the top. As the mechanics of throwing from the outfield are much the same as those of pitching, your pitching coach will be helpful in this drill. This is a good exercise for outfielders who tend to open up too soon and/or throw out over their front foot.

BREAK DRILL:

Designed for players who get a slow break on balls to either side or over their heads. Stand 10' from the player with a ball in each hand. Toss balls under-handed to the right and left, noticing if the player crosses over on the first step. Whenever possible, the player should get in good catching position and get the ball out of his glove as if making a throw. Some balls will be tossed directly over his head or shoulders. In these instances, you're looking for the player to make a drop-step rather than a cross over.

LONG TOSS:

Each outfielder should long-toss two or three times a week. Players should pair off, throwing softly from about 60' and gradually (5 minutes) work out to 200-250'. Throws should be kept on an arc, with no more than five throws being made at the maximum distance. A good drill for stretching the arm muscles and increasing the length of the throws.

FENCE DRILL:

The key to this drill: Outfielders must communicate during the play. Hit long fungoes to the fence in the gaps. One player must try for the catch while the other has to get in position to play any carom off the fence. Another part of the fence drill is hitting balls over the player's head. Have him find the fence, then come in or over to make the catch.

ALL PURPOSE DRILL:

This is a daily drill that all the outfielders should do after throwing in infield practice. All throws should be short and at a designated spot (a hat) on the ground. This will help keep the throws over the top and the release point out in front. Do this drill as follows:

1. Base hit directly at outfielder with no one on base.

2. Base hit directly at outfielder with runner on 1st.

3. Base hit to the player's left.

4. Base hit to the player's right.

5. Fly ball to player's left.

6. Fly ball to player's right.

7. Fly ball over the player's head.

8. Line drive hit at the player.

9. Base hit directly at the player with the winning run on 2nd base.

DO THIS DRILL EVERY DAY!

INFIELD GROUNDERS:

Outfielders who have bad or hard hands should take ground balls *every day* with the infielders.

CATCH AND RELEASE:

Release time can be speeded up if the player learns to catch a fly or ground ball with a low center of gravity. This is achieved by having him keep his rear-end down as he is making the catch; he's already getting his legs and shoulders into the optimum throwing position. If done correctly, he should be able to throw with only two steps after the catch.

USING SUNGLASSES:

Besides learning how to use glasses properly, the player must learn to block the sun with his glove or bare hand. Throw or hit balls directly into the sun. Each player should learn to look away from the sun by turning sideways or even by turning his back to the infield.

PICK-OFF AND RUN DOWN PLAYS

Runners on 1st, 1st and 2nd, or bases loaded—1st baseman behind the runner*

RHP: He gets the sign, comes set and looks back to 2nd. When he sees the 1st baseman break, he turns and throws to 1st base, giving a not-too-hard *chest high throw.*

LHP: The pitcher gets the sign and comes set. When he lifts his leg, the 1st baseman races toward the bag and makes the tag. The throw should be the pitcher's best move, *chest high,* and not too hard.

*The 1st baseman must not play too deep.

THE DAYLIGHT PLAY—RUNNERS AT 2ND, 1ST AND 2ND, OR BASES LOADED:

The SS moves into a position behind the runner. When he feels the runner is far enough off the bag, he flashes an open glove so the pitcher can see it, and then breaks hard for the bag. The pitcher then wheels and throws a chest high throw over the bag. *The pitcher must give the SS a throw he can handle!*

THE PICK-OFF PLAY WITH THE 2ND BASEMAN:

This play is given by the 2nd baseman to the pitcher. The 2nd baseman closes his glove or wiggles his glove fingers. The pitcher acknowledges the sign by tapping his foot on the rubber; the 2nd baseman then alerts the CF that the play is on so he can charge.

The pitcher comes set, checks the runner. When he turns his head toward home, the 2nd baseman races to the bag. The pitcher wheels and throws a *chest high throw.* The CF is charging hard. *It is imperative that the pitcher gets the sign!*

THE 3RD TO 1ST PICK-OFF PLAY:

Done by RHP's only! Runners at 1st and 3rd, pitcher gets the sign from the 3rd baseman. Again, the sign used is a wiggle of the glove.* The pitcher acknowledges the sign by tapping on the rubber. *The 3rd baseman is the key to this play.* The pitcher comes set, steps toward 3rd. If the 3rd baseman's hands are down, the pitcher wheels and throws back to 1st. If his hands are up, he is telling the pitcher that the runner at 1st has broken for 2nd. The pitcher then wheels and locates the runner. *The pitcher should not hold the ball too long.*

THE WHEEL PLAY AT 2ND BASE:

The SS gives the sign to the pitcher. (The sign is a circular movement of the index finger on the throwing hand.) The pitcher acknowledges the sign by tapping on the rubber. The SS alerts the CF by placing his glove on the back of his head. The pitcher comes set, checks the runner at 2nd. When he lifts his leg, the SS breaks toward 2nd; the CF races in and the pitcher turns back toward 2nd. He *doesn't wheel around,* as in his normal move. (Example: The RHP wheels to his *right,* the LHP wheels to his *left.*) He gives the SS a *chest high throw.* This play is used with runners at 1st and 2nd, 2nd and 3rd, or with the bases loaded. It's a great play when the count is 3-and-2 and the runners are going.

*You will notice that, in most cases, the "signs" are not given. This was done to encourage each team to develop their own system for giving signs. Signs are easily picked up by the opposition so, obviously, each team's should be different.

DEFENSIVE ASSIGNMENTS

Men on 1st & 2nd—man on 1st
is picked off

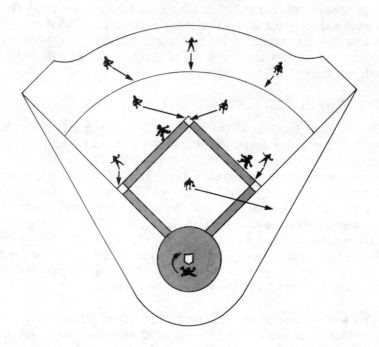

P: Back up 1st.

C: Cover home.

1ST. Cover 1st; be the tag man.

2ND: Cover 2nd; be the run-down man.

SS: Back up and cover 2nd with the possibility of being run-down man and tagger.

3RD: Cover 3rd to keep runner on 2nd from advancing.

RF: Come in to help back up 1st base.

CF: Help back up 2nd.

LF: Help back up 2nd.

Men on 1st & 2nd—man on 2nd is picked off

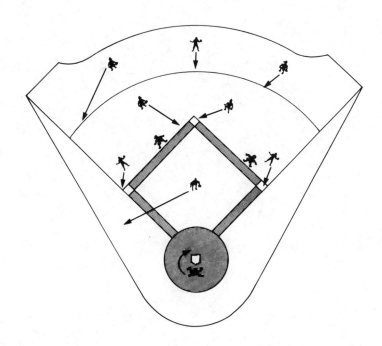

P: Back up 3rd.

C: Cover home.

1ST: Cover 1st.

2ND: Cover 2nd, with possibility of being run-down man and tagger.

SS: Cover 2nd; be tag man.

3RD: Cover 3rd; be the run-down man.

RF: Back up 2nd.

CF: Back up 2nd.

LF: Back up 3rd.

Men on 1st & 3rd—man on 3rd is picked off

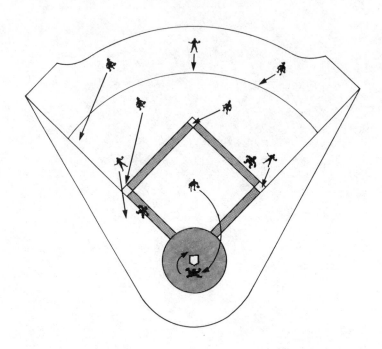

P: Cover home, back up catcher.

C: Cover home; be run-down man.

1ST: Cover 1st to keep the runner from advancing.

2ND: Cover 2nd; keep runner on 1st from advancing.

SS: Back up 3rd.

3RD: Cover 3rd; be the tag man.

RF: Back up 2nd.

CF: Back up 2nd.

LF: Back up 3rd.

RUN DOWN—INFIELD IN
(The follow-in play by the 3rd baseman.)

Man on 3rd tries to score on ground ball to the infield—infield is in

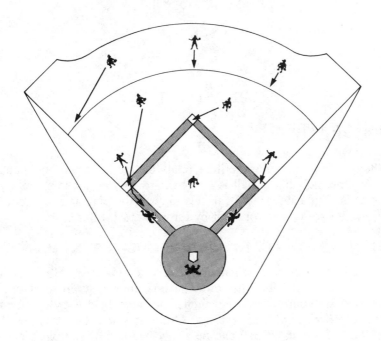

P: Cover home.

C: Cover home; be the run-down man.

1ST: Cover 1st.

2ND: Cover 2nd.

SS: Cover 3rd.

3RD: Follow about 10' behind runner off 3rd to make a quick tag; keep the batter from going to 2nd base.

LF: Back up 3rd.

CF: Back up 2nd.

RF: Back up behind 1st base.

BUNT SITUATIONS

MAN ON 1ST BASE:

1st or 3rd baseman:
When anticipating the sacrifice bunt, charge in when the pitcher throws the ball. If the ball is bunted hard to you, make the play to 2nd base. The catcher will call this play. If the play at 2nd is doubtful, make sure you get one out by throwing to 1st base.

RUNNERS AT 1ST AND 2ND—REGULAR BUNT PLAY:

The 3rd baseman's judgment is the key to this play. He is in full charge. Position is just inside of the line, four steps in front of the bag, and stationary. Tell the pitcher he must field the ball. *Know your pitcher's fielding ability!* One out *must* be made in this situation. The bunted ball can be easily handled by the pitcher. The 3rd baseman covers the base without taking his eyes off the ball. Tag the base with your right foot for better balance; be in position to make the throw to 1st.

On balls bunted down the line, the 3rd baseman charges the ball and runs the pitcher off. The play to 1st base is much easier for the 3rd baseman in this situation.

RUNNERS ON 1ST AND 2ND—USED IN LATE INNINGS:

This is a designed play and must be controlled by a sign. The pitcher, 1st baseman and 3rd baseman charge toward the batter. The SS shortens the distance, then races to cover the 3rd base bag. The 2nd baseman bluffs the runner, then covers 1st.

CHARGE PLAY:

Runner at 1st, RHP: He comes set, lets the 1st baseman take two steps toward home, then delivers a strike with something on it.

Runner at 1st, LHP: He comes set, lets the 1st baseman take two steps, then delivers a strike with something on it. The 1st baseman should be at least half-way before the ball is bunted. The sign used is the bill of the hat. *The 1st baseman must make sure the pitcher has the sign.* If he doesn't acknowledge the sign, call time out and tell him!

THE PICK-OFF PLAY IN A BUNT SITUATION:

This works better with a lefthanded pitcher and is usually used late in the ball game with the bunt in order. *RHP:* He comes set, lets the 1st baseman take two steps toward home, then turns and throws a *Chest high throw* to the 1st baseman. This is a *timing play* and must be practiced!

LHP: This is an outstanding play and should be used frequently. The pitcher comes set, allows the 1st baseman to take two steps toward home, and then gives his *best move* toward 1st. This is also a *timing play* and must be practiced! *The 1st baseman must make sure the pitcher has the sign.*

THE PICK-OFF IN A BUNT SITUATION WITH MEN ON 1ST AND 2ND:

Play #1: Use regular bunt defense.

Play #2: Pick-off at 2nd base: The pitcher comes set, lets the SS break toward 3rd. The 3rd baseman takes two steps toward home and so does the 1st baseman. The 2nd baseman breaks when the pitcher (after checking the runner) turns his head toward home. *Timing is essential;* this must be *practiced.* The 2nd baseman must cheat a little toward 2nd. He must also alert the center fielder that a pick-off play has been called.

THE RUN DOWN PLAY:

Important: Always run the runner back to the bag from which he came!

Try to start this play when the runner is half-way between the bases. Give the ball to the forward man and let him run the runner back to the base from which he came. The forward man should run hard at the runner, but not with a fake motion of the arm. The tagger should stay in front of his bag, and inside the baseline. This will give him the proper angle for the throw.

When the runner is about 10' from the tagger, the tagger should make a *break* toward the runner. This is the sign to the thrower that he should give the ball to the tagger on his first step. The thrower makes an *easy, chest-high toss*. When the play is executed correctly, one throw is all that's needed to get the runner at any base. The man without the ball must avoid interfering with the runner.

REMEMBER:

1. *Run the runner back to the bag from which he came.*

2. *Run the runner hard.*

3. *The tagger and the thrower stay inside the baseline.*

4. *The tagger must stay in front of his bag until making his break.*

5. *The thrower should make an easy, chest-high toss. Don't throw quick and hard!*

DEFENSIVE ASSIGNMENTS

BUNT SITUATIONS

Runner on 1st

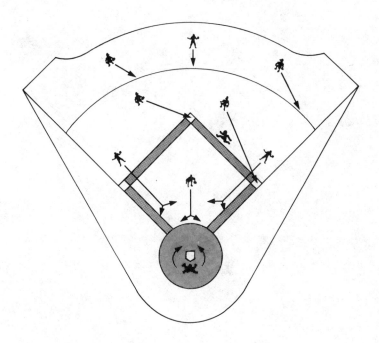

P: Break toward the plate after delivering the ball.

C: Field all bunts possible; *call the play.* Cover 3rd when 3rd baseman fields the bunt close to home.

1ST:* Cover the area between 1st and the mound.

2ND: Cover 1st; shorten position.

SS: Cover 2nd.

3RD: Cover area between 3rd and the mound.

RF: Back up 1st.

LF: Move in toward 2nd base.

CF: Back up 2nd.

*Lefthanded first baseman: Charge toward home, staying close to the foul line. *Always keep the bunted ball to your right.*

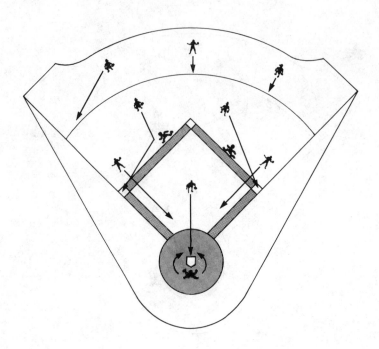

P: Break toward the plate.

C: Field bunts in front of plate or *call the play.*

1ST:* Charge toward the plate.

2ND: Bluff the runner, cover 1st base.

SS: Shorten distance toward 3rd. Get closer to the line, just over the shoulder of the runner, then race to cover 3rd.

3RD: Charge toward home.

Outfielders: Move to the infield area on *all* bunt situations.

Righthanded first baseman: Charge the bunted ball, keeping it to your left. This is done by charging toward the mound, then looping to your left.

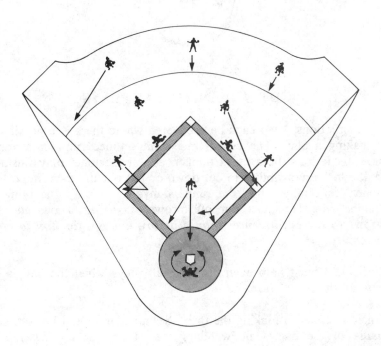

P: Break toward 3rd base line upon delivering the ball.

C: Field bunts in front of the plate; *call the play.*

1ST: Be responsible for all balls in the area between 1st in a direct line from the mound to home.

2ND: Cover 1st.

SS: Hold runner close to the bag before the pitch; cover 2nd.

3RD: Take position on the edge of the grass; *call the play,* whether the pitcher or 3rd baseman is to field the bunt.

RF: Back up 1st.

CF: Back up 2nd.

LF: Back up 3rd.

Your first objective is to retire the runner at 3rd, but one runner *must* be retired.

CUT OFF AND RELAY PLAYS

In all situations, keep each base covered where there is a possibility of making a play. The cut-off man's importance can't be stressed enough. He must be a quick thinker, able to decipher plays instantly. It's his responsibility to cut down or put out the most important runner, especially when the runners involved signify the tying or winning run. He must cut off throws, *assuring* a put-out. *All throws to the cut-off man should be low enough for him to handle easily.*

Outfielders must help each other on all plays when the ball is hit between them.

When a runner is making the turn, the infielder should be stationed *inside* of the bag while watching the runner tag the base. This makes the runner take a wider turn and increases the distance he must travel toward the next base. *Don't interfere with the runner by being too close to the base.*

CUT-OFF ASSIGNMENTS:

FOR THE 1ST BASEMAN:

You are the cut-off man on all base hits and fly ball scoring situations to *right and center field except* in these situations:

1. Single to right field between 1st and 2nd basemen with a runner on 2nd.

2. Single to right field between 1st and 2nd basemen with runners on 1st and 2nd.

3. A double, or possible triple down the right field line with a runner on 1st.

When 1st base is occupied, you are the cut-off man on *all extra base hits, except* when you have a double or possible triple down the right field line with a runner on 1st. In this situation, you are a trailer.

FOR THE 2ND BASEMAN:

You must cover 1st on these situations:

1. Single to right field with a runner on 2nd.

2. Single to right field between 1st and 2nd.

3. Single to right field between 1st and 2nd basemen with runners on 1st and 2nd.

FOR THE 3RD BASEMAN:

You are the cut-off man in these situations:

1. Single to left field with runner in scoring position.

2. Single to left field with runner in scoring position, judgment play, the throw should go to 2nd base.

3. Fly ball situations to left field with a runner on 3rd base.

FOR PITCHERS:

You are the cut-off man in two situations:

1. Pop fly in right field area.

2. Pop fly in left field area.

DEFENSIVE ASSIGNMENTS

SINGLE TO LEFT FIELD

No one on base

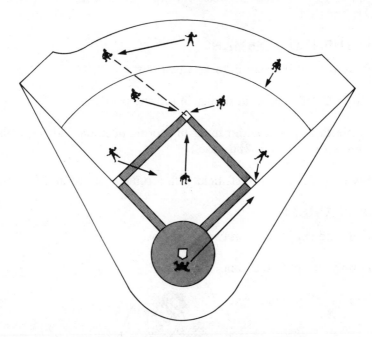

P: Move half-way between mound and 2nd.

C: Follow runner to 1st base.

1ST: Make sure the runner tags the base, then cover 1st.

2ND: Back up Lf's throw to SS.

SS: Cover 2nd; take throw from LF when possible.

3RD: Protect area around 3rd base.

LF: Get the ball.

CF: Back up LF.

RF: Move in toward 1st base.

SINGLE TO LEFT FIELD

Man on 1st

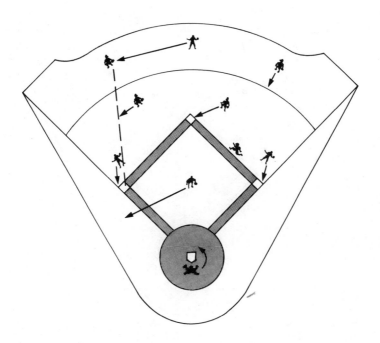

P: Back up 3rd.

C: Protect home.

1ST: Cover 1st.

2ND: Cover 2nd.

SS: Move into position to be cut-off man on throw to 3rd base.

3RD: Cover 3rd.

CF: Back up LF.

RF: Move in toward the infield.

SINGLE TO LEFT
(This is a judgment play.)

Man on 2nd, hitter is tying run

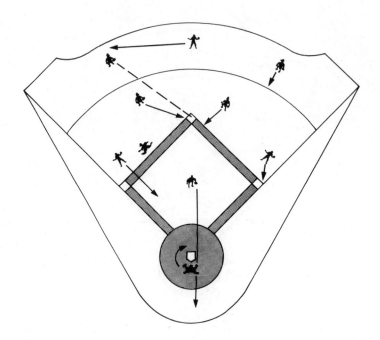

P: Move off mound to back up home in case the LF'er makes the throw to the plate.

C: Cover home.

1ST: Cover 1st.

2ND: Back up 2nd.

SS: Cover 2nd base.

3RD: Move to position to be cut-off man in case the LF throws home.

LF: Make low throw to 2nd to keep the batter from advancing to scoring position.

CF: Back up LF.

RF: Help back up 2nd base.

Never let the tying run into scoring position at 2ND base by making a foolish throw to the plate!!

SINGLE TO LEFT
(Ball hit between SS & 3rd base)

Man on 2nd, or 2nd & 3rd

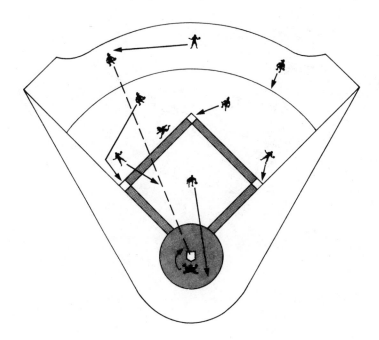

P: Back up home.

C: Cover home.

1ST: Cover 1st.

2ND: Cover 2nd.

SS: If the 3rd baseman can't recover, you become cut-off man. Otherwise, cover 3rd base.

3RD: Cut-off man. Take position about 45' from home in line with the LF'er and home plate.

LF: Throw to the plate.

CF: Back up LF.

RF: Back up 2nd.

DOUBLE, POSSIBLE TRIPLE
DOWN LEFT FIELD LINE

Man on 1st

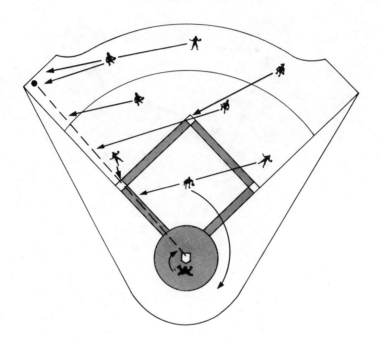

P: Back up home.

C: Cover home.

1ST: Cut-off man.

2ND: Become trailer behind the SS.

SS: Relay man.

3RD: Cover 3rd.

LF: Get the ball.

CF: Back up LF.

RF: Cover 2nd.

DOUBLE POSSIBLE TRIPLE
TO LEFT CENTER
No one on, man on 2nd or 3rd, or men on 2nd & 3rd

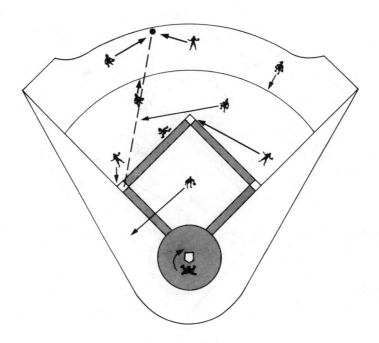

P: Back up 3rd in line with throw.

C: Protect home.

1ST: Trail runner to 2nd, cover the bag. Be ready for a play if the runner rounds the base too far.

2ND: Trail 30' behind the SS in line with 3rd.

SS: Go to a spot in left center, become the relay man.

3RD: Cover 3rd; stand on left side of the bag.

LF: Get the ball.

CF: Back up LF.

RF: Move in toward 2nd base.

DOUBLE, POSSIBLE TRIPLE TO LEFT CENTER

Man on 1st, 1st & 2nd, or bases loaded

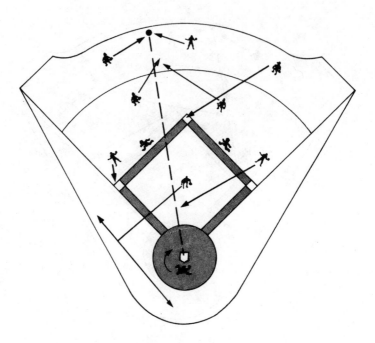

P: Go half-way between home and 3rd, then back up the base where the throw is going.

C: Protect home.

1ST: Cut-off man.

2ND: Trail 30' between the SS in line with 3rd base.

SS: Go to a spot in left-center and be the relay man.

3RD: Cover 3rd; stand on left side of the bag.

CF: Back up LF.

RF: Cover 2nd.

SINGLE TO LEFT FIELD

Man on 2nd, 1st & 2nd, or bases loaded

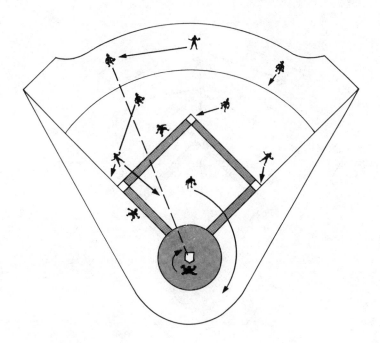

P: Back up home.

C: Cover home.

1ST: Cover 1st.

2ND: Cover 2nd.

SS: Cover 3rd.

3RD: Cut-off man.

CF: Back up LF.

RF: Move in toward 2nd base.

SINGLE TO CENTER FIELD

No one on base

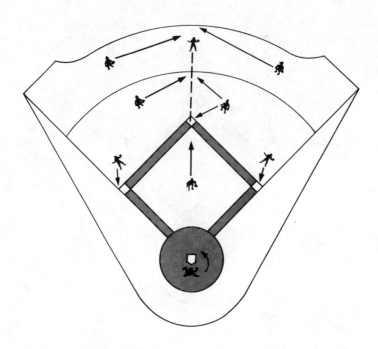

P: Move half-way between the mound and 2nd base.

1ST: Make sure the runner tags the bag, then cover 1st.

2ND: Back up the CF's throw to SS, then cover 2nd.

SS: Follow the ball, take the throw from the CF'er. You should be 30-40' from the bag.

3RD: Protect 3rd.

CF: Get the ball.

RF & LF: Back up the CF'er.

SINGLE TO CENTER

Man on 1st

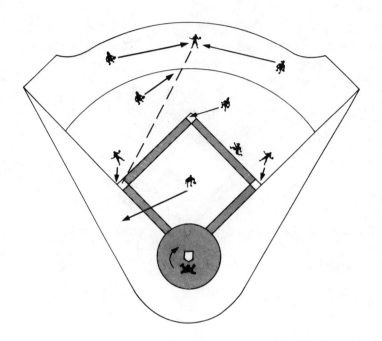

P: Back up 3rd.

C: Protect home.

1ST: Cover 1st base.

2ND: Cover 2nd base.

SS: Cut-off man on throw from CF to 3rd.

3RD: Cover 3rd base.

LF & RF: Back up CF.

SINGLE TO CENTER FIELD

Men on 1st and 2nd or bases loaded

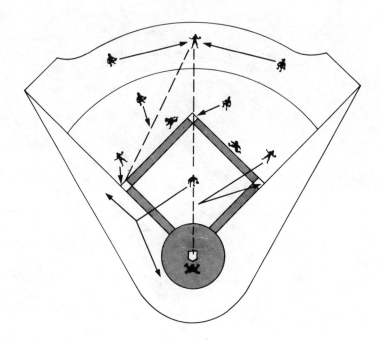

P: Go half-way between home and 3rd, then back up the base where the throw is going.

C: Cover home.

1ST: Move into a spot 45' from home in line with the throw; be the cut-off man. If throw goes to 3rd, go back to cover 1st.

2ND: Cover 2nd base.

SS: Cut-off man for possible throw to 3rd base.

3RD: Cover 3rd base.

LF: Back up CF.

RF: Back up CF.

SINGLE TO CENTER FIELD

Man on 2nd, men on 2nd & 3rd

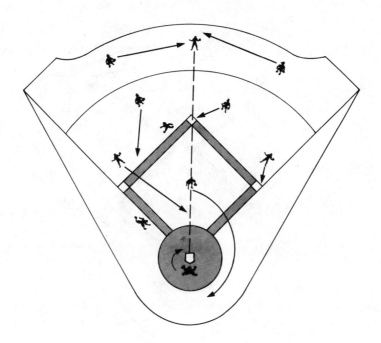

P: Back up home.

C: Cover home.

1ST: Cover 1st.

2ND: Go after the ball; then go back and cover 2nd.

SS: Go after the ball; then trail the runner to 3rd.

3RD: Cut-off man.

LF: Back up CF.

RF: Back up CF.

SINGLE TO RIGHT FIELD

No one on base

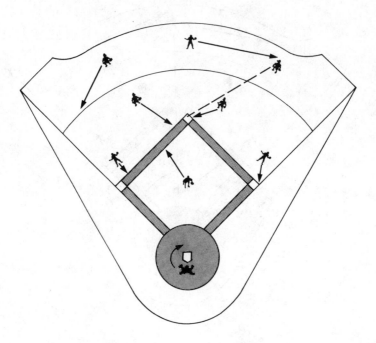

P: Move half-way between the mound and 2nd base.

C: Protect home.

1ST: Make sure the runner tags the bag when making the turn, then cover 1st.

2ND: Cover 2nd to take throw from RF.

SS: Back up RF throw to the 2nd baseman.

3RD: Protect 3rd.

CF: Back up RF.

LF: Move in toward 3rd base.

SINGLE TO RIGHT FIELD

Man on 1st, or 1st & 3rd

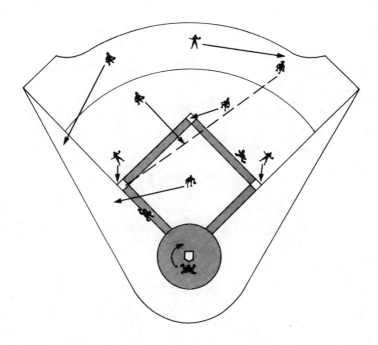

P: Back up 3rd, in line with the throw.

C: Protect home.

1ST: Cover 1st. Make sure the runner tags the bag.

2ND: Cover 2nd. Make sure the runner tags the bag.

SS: Station yourself about 45' from 3rd base, in a direct line from 3rd to the outfielder fielding the ball.

3RD: Cover 3rd.

LF: Move toward 3rd.

CF: Back up RF.

SINGLE TO RIGHT FIELD

Man on 2nd, men or 2nd & 3rd

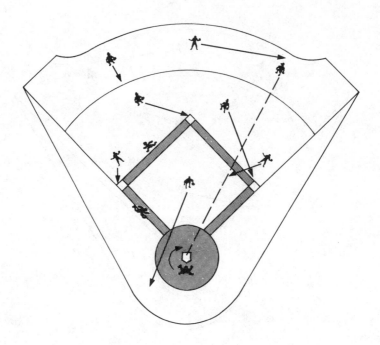

P: Back up home.

C: Cover home.

1ST: Go 45' from home plate to become cut-off man.

2ND: Cover 1st.

SS: Cover 2nd.

3RD: Cover 3rd.

LF: Move in toward 2nd base.

CF: Back up RF.

SINGLE TO RIGHT FIELD
(Between 1st & 2nd)

Men on 1st & 2nd, or bases loaded

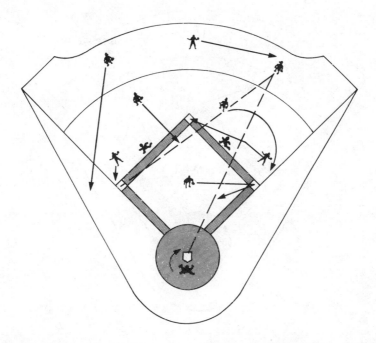

P: Start to cover 1st, when the ball goes through, retreat to be the cut-off man.

C: Cover home.

1ST: When you can't field the ball, go on and cover 2nd.

2ND: When you can't field the ball, go on and cover 1st.

SS: Cut-off man for possible throw to 3rd base.

3RD: Cover 3rd.

LF: Move into area behind 3rd to back up.

CF: Back up RF.

SINGLE TO RIGHT FIELD
(Between 1st & 2nd basemen)

Man on 2nd, or men on 2nd & 3rd

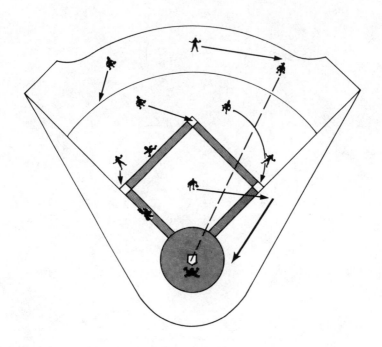

P: Start to cover 1st, then back up home plate

C: Cover home.

1ST: After attempting to field the ball, become the cut-off man.

2ND: After attempting to field the ball, continue to cover 1st base.

SS: Cover 2nd.

3RD: Cover 3rd.

LF: Move into the area behind 3rd.

CF: Back up RF, move in toward 2nd after the ball is fielded.

SINGLE TO RIGHT FIELD

Men on 1st & 2nd, or 1st, 2nd & 3rd

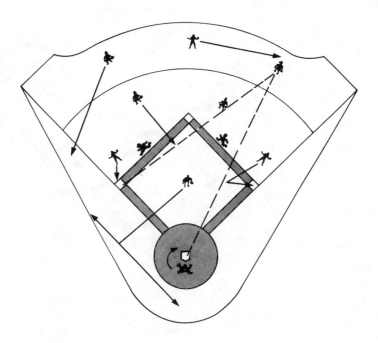

P: Go half-way between 3rd and home to see where the throw will go.

C: Cover home.

1ST: Cut-off man if throw is made to the plate. If throw goes to 3rd, cover 1st.

2ND: Cover 2nd.

SS: Cut-off man for throw to 3rd base.

3RD: Cover 3rd.

LF: Move to a point near the line and back up 3rd base.

CF: Back up RF.

RF: Make a low throw to the SS to keep the tying or winning run from going to 3rd.

Always keep the tying run from going to 3rd with less than two out. Give the opposing teem two runs to keep the tying run at 2nd. *Never make a foolish throw to the plate!*

DOUBLE, POSSIBLE TRIPLE
DOWN RIGHT FIELD LINE

No one on

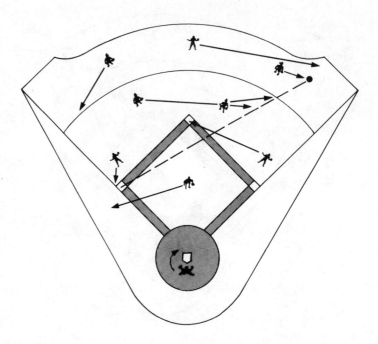

P: Back up 3rd.

C: Protect home.

1ST: Trail runner to 2nd base.

2ND: Relay man.

SS: Trail relay man.

3RD: Cover 3rd.

LF: Move into area behind 3rd base.

CF: Back up RF.

DOUBLE, POSSIBLE TRIPLE
DOWN RIGHT FIELD LINE

Man on 1st

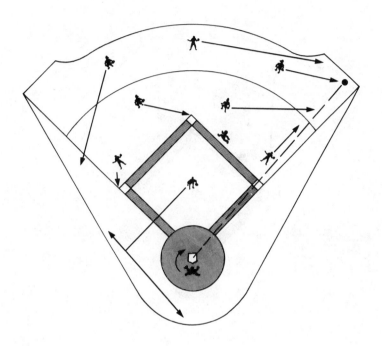

P: Go half-way between 3rd and home to see where the throw is going.

C: Cover home.

1ST: Trail 2nd baseman; stay about 30' behind him.

2ND: Relay man. Go to a spot in RF along the foul line, in line with the RF'er and home.

SS: Cover 2nd.

3RD: Cover 3rd.

LF: Move in toward 3rd base.

CF: Back up RF.

DOUBLE, POSSIBLE TRIPLE
TO RIGHT CENTER FIELD

No one on, man on 3rd, or men on 2nd & 3rd

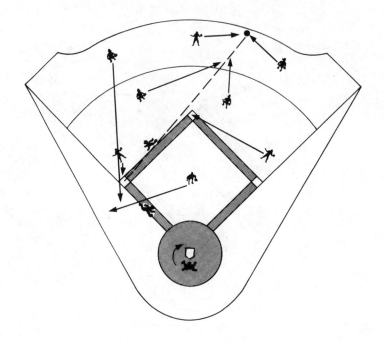

P: Back up 3rd, get as deep as possible.

C: Protect home.

1ST: Trail runner to 2nd, cover the bag. Be ready for a play at that base.

2ND: Go to a spot in CF (in line with 3rd) to become relay man.

SS: Trail 30' behind the 2nd baseman, in line with 3rd base.

3RD: Cover 3rd.

LF: Move in toward 3rd.

RF: Back up CF.

DOUBLE, POSSIBLE TRIPLE, TO RIGHT CENTER

Man on 1st, & 2nd, or bases loaded

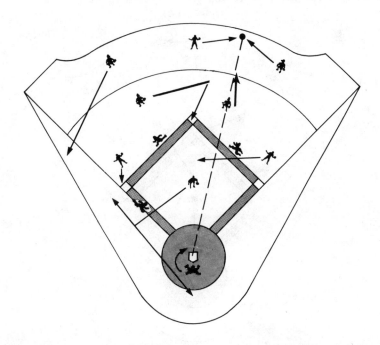

P: Go half way between 3rd and home to see where the throw is coming, then back up either base.

C: Cover home.

1ST: Cut-off man.

2ND: Relay man.

SS: Trail relay man then return to cover 2nd base.

3RD: Cover 3rd.

LF: Move into area behind 3rd base.

RF & CF: Go after the ball.

POP-FLY SITUATIONS

FOUL HIT BEHIND THE PLATE

Runners on 1st & 3rd, less than 2 out. Both runners tag up; runner on 1st breaks for 2nd. If there's no cut-off man, the runner on 3rd will score when the catcher makes his throw to 2nd.

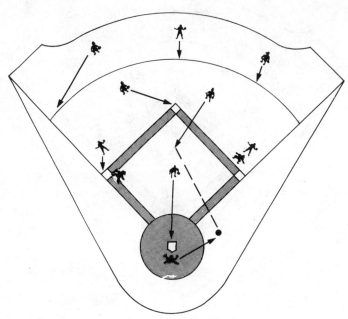

P: Cover home.

C: Catch pop-up; throw to cut-off man.

1ST: Help on pop-up.

2ND: Cut-off man behind the pitcher's mound.

SS: Cover 2nd.

3RD: Cover 3rd base.

LF: Come in, help back up short and 3rd.

CF: Back up 2nd.

RF: Cover 1st base.

POP-FLY HIT BEHIND 1ST BASE

Runners on 1st & 3rd, no outs; both runners tag up. The runner on 1st breaks for 2nd.

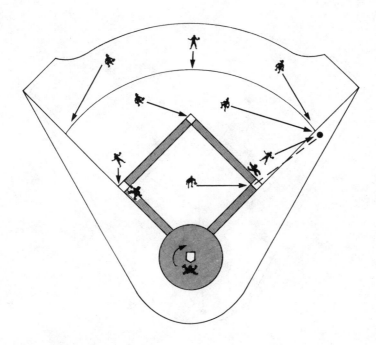

P: Come to a point near 1st base and be the cut-off man.

C: Cover home.

1ST: Catch the pop-up; throw to pitcher.

2ND: Also go after pop-up, then hustle to cover 1st.

SS: Cover 2nd.

3RD: Cover 3rd.

LF: Move to area behind 3rd for back-up man.

CF: Back up 2nd.
RF: Move in, help catch the pop-up.

DEFENSIVE ASSIGNMENTS

WILD PITCHES AND PASSED BALLS
Runner on 3rd, 1st, & 3rd or Bases Loaded

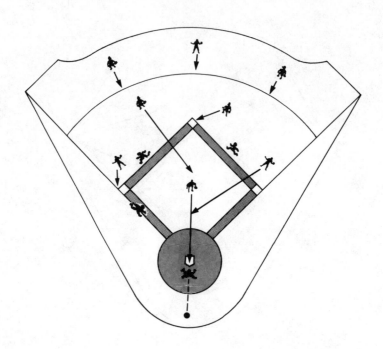

P: Cover home plate.

C: Retrieve the ball.

1ST: Back up home plate.

2ND: Cover 2nd base.

SS: Back up behind the mound.

3RD: Cover 3rd base.

Outfielders: Move toward the infield area to help where needed.

COMMON BASEBALL TERMS

BALK:

A "balk" is an illegal move by the pitcher with one or more runners on base. Although there are thirteen different ways a pitcher can balk, here are the two most common examples for right and left handed pitchers:

1. Righthanded pitcher: The most common balk is an exaggerated shoulder movement in and attempt to deceive the runner into thinking the pitcher's going to throw either to home or to a base.

A form of deception which is now illegal is knee movement by the pitcher. For example, Don Drysdale would come to the set position, and by bending his left knee (which, to a base runner, looked like he was going to throw to the plate), he would then spin on his back foot and throw to first base in an attempt to pick off the runner.

To avoid this type of deception on the rubber, the National League initiated a rule that states the right foot must clear the rubber, and the pitcher must step towards first base or a "balk" will be called.

2. For a left-handed pitcher: The pitcher comes set, steps toward home and throws to first. Another form of deception for a left handed pitcher is that when he comes set, his foot crosses the plain of the rubber. The rule states that he must now throw home. However, a lefthander with a good move can come close to crossing the plain and then throw to first in an attempt to pick off the runner. This is always a contraversial call because it is the umpire's decision whether or not the pitcher actually crossed the plain.

Whether a pitcher is right or left handed, the official rules of baseball dictate that it is illegal to change or alter one's delivery time to the plate in an attempt to decieve a baserunner. For example, once the pitcher has received the signal from the catcher, he must make a legitimate pause before he throws to the plate.

From the time the pitcher begins his movement toward the plate, a right handed pitcher should be 1.3 to 1.35 seconds to the plate, in order to give the catcher a decent opportunity to throw out a base-stealer. For a left handed pitcher with a decent move to first, 1.4 seconds to the plate is sufficient.

BATTING AVERAGE:

The "Batting Average" shows the percentage of times a batter gets a hit. To find a player's batting average, divide the number of hits by the number of official times at bat. Carry the answer three decimal places.

Example: In four games, Tom came to the plate fifteen times. He walked twice and he sacrificed once, leaving him with twelve official at-bats. He struck out twice, and flew out once, making three outs in twelve official at-bats. The number of hits Tom had (9) divided by the number of official at-bats (12) equals 0.750. Carried three decimal places, gives Tom an official Batting Average of 750 for that game.

DOUBLE PLAY:

A "Double Play" occurs when fielders put out two opponents in one play. For example, with a runner at first base, the batter hits a ground ball to the shortstop who fields the ball, and throws to the second baseman. The second baseman then steps on the bag for the first out and throws to first base to complete the double play. If you were to score that play, it would be "6-4-3".

EARNED-RUN AVERAGE:

"ERA" is the average number of earned runs scored against a pitcher every nine innings. An earned-run is a run that is scored without the aid of an error. To find a pitcher's ERA, divide the number of innings he pitched by nine. Now, divide that total into the number of earned runs the pitcher allowed. Carry the answer two decimal places.

For example, Tom pitched six innings and gave up two earned runs. Divide six (the number of innings pitched) by nine (the total number of innings):

$$\frac{0.67}{9 \overline{\smash{\big)}\, 6.00}}$$

Now, divide that answer (0.67) into two (the total number of earned runs the pitcher allowed):

$$67\overline{\smash{)}2.00}^{\displaystyle 2.99}$$

Tom's ERA is 2.99.

HIT AND RUN PLAY:

A hit-and-run play happens when the runner on first base breaks toward second as soon as the ball is released by the pitcher, thus forcing the second baseman or shortstop to cover second base. The batter then attempts to hit a ground ball through the "hole" left open by the infielder. A hit and run play is used primarily with contact hitters. The hitter is usually ahead in the count, (2 and 1) so the pitcher has to throw a strike.

SQUEEZE PLAY:

A squeeze play occurs when the batter bunts the ball in order to score a runner from third base.

RUN BATTED IN:

If a run (or runs) score because of a batter's base hit, out (except a double play), sacrifice, walk, or because he is hit by a pitch, the batter receives an RBI, or "run batted in". A batter does NOT receive an RBI when the run scores as a result of an error or passed ball.

SACRIFICE:

A Sacrifice occurs when a batter bunts a ball and is put out but still enables a base runner to advance. If the batter flies out and a run scores from third base AFTER the catch is made, the batter receives a Sacrifice Fly. When determining batting average, a sacrifice does not count as an official time at bat.

FIELDER'S CHOICE:

When a ground ball is hit with a man on base, a fielder may choose to put out the on-base runner instead of the batter, allowing the batter to reach a base safely. If a run scores on a Fielder's Choice, the batter receives an RBI.

KEEPING SCORE

Baseball is more interesting to watch if one knows how to keep score correctly. An accurate account of the play-by-play enables a player, coach or spectator to study individual hitters and pitchers performances even weeks after a game is played.

Below are the most common abbreviations and numbers used by professional Sportswriters when keeping score:

ABBREVIATIONS FOR ACTION DURING PLAY

W "Walk"	E "Error"	R "Runs"	
B "Balk"	O "Out"	F "Foul Out"	
FO "Force-Out"	PB "Passed Ball"	WP "Wild Pitch"	
HP "Hit by Pitch"	DP "Double Play"	TP "Tripple Play"	
SB "Stolen Base"	OS "Out Stealing"		
H "Hits"	RBI "Runs Batted In"		
Sac "Sacrifice"	SF "Sacrifice Fly"		
G "Ground Ball"	FC "Fileder's Choice		
(An unassisted	K (Backwards) "Called Third Strike"		
infield out.)	K "Strike Out"		

POSITION NUMBERS OF PLAYERS

1 Pitcher	4 Second Baseman	7 Left Fielder
2 Catcher	5 Third Baseman	8 Center Fielder
3 First Baseman	6 Shortstop	9 Right Fielder

Most Sporting Goods stores sell official Baseball Scorebooks. An example of official game-scoring, and a play-by-play explanation of each inning is on the following pages.

PLAYERS	POS	B/T	1	2	3	4	5	6	7	8	9	10
1. McKay	3		(2B)		RBI 1; (1B)		K (1)	G-3 (2)		RBI 1; (1B)		
SUB.												
2. Stanley	6		RBI 1; (3); (1B)		K (1)		(BB)	F7 (3)		(2); FC		
SUB.												
3. Donnenfield	4		K (1)		RBI 1; (3B)		(1B)		4-3 (1)	6-4-3 (2) (3)		
SUB.												
4. Snuffer	2		ꓘ (2)		5-3 (2)		RBI 1; (SAC); G-3 (2)		(BB)		WP	
SUB.												
5. Hardin	7		G-4 (3)		ꓘ (3)		E5		F8 (2)		(1B)	
SUB.												
6. Lindley	8			(1B)		(1); E6	K (3)		6-3 (3)		(SAC); G-3 (1)	
SUB.												
7. Lolli	5			6-4-3 (1) (2)		6-4-3 (1) (2)		RBI 1; (HR)		(BB)	RBI 2; F8 (2)	
SUB.												
8. Zabek	9			K (3)		ꓘ (3)		(1B)		(2B)	G-3 (3)	
SUB.												
9. Bolton	1				(2B)			F8 (1)		(SAC); F9 (1)		
SUB.												

PLAY-BY-PLAY

FIRST INNING:

McKay hits a double and scores on Stanley's single.

Stanley gets a single, and one run-batted-in (RBI).

Donnenfield strikes out swinging for the first out of the inning.

Snuffer strikes out looking, causing out number two.

Hardin hits a ground ball to the second baseman and Stanley's tagged out at second base for the third out of the inning.

At the end of the first inning, one Run scores on two Hits; there is one man Left On Base and there were no errors.

SECOND INNING:

Lindley singles.

Lolli hits into a double play: Lindley is tagged out at second for the first out of the inning. The second baseman throws to first and the first baseman, who gets Lolli at the bag for the second out of the inning.

Zabek strikes out to end the inning.

In the second inning, no Runs scored. There was one Hit, one man Left On Base and no Errors.

THIRD INNING:

Bolton leads off the inning with a double and scores on McKay's single.

McKay singles and gets an RBI.

Stanley strikes out swinging for the first out of the inning.

Donnenfield triples, scoring McKay; he gets an RBI.

Snuffer hits a ground ball to the third baseman, who throws to first for the second out.

Hardin strikes out looking to end the inning.

In the third inning, two Runs scored on three Hits. There was one man Left On Base and no Errors.

FOURTH INNING:

The shortstop commits an error, allowing Lindley to go to first base.

Lolli hits into a double play. The shortstop fields the ball and throws to the second baseman, who tags Lindley for the first out. The second baseman throws to first to get Lolli for the second out.

Zabek strikes out looking to end the inning.

In the fourth inning, there are no Runs, No Hits, no one Left on Base, and one Error.

FIFTH INNING:

McKay strikes out.

Stanley walks and goes to second base on Donnenfield's single.

Donnenfield singles.

Snuffer sacrifices the runners for the second out. Stanley advances to third, Donnenfield to second.

Hardin reaches first on an error by the third baseman and Stanley scores. Donnenfield goes to third on the error.

Lindley strikes out to end the inning.

In the fifth inning, one (unearned) Run scores on one Hit; there are two men Left On Base and there was one Error.

SIXTH INNING:

Lolli hits a Home Run, receives an RBI.

Zabek singles.

Bolton flies out to center field for the first out.

McKay grounds out to the first baseman for the second out.

Stanley flies out to left field.

In the sixth inning, one Run scores on 2 Hits; there was one man Left On Base and no Errors.

SEVENTH INNING:

Donnenfield hits to the second baseman, who throws to first for the first out.

Snuffer triples.

Hardin flies out to center for the second out.

Lindley grounds to the shortstop who throws to first base to end the inning.

In the seventh inning, no Runs scored. There were no Hits, one man Left on Base, and no Errors.

EIGHTH INNING:

Lolli draws a walk, and goes to third on Zabek's double.

Bolton hits a Sacrifice Fly to right field, scoring Lolli. Bolton makes the first out, but is credited with an RBI because Lolli scores on his Sacrifice.

McKay singles, scoring Zabek; he also receives an RBI.

Stanley reaches first on a fielder's choice, McKay advances to second base.

Donnenfield hits into a double play. Stanley is tagged out at second for out number two, the second baseman throws to first to get Donnenfield for the third and final out.

In the eighth inning, there were two Runs on two Hits, there was one man Left on Base and no errors.

NINTH INNING:

Snuffer is Hit by a Pitch (HP) and takes first base.

Hardin singles, advancing Snuffer to second.

Lindley bunts, sacrificing the runners to third and second respectively.

Lolli flies out to the center fielder. This is a sacrifice fly and does not count as a time at bat. Lolli receives two RBI's.

Zabek grounds out to the first baseman to end the inning.

In the ninth inning, two Runs scored on one Hit. There was no one Left On Base and there were no errors.

NOTES

NOTES

NOTES

NOTES

Please send me_____copies of THE COMPLETE INSTRUCTIONAL BASEBALL MANUAL. I have enclosed $9.95 per copy, plus $1.00 per copy for postage and insurance.

NAME_____

ADDRESS_____
        (Number)   (Street)

_____
(City)   (State)   (Zip)

I WOULD LIKE INFORMATION ON QUANTITY DISCOUNTS_____

SEND CHECK OR MONEY ORDER TO:

THE COMPLETE INSTRUCTIONAL BASEBALL MANUAL
THE STANLEY COMPANY, INC.
8711 EAST PINNACLE PEAK ROAD
SCOTTSDALE, ARIZONA
85255

Please allow two weeks for delivery. Arizona residents add 6% sales tax.

This Large Print Book carries the
Seal of Approval of N.A.V.H.

Center Point
Large Print

thirsty

fallen, resting her cheek against her arms. Markus hung back, still watching. He doubted she'd be much trouble for him in her current state.

Black hair slid over her shoulder, reminding him so much of the one he loved. He tried to shove away the image of the perfect face, sweet smile, supple skin. Each time he remembered her, it drove him deeper into despair. This girl looked so much like her he could hardly keep from calling out her name.

Kimana.

There, in the dim of twilight, he remembered her lovely face and couldn't bury his longing.

"Nina!" The shout came from a male who, judging from the crack in his voice, wasn't quite through puberty. Only sixteen or seventeen.

Markus tensed, his reflexes poised for response, but thankfully the control he'd cultivated over years returned.

"Ugh. Stephan," the girl mumbled without lifting her head or opening her eyes.

Markus moved quickly into the shadow of an evergreen as a boy crashed through the trees and stumbled over the girl. He caught his balance, then knelt beside her. "Nina, are you okay?"

"Go away."

"I'm not leaving you out here alone." The boy touched her shoulder.

She slapped at him without landing a blow. "Keep your hands off me."

11

The boy reached out again. She shot up to her knees and stared at him, her eyes wild, her hair tangled. The combination made her look untamed. His stomach tightened.

"I said stay away!"

The kid raised his hands in surrender. He stood slowly, as though a string attached to his shoulders pulled him to his feet. "I'll take you back to the river."

"I don't need your help." She used a couple of slurred profanities to articulate her opinion of him.

He paused. "I can't leave you here all by yourself."

"A little late to care about me now, isn't it?"

Shoving his hands into the front pockets of his loose-fitting jeans, the boy released a frustrated sigh. "Nina . . ."

"Just go!"

Anger flashed across his half-man, half-boy face. "Fine. I'm going."

Markus watched them. She was behaving foolishly. The boy genuinely wanted to help her, Markus believed. He couldn't feel that way about his own motivations.

The girl lay back, clearly dismissing the kid. Markus almost felt sorry for him. Shaking his head, the boy backed away reluctantly.

When he had disappeared from sight, Markus stepped softly across the crackling leaves and branches. The girl's even breathing indicated she'd either passed out or fallen asleep. Either way, she was unconscious. Markus squatted next to her.

The girl sighed, and Markus's gaze darted to her round face. Dark, straight hair streamed down her neck, sticking to her wet cheeks. His pulse thudded in his throat as he stared at her. Long, wet lashes grazed the tops of her cheeks.

The lines of time converged, and he saw his Indian princess lying there on the forest floor. He longed for her in a way that made his gut tighten and his heart reach out to this girl who reminded him so much of her.

Perhaps for that reason, he scooped her into his arms and began to walk toward his cave. She couldn't have weighed more than a hundred pounds. So small and helpless. Her head lolled back over his arm, exposing the full length of her neck. A long, slow shudder made its way up his body. With discipline cultivated over many years, he forced his attention to the path before him.

He reached his cave quickly and moved through the dark to a thick pallet of down-filled sleeping bags and quilts. Gently, almost reverently, he lowered the girl. Her lips parted, releasing a sigh.

He held his breath. If she woke and started screaming, he'd have no choice but to kill her. The thought repulsed him. Kimana's face seemed to mold into hers, and he fingered a strand of the silky black hair. If only he'd had this control back then.

She reeked of booze. He'd never cared for the smell or taste of alcohol, but the other scent wafting from her played havoc with his senses.

He paced the cave, struggling for control, his resolve slipping. A man could only take so much. Instinct, strong and without reason, took over, and he lost his battle. He knelt over her, reached out his forefinger, and drew a line down the side of her neck. His heart rate picked up in anticipation, like a young lover preparing for a first kiss.

Her eyes opened and looked up at him, dulled and confused. She moaned and her eyelids fluttered, then closed once more.

Easy, compliant prey. So why did he hesitate?

Her high cheekbones and full lips reminded him so much of Kimana, he hurt.

He drew back his emotions. He was being a fool. This girl was not the love he'd lost. She was nothing more than a child who'd had too much to drink and gotten herself into a situation she could not control. It was time to end this.

In the distance, he heard frantic cries. "Cops! Get out of here!" Engines fired, and he heard the sound of tires spitting gravel and sand as the teens abandoned the party. He glanced back at the girl. Didn't they know she was missing?

14

He made a quick decision—not at all difficult —and took her in his arms once more. She whimpered and snuggled closer. Her breath seeped through his shirt, warming the flesh just above his heart. Pressing her head close to his chest, he sped down the ravine to the riverbank and laid her next to the still burning campfire. The police would find her. She might get into some trouble, but if he kept her with him much longer, he wouldn't be able to control his hunger. As it was, he'd spent too much time watching her. Her scent lingered on his arms, his chest.

Moments later, he watched from the trees above the bank as two police cars skidded to a halt and four officers jumped out. They looked around, clearly disappointed to have been thwarted in their effort to bust the group of wayward teens. A middle-aged male officer noticed the girl.

"Who is it, Dan?" another officer called out.

"One of the Parker girls."

"She alive?"

"Just passed out."

One of the cops snorted. "Apple don't fall far from the tree."

"She's just a kid, Tony. Lots of kids party and drink too much. Doesn't mean they're going to be the town drunk."

"Don't mean she ain't, either."

"You two shut up and call the paramedics. She

15

isn't moving at all. I want to get her checked out before we send her home to sleep it off."

From his perch, Markus waited, watching over the beautiful girl. He stayed until the lights of the ambulance flashed through the trees as it sped away.

Long after she was gone, her scent lingered in his clothing, and he could still feel her warm breath and the weight of her small body in his arms.

CHAPTER ONE

*I went up in a hot-air balloon once,
when I was ten. The fair had come to
Abbey Hills, and all the kids were
buzzing about the ride. Everyone
would be talking about it the next
day, and I was determined that, for
once, I'd have something to talk about
too.*

*The thing was, I knew I'd never get
to go if I asked, so I snatched five
dollars from Mom's purse and went
anyway. Mom blamed Dad. He'd
taken her last five dollars before
when the shakes got the better of him
and the call of whiskey grew too loud
to ignore. He never even defended
himself against the accusation. Just
apologized and promised to do better.
I felt a little guilty about that, but
nothing could have kept me from that
balloon ride.*

*I knew I'd made a mistake the
second I climbed into the basket and
outrageous fear took hold of my gut.
I could have gotten off before the*

*rope released and lift took over, but
I didn't.
Good choices aren't my strong suit.*

F unny how much a person could sober up
between last call and time to call a cab. An
hour ago, when Nina had devised the brilliant
idea of surprising Hunt and spending Christmas
with him and the kids, she'd confidently imagined
the warmth of his open arms. But now, as she
stood on his doorstep watching the cab drive
away into the dark, wee hours of the morning,
she realized it had been an incredibly dumb
idea. That was the problem with being only a
little drunk—a girl was clear enough to see how
stupid she was but not clear enough to make a
smart decision.

An icy splash of wind shot across the porch,
making her shiver as she waffled between knocking and risking the disgusted look on Hunt's face
and running down the street in three-inch heels
after the cab that had just rounded the corner.

Resolute, she ignored the voice telling her to
sit on the porch all night and freeze to death. In
the morning, Hunt would find her frozen corpse,
and then wouldn't everyone be sorry for the way
they'd treated her?

She knocked, taking extra care to avoid brushing against the eleven-year-old Christmas wreath
—still as ugly as the day Hunt's mother had given

it to her. Stomping her feet on the porch, she hugged her body to ward off the cold. Patience had never been her thing. And at thirty-four years old, she wasn't likely to develop any, so everyone could just deal with it.

Come on, Hunt. It's the North Pole out here.

She raised her fist again. The porch light snapped on just as she was about to knock a second time.

Relief poured through her, feeling a lot like that first warm rush of a semi-dry white wine. Pushing back her hair, she arranged her mouth into the smile she knew showed off her dimple best.

Please be happy to see me. A foolish hope, she knew, considering he had divorced her six months ago.

In view of that, she'd settle for *not ticked.*

The door opened. Nina's stomach took a dive at Hunt's dark, sleep-tossed hair. Why did he have to look so good?

He leaned against the door frame, arms crossed. "It's two in the morning. What do you think you're doing?"

Not the greeting she'd been praying for, but then prayer wasn't really her thing. "You invited me for Christmas Eve." Her hands trembled. She shoved them into the pockets of her black leather jacket. It had been a Christmas present from him last year, just before he'd finally ended things between them for good. Nice consolation prize.

She raised her chin. *Buck up, Nina. Never let him see you cry.*

"The party's been over for a long time. You missed it." His eyes raked up and down her body, and not in a flattering way. "Looks like you made a party somewhere else, though."

She shrugged.

"Well, you missed out. Meagan and Adam are in bed. Sleeping."

"I figured. Guess I shouldn't have come."

"Probably not."

"Okay." An awkward silence thickened the icy air between them. "So I shouldn't have come." Nina dimpled. Time to turn on the charm. "But now that I'm here, do you think I can stay? I'd like to be here in the morning when the kids wake up."

"No, Nina. Not when you've been drinking."

"I jus' want to see them open their presents." Nina bit her lip hard. She'd slurred. Hunt hated that.

His mouth tightened, eyes cold. He didn't bother to respond.

She waved toward the street. "Well, my cab seems to have gone, so I really don't have any choice but to stay."

He drew a long, drawn-out breath. His *God, give me patience* breath. "The cab may be gone, but you've still been drinking."

20

"You don't have to keep saying that!" Nina closed her eyes and gained control. "I know I've been drinking a little, but I know better than to come over when I'm drunk. See?" She took three steps across the porch, then three steps back. Too bad her legs had crossed as she walked. Twice. Her lips curved. A conscious effort. "Dang heels."

"Right." He rubbed his chin, his sign of weariness. "I'll call another cab."

She grabbed his arm before he could turn away. "Hunt."

Heat radiated from the touch, and their eyes met. His beautiful pools of blue, so honest in their search. He seemed to always be searching. For the woman she used to be? Nina wondered if he was remembering when he still cared. Every second of their relationship replayed in her mind. A heartbeat, a lifetime. Christmas mornings around the tree, peals of excitement, loving. Each wonderful second of joy. The heart-ripping torture of a home torn apart with her own hands. Nina softened her grip to a light touch. "Pretty please? Just this once. For me?"

She knew she'd said the wrong thing even before his face hardened and his eyes lost the softness that only a second ago had weakened her knees.

"No," he said, his voice ice, even colder than the god-awful air. "You can come in and wait for the cab if you want."

In the face of such blatant and harsh rejection, sarcasm worked its way into her tone. "I thought you didn't want me in your precious house."

"I don't. But I don't want you getting sick out here in the cold either." He stepped aside to let her in. "Come on."

"No, thanks." Too bad she'd given up smoking. Now would have been a great time to nonchalantly light a cigarette and blow smoke in his self-righteous face.

"Suit yourself. But try not to make a scene. I saw Mr. Taylor staring out his window. You don't want him calling the cops again."

Nina turned and looked up at the second-story window in the house across the street. The curtain fluttered. "Nosy old piss ant."

Hunt grinned. "I'll be right back." He peered closely at her, and Nina's breath stilled at the softness in his face. "Be good."

"Please let me stay," she whispered.

His lips flattened into a grim line, and his guard flew back up. "You just can't leave well enough alone, can you?"

Nina's eyes swam as he stepped inside and closed the door. She stared at the big, blurry wreath bow in front of her as she tried to wrap her foggy brain around the facts. Instead of sinking into the pillow-top mattress in the guest bedroom at the top of the stairs and waking to happy squeals from her kids, she'd be waking up to a messy studio apartment and *A Christmas Story* marathon on cable.

Hunt wasn't being fair.

She shook as anger ignited in her gut. The elaborate wreath stared back at her, a mocking reminder that she'd never been good enough for Hunt.

She'd always hated that ugly, gaudy thing. Hunt's mother had given it to them their first Christmas together. "Now don't be offended, hon, but Christmas just isn't Christmas without a wreath hanging on the front door."

Well, when you'd been working three jobs to pay for school and raising a daughter alone, there wasn't much leftover for fancy lobster dinners and fifty-dollar wreaths, was there?

Every Christmas of their eleven years together, Nina's sense of duty had walked her to the door and lifted her arms as she hung the wreath on it. Well, guess what?

She reached up, snatched the ugly, fake-pine, bell-and-bauble-laden monstrosity from its nail and began ripping it apart. She yanked and pulled, tore and tugged until all that remained in her hand was the shredded bow. Elation exploded through her, shooting a flood of laughter from her lips.

"Nina!"

She hadn't heard Hunt open the door. Still reeling with guilty pleasure, Nina turned to face

23

him, but he wasn't looking at her. Instead, his bewildered gaze rested on the remnants of the wreath. Slowly, he raised his head and looked at her.

Fever rose to her cheeks. "You know I always hated it."

His silent stare shouted through the foggy mist in her brain.

"Don't look at me like that." Like she was something to be pitied.

"Nina, this has to stop. What's it going to take? You need—"

"No, don't tell me. Let me guess. I need religion." Nina threw the wrinkled bow onto the porch. It landed in the middle of the mangled wreath.

"I wasn't going to say that." Hunt's quiet voice made Nina's chest tighten.

"Good. Because I tried that once, remember? That God of yours never bothered showing up."

"What do you want me to say?" He shook his head, helpless.

"Nothing, Hunt." Hunt opened his mouth, but she held up her hand. "I mean it. I don't want you to say anything."

He crossed the threshold and stepped onto the porch. "At least come inside and wait for the cab."

She lifted her chin, but a shiver claimed her body. Why couldn't she catch a break?

"Come on, Nina. It's starting to ice again."

"No, thanks. I'd rather wait out here. I'm too mad to feel the cold."

"Your teeth are chattering. Stop being so stubborn."

"I said no." She glared at him. "Why can't you just take no for an answer? We're divorced, remember? I don't have to follow your every command."

His nostrils flared and his eyes glinted. Angry calm. He was good at it. "No one expects you to follow my command. Least of all me. And you might want to lower your voice." His fingers closed around her arm.

Nina yanked free of his grasp and stumbled down the steps. Her three-inch heel turned. She fought for balance but fell hard onto the gravel path.

"Nina!" Hunt rushed from the porch, skipping the last two steps. He knelt at her feet and unbuckled her strappy sandals.

"Leave me alone." She kicked at the air, a warning that the next one would make contact with him.

"Stop being stupid."

"Please, Hunt," she whispered through a lump in her throat. Couldn't he see she was humiliated?

He sat back, palms forward in surrender. "Okay, fine." She could hear his weariness.

Nina hauled herself up and stumbled, barely

avoiding crashing back to the ground. Hunt's warm, familiar arm slid around her waist. Nina closed her eyes and tried not to give in to the desire to bury her face in his neck and take in his scent.

"Come inside and let me take a look at it," he said.

She fought the darkness rushing in around her eyes. Steeling herself against the pain, she pushed her words through clenched teeth. "Not even if there were a bone sticking through my skin and blood gushing on the ground, *Dr. Hunter.*"

"Nice dramatics. I'm impressed."

Panic clutched at her as Hunt shoved her shoes into her hands and lifted her into his arms without waiting for permission. She knew that look in his eyes. He was like the Terminator. She'd need a vat of acid to stop him when he was committed to something.

Ironic. She'd been the acid in their relationship.

Headlights beamed toward them from the end of the street. With Nina still in his arms, Hunt turned toward the vehicle. "That must be your cab. Go home and sleep this off. You can come for dessert tomorrow night after the kids and I get back from my parents'."

"Thanks for the crumbs off your table."

Hunt shrugged. "Take it or leave it."

"Put me down."

26

He obliged. "Want me to help you to the cab?"

"No."

"Okay then. Meggie and Adam will be awake in a couple hours. I'm going to bed."

"I can't believe how mean you're being, Hunt. They're my kids too."

"I never said they weren't." His tone had reverted back to caution, ready to defend himself if necessary. "But when you've been drinking, you will not see them. I'll never give in on that point. It would be best for everyone involved if you'd save yourself the trouble of even trying."

A comeback was out of the question. She didn't have it in her to mentally spar with him. She wrapped her fist around her shoes. Who cared if he didn't want her? Who needed Hunt, anyway?

Her mind didn't have time to catch up with her action as she lifted and flung both shoes away from her. One landed harmlessly on the porch. But the other . . . Nina gasped at the shatter of glass.

Her wide eyes found Hunt's profile. He stared at his obliterated front window, the muscle in his jaw jumping as he clenched and unclenched his back teeth. Blue and red lights flashed in the driveway, accompanied by the blip of a warning siren.

"Mommy? What crashed?"

Nina turned, her mind barely registering the

27

police car at the sound of her son's voice. Seven-year-old Adam stood in the doorway, his eyes sleepy and confused.

"It was nothing, baby." She limped forward despite her screaming ankle. "The dumb window just broke on accident. But Daddy's going to cover it up in a minute." She stopped before the steps, not wanting to chance a stagger. Forcing gaiety into her voice, she grinned. "You best get back to bed. Santa's going to be here soon, and you know what'll happen if he finds you awake."

Adam's blue eyes widened as he looked toward the sky for signs of the jolly elf, then back to Nina. "Will you tuck me in?"

Hunt spoke up before Nina could respond. "Mommy has to go, sport, but I'll be up in a second."

Adam's face clouded with disappointment, and he turned to go back upstairs. Then his eyes hit the shredded bow and mangled fake pine. "The wreath!"

He raised a chubby foot. Anticipating the move, Nina sprang forward, but Hunt was a beat ahead of her.

"Don't move, Adam!" Hunt rushed barefoot up the steps and snatched up their son before Adam could bring his foot down on the broken glass that covered the porch.

Once again, Hunt had saved one of their children from her stupidity.

The sound of boots crunching on the gravel driveway made Nina turn away from the sight of her son being cuddled in his father's arms.

"Good evening, folks." A police officer strode toward them, his hand resting on his belt. "What seems to be the problem?"

Nina stared at Hunt. "I thought you were calling a cab."

"I did call a cab. Mr. Taylor must have called the cops. He did warn you last time."

"He didn't call," said a new voice. "I did."

Nina and Hunt turned.

"Meg?" Nina said, her voice suddenly small. "You called them?"

Their fifteen-year-old daughter stood in the doorway, wearing a pair of flannel pants and a T-shirt, shivering and wrapped in her own arms.

Nina expected Hunt to chastise the teen, but instead he spoke in the soothing tone he'd used when Meg was little and woke up screaming from night terrors. "It's okay, Meg."

Nina tried to hang on to her resentment, but Meggie did look a little white. She had probably awakened to their arguing and gotten scared. "Yeah, it's okay, Meggie."

No matter who called the police, Nina just wanted to get rid of this guy so she could help with damage control for the kids. Remorse flooded her. How could she have been so stupid?

Practicing her smile as she turned to the cop, she widened her eyes and concentrated on not sounding drunk. "Officer, there's been a bit of a mix-up here tonight."

"A mix-up, eh?" The officer smirked. Nina decided smirking at a person you're about to arrest should be illegal. What happened to protect and serve?

"The only mix-up is in her mind." Hugging Adam close, Hunt stepped forward. "My ex-wife came to my house drunk, destroyed my wreath, and as I'm sure you saw, threw her shoe through my window, scaring the kids half to death."

Nina's mouth dropped open. Hunt was throwing her under the bus?

The officer nodded, eyeing her sternly. "I saw."

Nina gave him a sheepish grin. "I was provoked. And it's not a very sturdy window. We—um—always said it was flimsy."

The officer stepped forward. "Place your hands behind your back, ma'am."

"You're arresting me?" Nina stared at Hunt. "You're just going to let him haul me off to jail like a common thug? In front of our kids?"

"Good night, Nina." Hunt walked toward the door, limping slightly.

"Good night? What are you talking about? Hunt!"

He ignored her, instead addressing the officer. "She hurt her ankle. Could you make sure someone takes a look at it? It looks fairly bruised and swollen. A sprain, most likely."

"Will do."

The icy air wrapped around Nina as Hunt cradled Adam and headed for the front door.

"How much have you had to drink tonight, ma'am?" the police officer asked.

"None of your business," Nina snapped. "Hunt, what's going on? Tell him you don't want me arrested."

Hunt waited for Meg to step aside so he could enter. As she turned into the house, Meg looked over her shoulder. Anger mottled her face, and her glare silenced Nina, filling her with shame.

"Is Mommy going to jail?" Adam's words trembled in his throat.

Nina didn't catch Hunt's reply as he stepped across the glass and entered the house. The door closed with a solid thud.

Bewilderment left Nina too weak to struggle against the cold steel circling her wrists. Pain pinched her right shoulder as her arms stretched unnaturally behind her back. Disbelief hauled her to the squad car, despite her screaming ankle. She didn't resist as the officer folded her like a lawn chair into the backseat.

She turned toward the house as they drove away, hoping to find some evidence that Hunt was watching. That he still cared.

The hallway light snapped off.

Turning, she settled into the seat for the silent ride to the police station. She'd been arrested twice before but had never made it to lockup. Still, she'd watched enough Lifetime movies to know what went on, and shards of fear sliced through her as her imagination went wild. But those violent images weren't the worst things that could happen.

Her shoulders slumped, and she blinked away a tear. If she'd really, truly driven Hunt to the end of his rope—if he truly didn't care anymore—then they might as well give her the chair, because her life was over.

CHAPTER TWO

When I was ten, my older sister Jill won a chance to go to the state singing competition. She and Mom were going to be gone all day, so my dad decided to take me on one of our fishing expeditions. Just the two of us. Mom made him promise not to leave the house or drink. Dad winked at me as he promised, and I knew he was pulling her leg.

I remember feeling special, like I did whenever my daddy paid attention to me. We climbed into the fishing boat and rowed to the middle of the pond. Dad baited his hook and mine, and we cast out. He told me stories about fishing with Grandpa, how Grandpa would always say, "Time to get in my boat, fish!" whenever he had something on the line. Then Dad popped open his first beer and waited for the fish to bite. A couple of hours later, when he passed out, I rowed us to shore. I got Dad into the car somehow and drove us back to the house. I

33

was only ten, but what choice did I have?

Mom and Jill came home two hours later. By then Dad was snoring on the couch where I'd left him, and I'd gutted the fish and cleaned up the mess. I pretended to be asleep when my mother tiptoed into my room to kiss me good night. I wiped off the wet spot on my forehead as soon as she left the room.

We ate fried catfish the next night for supper. If Mom ever wondered where they came from, she never said a word.

Moonlight splashed lazily across the deck as Meagan stretched out on the lounge chair next to her best friend, Izzy. They'd grown up together as neighbors. They'd been through grammar school together, junior high, freshman year, sophomore year, and now they were almost to the end of their junior year.

Izzy lifted her glass of soda and toasted the air. "New Orleans, here we come!"

A soft breeze carried Meg's sigh into the night.

Izzy turned, a frown creasing her brow. "What?"

"I can't go, Izzy."

The light from the kitchen window behind the

deck illuminated the scowl on Izzy's perfect Halle Berry–reminiscent face. "What do you mean you can't go? We've only been planning this trip forever."

"Right. But Nina's coming home tomorrow."

"I thought that was next week, after we get back."

Meg shrugged, trying to choke back tears. "Dad had the dates all mixed up." Although according to him, Meg had told him the wrong ones in the first place. Whatever. That was just his way of backing out on a promise, blaming her as usual.

Izzy smacked her palm against the wooden arm of her chair. "What about your spring break? And how come you're just now letting me know? We've been planning this trip for months."

"I found out about ten seconds ago, Iz." The blowup at supper had been apocalyptic. Especially when Dad had informed her just where she would be spending her break. "He's making me go with Nina to Abbey Hills."

"No way!"

"Would I make up something this awful?"

"Why is he making you do that?"

"Punishment for not going to see her during her rehab, most likely."

"Your dad said that?"

Meg brushed away a mosquito. "No, but what

35

else? According to him, Nina and I need time to rebuild and all that. She asked him to let me come. And he said yes."

"Without even asking you?"

"That's the way she is. Who cares what anyone else wants? As long as she gets her way." What more should Meg expect from a drunk?

"What am I going to do for a whole week without you?" Izzy's tone bordered on whining, but it made Meg feel better. "Now it's just going to be boring family stuff."

Yeah, right. Nothing to do in New Orleans but hang out with family. That was the thing about best friends. They would lie to make you feel better.

"You could always come to Abbey Hills with me." Meg grinned.

Izzy grinned back. "But how would that help all that mother-daughter bonding?"

Meg sighed. "This week is going to seem like a hundred years."

Nina hadn't wanted Meg around for most of her life, so why did she have to pick this week of all weeks to try out motherhood? Meg knew it wasn't going to last, so why bother? Especially when it meant ruining spring break.

"Hi, I'm Nina, and I'm an alcoholic." She swallowed and forced herself to continue. "It's been ninety days since my last drink."

36

"Hello, Nina."

The admission, the response. You'd think it would be easy to feel strong when there were fifty other people in the room who knew exactly where you were coming from.

But it wasn't. After three months of sobriety—three months of court-ordered rehab, an alternative to jail time—Nina was terrified. Today was the day. The real world beckoned. The world, with a liquor store on every corner and more problems than she had solutions.

She gripped the sides of the podium, hanging on for dear life. She, Nina Parker, was an alcoholic and couldn't be trusted alone with a bottle of anything with the slightest alcohol content—not even liquid cough medicine.

"I don't know if I ever would have admitted that I'm an alcoholic if the judge hadn't forced me to come here." She bit the inside of her lip for control. "Losing my business, not to mention my husband and kids, wasn't enough to open my eyes. My life was all about when I could get that next drink."

She scanned the room. Brad Sommers nodded at her from the front row. Brad knew all about loss. He knew what it meant to be at the top of his game as one of the most highly sought-after neurosurgeons in Texas. He'd been a functioning drunk for years, only drinking a little during the day to take the edge off. Never anything before lunch. But the day his wife finally got fed up and walked out, he'd needed the shot of bourbon too badly to hold off until a respectable time, and then he'd needed another and another until he filled his glass one too many times. A full day and night. He should have taken the next day off, but brain tumors rarely waited for storms to die down before smothering the life out of an otherwise beautiful brain.

His hands shook as he scrubbed up that morning after the twenty-four-hour bender. An hour later, he was escorted from the premises. Today he thanked God that his nurse, a twenty-two-year-old just out of nursing school, had smelled his breath and noticed his slurred speech before he could saw open the tiny skull of a two-year-old boy to get to the gray matter inside. He thanked God but couldn't forgive himself.

Nina hated baring her soul. She'd never been a joiner. But this was her last chance to share her story with a group that understood. Outside these walls, she'd get nothing but dirty looks and comments about control and just saying no. *No* was the hardest word in the human vocabulary, and only these people understood that.

"I never meant to turn out like my dad. Never even considered the possibility. I've hated him as much as I've adored him. Because of him, I was the girl from the other side of the tracks. I never understood why he couldn't get a handle on this thing and just stop." She gripped the podium. "Now I get it.

"I had to lose everything to get it. But I get it." She thought of her veterinary clinic, the one she'd dreamed of from the moment she saw the General deliver a foal in his barn at the animal reserve back home in Abbey Hills and a dream seed was planted in the center of her heart. Hunt's presence in her life had been a turning point of possibilities, and she had wondered if maybe dreams did come true.

The Hunter Clinic for Animals opened in September 1999 and closed four years later after she'd neutered a prize-winning stud horse, Granger, belonging to the second largest horse farm in Texas and her best client. As personal veterinarian for Myles Jackson, she'd enjoyed a certain amount of prestige and was booked months ahead, catering to the Texas elite.

In one dreadful moment, she lost it all. Her negligence had affected not only her, her family, and the poor horse, but others as well. She'd lost three great employees, who were immediately out of work and unable to use her as a reference on their résumés if they wanted to be hired again.

Her stomach tilted with regret as she shared her story.

"I—um—I leave in a little while. And I'm scared. My apartment and job are both gone. I'm going home to Missouri with my sister." An ironic grin slipped across her mouth. "She's a cop, of all things."

Sympathy laughter flittered around the room.

"Anyway. I'm leaving my two kids here with my ex-husband because the court gave him full custody. I don't know how I'll live three states away from my babies and not drink to ease the pain of it.

"In thirty minutes I walk out the door." She drew a long breath and exhaled. "What if I can't handle the real world?"

A smattering of support lifted from the audience.

"You'll do it, girl."

"One day at a time."

"Don't forget your sponsor."

"Call on your higher power."

"Amen!"

She sat down amid the thunder of fifty pairs of hands. Fifty minds that understood. Fifty hearts rooting for her. These people understood her fear that even after ninety days of sobriety, she might fail. Many of them had failed before, but she couldn't think too much about that.

She made it through the rest of the meeting, wishing time would slow down. Give her a chance to catch her breath.

Her suitcases sat near her feet as she waited on the bench outside New Haven Rehabilitation

Facilities for Hunt to pick her up. She hadn't seen him since midway through her rehab, when she'd been forced to face him and apologize for all the pain she'd caused. He'd been gracious, but Nina could tell that whatever love he'd once felt had slipped away.

That was the worst day of her rehab. She'd asked Hunt not to come back for the duration. She needed to get through the process without the pain of lost love. Until that day, he'd been to see her each week, bringing Adam with him. Meagan refused to come. Hunt hadn't been happy about their daughter's refusal . . . even on her sixteenth birthday in January, but had respected her wishes. Nina would have given anything for a glass of wine that night.

She sat alone, sweat trailing down her spine. Eighty degrees at the end of March. She'd missed most of the winter while in rehab, and apparently spring had stepped back and allowed summer to barrel right over it. She knew the feeling.

The thought of facing Hunt tugged on the knot in her stomach, threatening to unravel her fragile emotions. All she had to do was walk away, find the nearest bar, and forget about the pain of recovery. What did she have to go back to anyway? Abbey Hills, the town that made her who she was today, wasn't a beacon of welcoming encouragement, calling her home. Her ghosts lived there.

Her legs shook as she stood. *Walk away, Nina. Anything's better than going back to Abbey Hills.*

Hunt's silver Durango pulled into the circle drive.

One day at a time. It felt like a cliché, but it was all she had. Hopefully it would be enough.

The Durango stopped in front of the bench. Hunt exited and walked toward her, his smile tentative at best. She didn't blame him for being guarded. Nina felt the same way.

He leaned forward and kissed her on the cheek. She closed her eyes and surrendered to a subtle inhale, taking in the heady scent of freshly showered skin and sunshine. It would have been so easy to lean into him, wrap her arms around his neck, press against him, and hope with the small amount of hope she had left that he didn't push her away. But she was too self-conscious to put either of them in that situation.

She clenched her duffel bag so tightly the leather handle pinched the skin on her palm. Suddenly shy, she peered up at him through hooded eyes.

Hunt looked her up and down. "You look good."

"Thanks." She knew he meant it. She'd dropped two sizes. "Who knew booze could pack on that many pounds?"

He nodded at her bag. "Let me take that for you."

"Thanks."

Hunt opened the passenger door and waited while Nina scooted onto the seat that was almost too high, then deposited her bag in the back.

They made small talk during the thirty-minute drive home. Nina's stomach grew tighter and tighter as they turned onto Hunt's street and finally into the driveway.

A Welcome Home Mommy sign hung over the door. Nina smiled. "Adam's handiwork, I take it."

"My mom bought the poster board and helped him with the paint."

"That was nice of her."

He cut her a quick glance.

"I mean it," she said. She held her breath, hoping he wouldn't say anything about the new Nina or the change in her. At the same time, she hoped he would acknowledge the difference.

He didn't.

She closed her eyes, trying to center herself, breathing deep from her core. When she opened her eyes again, Hunt was staring at her, his eyes filled with compassion. Compassion that burned a path of humiliation through her. What good was compassion when he didn't love her anymore? Once, she'd been too fogged up to care. Without that numbing fog, she cared so much she could hardly stand it.

She cleared her throat. "The new picture window looks nice."

His lips quirked. "Thanks."

"I'm sorry, Hunt. I'm sorry for everything about that night."

"We've already been over it, Nina. Let's just try to put the past in the past and move forward from here. Hopefully, you're not that woman anymore."

Nina squeezed her fist tight. *God grant me the serenity to accept the things I cannot change, the courage to change the things I can, and the wisdom to know the difference.*

She wasn't sure it helped, but she hoped if she said it enough, it might.

"Look who's waiting for you," Hunt said. "Make sure you notice his missing tooth."

Nina followed Hunt's gaze to the edge of the driveway, where Adam grinned and waved. Her arms ached for him.

"Does he know yet?"

Hunt shook his head. "You said you wanted to be the one to tell him."

Nina sighed. "I know. I guess part of me hoped you'd go ahead. Or that he'd overhear you telling someone."

"Nope. There's no taking the easy way out on this one."

Nina angled her head to look at him. "Is that a dig?"

Hunt averted his gaze. "Sorry. I'm having a hard time with your decision to move away."

Nina held a breath. What exactly was he saying? That he would miss her? That he didn't want her to be so far away from him? Was there a chance he still cared about her?

He released a breath. "It's going to be hard on Adam."

She exhaled and reached for the door handle.

"Don't forget to say something about his missing tooth."

Nina didn't respond as she shoved open the door and climbed down.

Adam greeted her with shy acceptance the second she exited the SUV. He grinned, showing off a gap.

Nina squealed for his benefit. "You lost another tooth?"

"Yep." His eyes brightened. "Kevin Thompson knocked it out."

Nina gasped. "What?"

"He means with a baseball," Hunt said, his voice thick with amusement. He ruffled their son's hair. "And it was so loose already that a good shaking would have knocked it the rest of the way out anyway."

Nina smiled down at her son. "Well, come and hug me, will you? I think you've grown about six inches since I've been gone."

"Really?"

"Almost." Nina closed her eyes and took him into her arms, relishing the feel of her warm, chubby little boy.

Nina looked over Adam's shoulder, and her stomach sank as she realized Meg was not outside waiting for her. She set Adam down, he slipped his warm hand inside hers. She wanted to stand there and savor that feeling, remember it second by second. Tomorrow would come much too soon.

Hunt opened the door, and Adam tugged her forward. Once they were inside, Nina had endured all of Meg's absence she was going to put up with. She looked at Hunt. "Where's Meg?"

Before he could respond, Hunt's mother, Ellen, entered from the kitchen. Her plastic smile settled firmly into place, and she gave Nina a high-society kiss next to her cheek. "Nina, honey," she said, "it's so good to see you."

Nina tried not to be obvious, but she stiffened in spite of herself when the woman threw skinny, too-tanned-for-sixty arms around her and squeezed. "Thanks, Ellen. How's Hal?"

Hunt's dad was salt of the earth and way too good for Ellen, even if he did keep a twenty-four-year-old ballet dancer in an upscale apartment down in Austin.

But Ellen preferred to pretend, so they all played the game. "Oh, you know that man. He's supposed to be retired, but will he slow down? No, he will not. He wanted to come welcome you home, but I'm afraid he was called away on

46

some consulting project or another."

The diamonds on her fingers were evidence of Hal's devotion. The new Mercedes in the driveway explained Ellen's ability to forgive and forget. Especially forget.

"Tell him I'm sorry I missed him," Nina said.

"I will, honey." Ellen turned to Adam. "Adam, sweetie, run along and tell your sister it's about time to eat."

Hunt motioned toward the stairs. "I'll go with Adam and make sure Meg doesn't bite his head off."

Nina grinned at him. "Good idea."

Adam raced up the stairs, Hunt close behind, and Nina and Ellen were alone. Outside a distant rumble signaled impending spring rain. Ellen smiled. "My bones have been aching all day. Guess now I know why."

"Yeah, I'd heard thunderstorms were in the forecast," Nina said.

An awkward moment of silence followed. Nina looked out the picture window, expecting to see the thick black clouds she felt inside her to be crowding the sky. Nina's skin crawled, and her stomach tightened. She'd give almost anything to escape.

"Well," Ellen said. "I best go check on our supper."

Nina released a breath. "Can I help with anything?" *Please say no.*

"Why, thank you, hon. You can cut up the salad if you want."

"Sure."

Nina followed Ellen into the kitchen. Everything was different. Even the floor. The old blue and white linoleum had been replaced by a laminate, something Nina had never liked in a kitchen. How could Hunt have just changed everything without telling her? She felt like a stranger in what used to be her favorite room in the house.

"The floor is different." She hadn't meant to say it aloud.

Ellen perked up. "I told Hunt this fake wood stuff is so much easier to take care of than anything I've ever had. And you know I've had everything under the sun. Tile, linoleum, you name it." She sent Nina a knowing look. "And a man without a wife? If anyone needs the easiest floor to keep clean, it's a single father. Know what I mean?"

The words cut deep and grazed Nina's defenses. She refrained from mentioning that Hunt was a surgeon and could afford to hire someone to mop a decent floor if he wanted. She was learning to choose her battles, even the ones where she knew she had the upper hand, and this wasn't the time to start anything with Hunt's mom.

Nina pulled out a crystal salad bowl and set it on the counter. "What are we having? It smells wonderful."

"Lasagna and homemade dinner rolls."

Nina didn't have to force her smile. "Sounds great."

"You've always liked it. I made sure there's enough for lunch tomorrow."

"Wish I could be here for leftovers."

"Why won't you be here?" The confusion in Ellen's eyes seemed real.

"Hunt didn't tell you?"

Ellen shook her head. "I haven't seen him all week. He's been on call. What's going on?"

"My sister, Jill, is coming to get me tomorrow. I'll be staying with her in Abbey Hills. I already have a job there." She wouldn't be starting until midweek, but it was good to know she would be employed, even if she was going to be waiting tables.

"Well, that is news, isn't it?"

Ellen's disapproval cut into Nina's fragile emotions, raising her defenses once again. "Yes, well, I lost both my job and my apartment here, so what choice do I have?"

"Surely you can find something here as easily as anywhere else."

"But I don't have a home here or a way to get started in a home."

"Well, you can come stay with me. Hal's gone most of the time anyway, and I could use some help in the store."

Interior design? Something Nina knew nothing

about and had zero interest in learning.

"It's a kind offer, Ellen. I appreciate your thoughtfulness, but you know I can't live with you."

"It would only be for a couple of months while you saved for a place of your own. I could even help you out. You could pay me twenty-five dollars a week or something until you've paid me back."

Nina slid a knife from the block and picked up the head of freshly washed lettuce from the counter. *Deep breaths. Deep, cleansing breaths.* "I'm grateful for the offer, Ellen. But no. No, thank you."

Ellen lifted her chin. "It was just an offer. I never really thought you'd accept." She turned her back and began pulling plates from the cabinet. "But my goodness, do you think it's a good idea to leave the kids again so soon after getting home?"

"I don't really have a choice. I've got to start bringing in an income right away. Anyway, Meg's coming with me for spring break, so at least I'll have her for a week."

Ellen frowned and faced Nina again, the stack of plates held against her chest. "Coming with you? But Meagan's been planning a trip to New Orleans with her friend next door."

Nina's stomach sank. "I didn't know about it. Hunt never said anything."

"It's all the two of them have talked about for the last six weeks."

"I didn't know."

"Oh dear." Ellen pulled her lower lip between her teeth, then released it. "I hope I haven't said something I shouldn't have."

So much for reconnecting with Meggie. Forced to give up New Orleans with Izzy for Abbey Hills? Nina turned to Ellen. "Do you mind finishing up the salad? I'd like to talk to Hunt before dinner."

Ellen waved her toward the door. "There's not much left to do anyway."

Nina found Hunt on the front porch. He looked up when she stepped across the threshold and patted the porch swing next to him. "Have a seat."

A light, cool breeze had replaced the oppressive heat of earlier as thunder rumbled closer. A strong storm would most likely hit within the hour, but for now the coming rain perfumed the air. Nina couldn't help thinking back to all the times she and Hunt had sat in this exact spot, allowing the coming storm to play over their senses, waiting until the last minute before heading inside to escape the violence of lightning, winds that blew branches off trees, and thunder so loud it made the heart race and stomach dive.

Hunt smiled at her, comfortable. "Seems like old times."

"Yeah." Nina didn't want to ruin the moment

by reminding him how far from old times this was. She sat next to him, and the swing rocked.

"The storm's going to be a gullywasher," he said.

"Spring in Dallas."

He nodded. "Something on your mind?"

"Yeah. Your mom said Meg had plans with Izzy for spring break."

"The dates were off. She told me the trip was over Easter vacation." He shrugged. "She'll have to learn to get things right."

"I just wonder if taking her vacation away from her is counterproductive. I'm not sure she'll warm to me if she feels punished."

Hunt frowned. "What do you suggest?"

"Let her go to New Orleans."

"Too late. Izzy and her folks left right before I picked you up."

"Is this why I haven't seen Meggie yet? Passive resistance? She's mad, isn't she?"

"Most likely. But don't worry. I didn't give her a choice about eating dinner with the family. She was headed to the shower when we went upstairs. You'll see her in a few minutes."

Nina scowled. "Great. So much for us catching up and reconnecting. She's going to hate me all week."

"Maybe not. Give yourself some credit."

Nina cut her gaze to his. "Why should I? I don't have much of a track record."

52

"I think you're too hard on yourself. You've been through a lot."

"I've put *her* through a lot. Her and everyone else." Nina pulled one leg up and hugged it to her chest, resting her chin on her knee.

Hunt slid his arm along the back of the seat, his fingers brushing her shoulder. "All you can do is build from here, Nina. That's the thing with kids. There's always a block of love somewhere down deep. You just have to lay one new block at a time until you get to the surface."

Nina couldn't help but notice he'd left himself out of the equation.

She turned her head toward the storm to hide the sudden rush of tears clouding her vision. She blinked them away, but not before wishing there was something left in Hunt's heart for her. A small block deep down. Something on which to rebuild what she'd shattered.

~

The first time I saw Nina, I was ruined for any other woman.

From my spot in Romey's Bar and Grill, I watched her glide from one end of the bar to the other, beckoning the sun with her smile, mesmerizing each patron with nothing more than a glance. She poured their drinks, completely unaware that she was the focus of every pair of male eyes in the room.

53

I tried not to be apparent, concealing my fascination as best I knew how. Without warning, she tilted her head and found me. For one long, gut-ripping second, our eyes locked, sending my brain into a spin. My breath stilled. The edges of her mouth tipped upward, and even when she glanced away, I couldn't stop staring.

Next to me, Chris Caulfield let out a low whistle. "My God, would you look at her?"

The way he ogled her clubbed something inside me. My inner Neanderthal roared, but I said nothing. That was the way things worked. Chris always got the girls, ever since sixth grade. Even the ones he didn't really like—the ones I did. It had never occurred to me that one of those girls might have been better off with me. Might actually have preferred me to Chris.

She walked toward us, her smile too beautiful to be real. Chris whistled in a breath. "Wish me luck."

I couldn't.

Chris and I had never had the same tastes in women. Chris liked the busty, blond types—Marilyn Monroes, Anna Nicoles. I—well, I liked this type. I couldn't blame Chris for being mesmerized. Olive skin that glistened even in the muted glow of the dim bar lights. Coal black hair with not one hint of wave, let alone curl, slipped delicately over tanned bare shoulders and just touched the low neckline of her tank top. Dark, exotic eyes slanted upward beneath arched, sculpted eyebrows. An Indian princess.

"What'll it be, fellas?"

Chris applied the classic line. "Are you on the menu?"

She rolled her eyes, then turned to me as though he hadn't spoken.

But Chris hadn't earned all those notches on his bedpost by being put off that easily. He persisted. "Hey, if you keep playing hard to get, you'll definitely catch me."

I felt offended for her, embarrassed for myself. How come I'd never recognized what a jerk Chris could be? Or maybe I had. Maybe this was the first time I'd ever cared. The hero in me sprang to life.

I smiled at her. "I'll have a beer. Draft. I don't care what brand."

"A low-maintenance man." Her eyes flashed interest. "Impressive."

"Hey," Chris piped in, pouting. "I'm low maintenance too. Give me the same as my friend here."

She gave him a dubious once-over. My heart beat faster as she patted the bar in front of me. "I'll be right back."

My throat tightened around my vocal chords, squeezing off my ability to speak, so I simply nodded.

Chris nudged me when she walked away. "Hey, what's the deal? I called her first."

I hadn't taken my eyes off her, and only my determination to stake my claim forced me to do so now. I turned and caught Chris's frown. In that moment, I didn't care if I lost my longtime friend. "Not this time, pal."

His frown deepened. His eyes narrowed, and for a minute I thought I might have to rough him up to make him understand that I wasn't backing down. Not like I had when Linda Pierce came to our school in tenth grade. Chris got Linda. I was going to have my shot with this one.

For a heavy second, tension punched through the space between us, then Chris shrugged and scooped up a handful of the germ-ridden snack mix on the counter. "Oh well. Not my type, anyway." He swiveled on his stool and scanned the room. "That one, however," he said with a lecherous grin, "is. And not a day over twenty-one."

I didn't have to look to know he'd spotted his Marilyn Monroe for the night. I was only relieved that he walked away from the bar.

"Hey, buddy," the bartender said, sliding two foaming mugs onto the bar. "Where'd your friend run off to?"

I jerked my head toward the smoky, dim corner where Casanova was making his move on a couple of coeds. "Just leave the beer." I wondered if I'd ever have the guts to ask her out. "If he doesn't come back, I'll drink them both."

"Don't get loaded," she said. She turned slightly, and I noticed a tattoo on her back, just off her shoulder. A foot with a delicately inked wing attached. Hermes' foot. "I'm out of here in an hour, and if you're drunk, I won't let you buy me a cup of coffee and breakfast down the street. I love warm glazed doughnuts. Don't you?"

She smiled, and a dimple flashed just below one corner of her mouth. I fixated on the spot, barely controlling my urge to reach out and touch it.

I nearly jumped when she stuck out her hand. "Nina Parker."

"Jordan." At the first touch of her fingers on mine, my stomach dipped. I'd never felt this way even once during my entire thirty years.

"Jordan what?"

"Hunter."

"Jordan Hunter. Jordan Hunter." She repeated my name several times, rolling the words around on her tongue, tasting each syllable.

Driving me crazy.

Finally, she stopped the torment and nodded. "Great name."

I couldn't resist a small laugh. "No one's ever told me that." It occurred to me that perhaps she was a little immature. Why hadn't I noticed her youth? *Please, God, let her be at least twenty-five.* I drew the line at a five-year age difference. No exceptions. Not yet anyway.

She wiped a rag over the bar. "So what do you do, Jordan?"

"Actually, everyone calls me Hunt."

"Even better." She grinned and that dimple tempted me again.

"I'm a resident at County."

"A resident. You mean like a doctor?"

"Yeah."

I liked the way her eyes widened, impressed. "Wow. Smart guy, huh?"

I couldn't tell if she was teasing me. My face suddenly went feverish, and I felt like an undergrad. "I don't know about that." I tried to hide my embarrassment behind a cough.

"I can tell. You have intelligent eyes." Her delicate hand reached across the bar and settled over mine. "And kind."

The weight of her hand felt so warm, so right, that I wanted to close my eyes and relish the sensation. But that would have meant shutting out the sight of her face, so I reached my thumb around, caressing the top of her fingers. "Thank you, Nina."

"Do you want to know what I do?"

The question took me aback. "Tend bar, I presume?"

A delighted burst of laughter sprang from her. "At night I tend bar. During the day I go to school. I'm studying to be a vet." Her voice shivered with excitement. "I still have a couple years though. Two classes a semester. It's what I can afford." She grinned. "We're both in the medical profession."

I soon learned that was the way Nina saw things. There were no levels with her, no caste system, no classes. No one was above Nina Parker, and there wasn't a single smug, snobbish bone in her beautiful body. What you saw was what you got.

In that moment, I made it my mission to win Nina Parker's heart.

Too bad winning her heart meant giving her the power to break mine into a million pieces.

CHAPTER THREE

I went up in a hot-air balloon once. I wonder—if I hadn't taken that crazy quilt ride, would my expectations, hopes, and dreams have stayed hidden inside, unexposed to a world that only wanted to keep me in my place?

I don't know. Maybe it was my destiny. Dane Williamson, the cutest boy in junior high and way out of my league, took my hand during that ride. He told me he had always thought I was cute and invited me to his birthday party the next week. I knew the gods were smiling on me. Like a fairy tale, my life was about to change forever. Dane Williamson liked me.

For fifteen minutes I was somebody. Then the ride ended.

My stomach hadn't stopped rolling from the second we lifted off the ground. When Dane turned to tell me good-bye, I threw up all over him.

Why can't God assign special angels to protect the self-esteem of little girls? That day was destined to change my life one way or another.

Dane took back his birthday party invitation. And from then on, I was known as Puke.

Awkward silence reigned at the table, and Nina felt the familiar guilt of ruining a family dinner. Meg's sullen glare and jerky movements attested to her displeasure at missing out on her vacation with Izzy. Even Adam had reverted from his effusive, talkative self to a quiet shell.

Nina stared at her plate. She'd taken a couple bites of the lasagna, but it had stuck in her throat like a blob of glue.

Ellen cleared her throat, breaking through the heavy veil of silence. "So, Nina. What time will your sister be coming tomorrow?"

Adam's head shot up. "Aunt Jill's coming?" The excitement in his voice nearly broke Nina's heart.

Meagan actually glanced up from her plate, pretending nonchalance, but her eyes widened in anticipation of the answer. Jill was Meagan and Adam's only aunt, and they had no uncles, so her presence was always cause for excitement. And maybe, just maybe, Meg was softening to the idea.

"She's coming tomorrow," Nina said.

Adam whooped, and Meagan gave in to a small smile—no visible teeth, but considering the lack of emotion she'd shown since Nina's arrival, she appeared positively giddy.

Adam still didn't know she was leaving. Nina would have much preferred that Hunt break the news to their son, but she supposed this was part of her growing process. Facing difficult things.

She gathered a breath for courage and turned to her little boy. "You know Mommy lost my job."

Meg scowled. "Yeah, we know."

"And my apartment."

"You can live here, Mom," Adam said, reaching over and taking her hand.

"Thank you, baby. But Daddy and I aren't married anymore, so it wouldn't be right for me to live here.

"Why?"

Meagan snorted. "You're such a spaz."

Clearly at the end of his rope, Hunt turned an icy stare in her direction. "Meg, either shut up or go upstairs."

Meg's chair scraped against the wood floor. "Fine." She turned to Adam. "Nina's trying to tell you that Aunt Jill is coming tomorrow to take her back to live in Abbey Hills where our grandma and grandpa live. The ones we've never seen. And Nina and Dad are making me go to Abbey Hills for spring break. Any more questions?"

Meg turned to Nina, gave a smug grin, and glided away as though she had all the time in the world.

Nina watched her go, her spirits drooping. She only hoped it wasn't too late for her to become Meg's mother again.

Meagan stuffed a week's worth of underwear into her oversized duffel bag and zipped it shut with a jerk that probably pulled a muscle. Abbey Hills instead of New Orleans. And what was with Nina, all motherly and calm? Meg liked her better with a few glasses of wine in her. At least then she was funny.

Her hoodie pocket vibrated. She pulled out her phone and checked the screen. "Hey, Iz."

"How you holding up?"

"Okay, I guess. You in New Orleans yet?"

"No. Some gross Shoney's restaurant. I don't even know what town. We won't be at my grandma's for about three more hours."

Meg sighed. She'd give anything to be eating at that gross Shoney's with Izzy and her parents instead of here with Nina. "I just can't believe my dad is sending me off with her. Hasn't he learned his lesson by now?"

"Well, you know, it's been a long time since she drank."

Meg let out a short laugh. "Yeah, because the judge forced her. This wasn't her first rehab, and I'd bet money it won't be her last. Anyway, let's drop it, okay?"

"Okay. Hey, Mom says we're coming back here

in July, when my aunt will be visiting from New York. If it's okay with your dad, you can come with us."

"I'll ask."

"Mom hopes you can. I think she wanted to show you New Orleans. The French Quarter and stuff. She was disappointed you didn't get to come."

The knowledge warmed Meg. Izzy's mom was the greatest. A real mom. The kind of mom a girl could count on.

Some kids had all the luck. And some got stuck with lousy drunks.

Nina held tight to Adam, fighting tears as they stood next to Jill's Camry. She didn't want to let him go. How could she ever have thought she could do this?

Hunt touched her shoulder. "We have to go, Nina. We'll be late for Sunday school."

Resentment came fast and fell hard. "He'll always have Jesus with him," she sneered. "His mother is leaving. Can't you bend the rules this once?"

Jill cleared her throat. "We should be getting on the road anyway, Nina. I have to work in the morning."

"Where's Meg?" Nina looked toward the house, hoping to see her daughter coming of her own accord. No such luck. Would she and Hunt have to drag Meagan, kicking and screaming, to Missouri? She hadn't come down for breakfast and wouldn't answer the knock on her door.

Hunt glanced up at Meg's window on the second floor. "I think this is her Alamo standoff. She'll be down in a minute."

Nina nodded, catching her lower lip between her teeth. She held her arms out to Adam. "One more hug for Mommy?"

Adam went easily into her embrace. His warm breath lifted a strand of hair, tickling her neck. She shivered. Over his shoulder, she detected movement. The storm door slammed. Meg jerked down the steps, muscling a duffel bag in one hand and a backpack in the other.

"So are we going, or what?" she asked.

Jill put her hands on her hips. "You don't say hi to your aunt?"

Meg's face turned pink. "Sorry." She accepted Jill's hug, relaxing against her until Nina felt a twinge of jealousy.

"What about me?" Hunt asked.

Meg shrugged and stayed planted where she stood next to the open trunk. Hunt walked across the driveway and held out his arms. Grudgingly, Meg suffered the embrace. Nina cringed at the hurt in Hunt's eyes.

"You're going to stay mad at me?" he asked.

Meg shrugged. "I just wonder why I have to go and Adam doesn't." She glared at Hunt but didn't give him a chance to reply. "I guess it's because you're his real dad and not mine. Who cares if I go with Nina, right? But you're not going to let your precious son spend a week with a drunk."

Her words forced all conversation to a halt for a minute as the three adults grappled to wrap their heads around the audacity of Meg's words.

Hunt found his voice first. "Is that how you truly feel, Meggie?"

"How else should I feel?"

Shoving down the hurt from Meagan's thoughtless words, Nina took charge of the situation. The attempt at manipulation was obvious, and if anyone should be able to recognize manipulation, Hunt should after years of living with an alcoholic. She shook her head, unable to believe Hunt was buying into Meg's baloney.

She touched his arm. "Can I talk to you for a second?" He followed her a few feet away, out of earshot. "Don't let her get to you, okay?"

His guard slipped, his eyes moist. "She said I'm not her real father."

"Fighting words, nothing more."

A crooked grin split his mouth. "Still hurts."

"That's exactly what she was going for. She wanted to hurt you as much as she's hurting over losing her vacation and being forced to bond with her deadbeat mother." Her lips turned up in a tentative grin. "Be glad you're still the favorite parent. She'll get over being mad at you as soon as she gets home. Who knows if she'll ever love me again?"

"She loves you. That's one of the reasons I wanted her to spend this week with you, Nina. It's time to work on this relationship. I remember how inseparable the two of you were when I first met her."

"That seems like an eternity ago." Nina caught her lip between her teeth.

"It wasn't. It was only eleven years ago." His smile was kind, compassionate. "There's a lot to rebuild, and it needs to start somewhere."

"What if pushing us together like this isn't the right way to do it?" She swallowed hard. She hadn't intended to vocalize that worry. "What if it backfires and she has even less respect for me by next weekend than she does now?"

"I don't think that'll happen, but it's a risk worth taking." He glanced over Nina's shoulder. "If you have reservations and prefer to let her get used to the idea of visiting, I guess we can let her stay home for spring break. Although that'll make her mad too, now that Izzy and her mom are gone." He grinned. "I bet she'd rather go to Abbey Hills."

Meg's impatient voice broke into their conversation. "You're going to be late to church, Dad. Plus, Aunt Jill's ready to go."

"I didn't say that," Jill called. "Take all the time

you need." She scowled at Meg. Meg gave her an impish grin.

Nina turned back to Hunt. "I guess she'll be okay. If nothing else, she'll bond with Jill and my parents." She shrugged, trying not to feel sorry for herself. "At least the week won't be a total waste."

"Okay. Meg's right. I have to get to church, and you three should be getting on the road."

He reached out and gathered her close. Nina hesitated a second, surprised he'd initiated the embrace. Then she wrapped her arms around his waist and rose onto her tiptoes, wishing she could stay in this place of safety and warmth.

"You can do it this time," he said, his voice low and husky, filled with emotion. "I believe in you."

She tried to find his face as he pulled away. She wanted to see a sign. But he was already herding Adam toward his Durango.

Her heart still soared moments later as she slid into the car, replaying that hug and his words over and over in her mind.

Hunt's Durango followed them down the street. He would turn in another block, but until then, Nina watched his Durango through the side mirror. Hoping to catch a glimpse of him.

Halfway down the block, Meg let out a howl. "Wait! Stop the car, Aunt Jill."

"What's wrong?" Jill asked, already braking.

"Stop!"

"I can't just stop in the middle of the road, Meggie."

"Jill," Nina said, her voice low. "Please pull over." Her heart sank. She couldn't force Meg to go on this trip when she was so upset. She wouldn't.

Meg leaped out of the car as soon as it came to a stop. Behind them, Hunt stopped his Durango and hopped out as Meg barreled toward him. His face was clouded in worry, but he held out his arms. Meg fell into them, sobbing.

Nina opened her door and walked toward the pair until she was close enough to hear Meg.

"I'm sorry, Daddy. I didn't mean what I said. You're the best dad in the world, and I know you love me."

"I forgive you, sweetheart." He pulled back and looked her in the eye. "If you truly don't want to go, your mother and I won't make you."

She shook her head. "No. I want to."

Nina gathered a sharp, cool breath.

"I've never met my grandparents," Meg said.

A split second of disappointment shot through Nina, but she shoved it aside. At least with Meagan in Abbey Hills, no matter what the reason, she would have the opportunity to add those building blocks Hunt had talked about. She only hoped Meagan would meet her partway. She wasn't asking for anything as ambitious as halfway, but if her daughter would take just a few steps in Nina's direction, that would be enough to sustain Nina's hope and strengthen her resolve.

~

The first thing that impressed me about Nina, after her beauty caught my attention, was her focus. She juggled three jobs—waitressing, bartending, and delivering pizza. Plus she was working on her degree in veterinary medicine. How could you not find that kind of determination attractive? This tenacity fueled her energy as she worked to make a better life than the previous generation had in her family. A family she rarely mentioned except in passing.

We dated for six weeks before she told me about Meagan. I respected her desire to protect her daughter, but after six weeks, I was pretty much gone on Nina. Breaking it off wouldn't have been an option.

That night Nina and I had our first fight.

I'd never been invited into her home before. I'd started to wonder if she was hiding a body. Or maybe just really bad housekeeping. I was relieved to discover neither was the case—until she haltingly showed me a photograph of a five-year-old girl with dark eyes and hair. The little girl could have been a younger Nina.

The soft glow of a floor lamp danced across Nina's sleek hair. I slipped my hand along her neck and felt her silky mane fall over my wrist and forearm. "Don't you think you should have told me about your daughter a little sooner?"

Nina quickly blinked her tears away. "Hey, no one's asking you to be Meggie's daddy." She put on what I now know is a practiced nonchalance, but back then I could never tell if she cared or not. She hid her feelings well.

"Take it easy. I'm not mad," I said. "You just took me by surprise, that's all. Give me a few minutes to get my head around it, okay?"

She refused to meet my eyes, so I cupped her chin and gently pressed until she had no choice. Her eyelashes glistened from unshed tears. "If you don't want to see me anymore, I'll understand."

I pressed a kiss to her forehead. "Don't talk that way." I felt the tension leave her body.

"I should have told you right away, but I don't share my personal life with many guys. How did I know you weren't going to be just a one-nighter or friends with benefits?"

Her words slapped at my heart like a whip, flaring my anger against her for the first time since we'd met. I dropped my hand from her neck and stepped away. "Have I ever treated you like this was a casual relationship?"

She followed me, closing the distance I'd created with my retreat. "How would I know how you treat your friends with benefits?" She smiled, flashing that crazy dimple and defusing my anger. She slipped her slim, sun-bronzed arms around my neck and pressed herself close, filling my senses with her perfume and the smell of her skin. She didn't leave me any choice but to wrap my arms around her, take her glossy mouth with mine, and imagine forever as a husband. And, I suppose, a father as well.

"So where is this little girl of yours?" I found myself asking.

Nina smiled. "Follow me."

She took my hand and led me across the room to the window seat. Her slender finger pressed against her mouth. Intrigued, I couldn't help but smile.

She lifted the padded lid, and inside was the most gorgeous little girl I'd ever seen. Nina reached down and rubbed her back to wake her. "Meggie?"

Meagan sat up slowly. She blinked and stared at me. The little girl was enchanting. Her brown ringlets were messy from sleep, her cheek lined from wrinkled fabric. She hugged a ratty brown bear that had seen better days and eyed me with wary scrutiny.

Meg lifted her arms, and Nina pulled her up.

"Meggie, honey," Nina said as the little girl wrapped her skinny five-year-old legs around Nina's waist like a spider monkey, "I want you to meet Hunt, Mommy's friend. I want you to be his friend too, okay?"

She offered her sweet little hand to me and gave a sigh. "Okay."

The kid stole my heart with one sweet breath. Every fatherly instinct that had lain dormant for thirty years sprang to life and sang her name.

The next day I bought Nina an engagement ring.

And I've never regretted it. Not once.

CHAPTER FOUR

Once when I was ten, I woke to a crash in the middle of the night. I sat up and stared wide-eyed into the darkness, listening for more sounds, something I could identify.

My dad stumbled down the hall. He knocked against the wall, cursed, and knocked against the wall again. Finally I heard him shove his way into the room he shared with my mom. In moments, I heard him snoring.

I turned to see what Jill thought, but she'd slept through the whole thing. Disgusted, I crept from my bed and tip-toed down the stairs. I had to make sure my fish tank wasn't the source of that crash. Relief wound through me when I noticed the broken lamp. I'll never forget the next three seconds.

Dad had done something he'd never done before.

Instead of draining his bottle and passing out, he'd stumbled to bed with half a bottle of vodka still sitting, lid off, on the coffee table.

I stared at the bottle. The liquid inside looked like water. Something more than curiosity took hold of me—a compulsion, almost like a craving, only I'd never had a drink, so how could I crave one? I couldn't take my eyes off the bottle. My heart raced in my chest, and I reached for it.

"Nina Parker!"

I screamed at the sound of my mother's voice.

"Daddy left it." My voice trembled. "I was going to dump it out."

A look flickered across her eyes as her brow furrowed. I thought for a second she might call me a liar and demand I confess. If she had, I'd have wept with remorse.

I held my breath as she fixed her attention on the lamp. "I'll clean up down here. Come give me a hug, and run on back to bed."

I brushed past her open arms, ignoring her hurt frown, and didn't stop until I was safe in bed.

I didn't sleep. I raged inside.

Why did she always ruin everything?

Nina's jaw hurt from clenching her teeth for the last two hundred miles. The nearer they got to her hometown, the more the road dipped and swayed. When her ears popped from the altitude, she knew she'd passed the point of no return.

All those years ago she'd promised herself she'd never come back.

She remembered running through the woods that last night in Abbey Hills, pain exploding in her head. Vomiting, hallucinating, then nothing. She woke up in the hospital, her nose and throat aching and raw. They'd pumped her stomach.

Her parents hovered over her hospital bed. Dad could barely look her in the eye. Mom skirted on the brink of tears, making Nina feel so small and ashamed that she finally begged the nurse to tell them visiting hours were over.

Staring out the window the next morning, Nina lay still, wishing she were dead rather than forced to spend one more day in Abbey Hills. She waited until she was alone, then yanked the IV from her hand, found her jeans from the night before, and snuck out. Twenty minutes later, she lucked out. An elderly couple just leaving Branson was headed back to Dallas. She slept every minute of the ten-hour trip.

Graduation was over. She was eighteen years old, an adult. Dallas seemed as good a place as any to begin her own life.

A switch had flipped. Something awful had happened in the woods, and she couldn't imagine another day in Abbey Hills. Her parents had Responsible Jill. They'd be fine.

Two months later, she missed her second period, threw up every morning, and couldn't wear any of her bras.

When she thought back to those days, she had no idea how an eighteen-year-old girl had fended for herself, carried a baby to term, and then taken care of the baby. She'd been stronger back then. Too much had happened in the years since.

"Everything okay, Nina?" Jill asked.

Nina swallowed the memories. "Trying to stomach memory lane."

"Bumpy road, huh?" Jill's voice was laced with sympathy.

"Potholes the size of houses."

"Mom is looking forward to finally meeting Meg."

Nina stiffened. She'd been trying to prepare herself for that inevitability, but as the miles melted away behind her, her dread rose. The reunion with her parents would be easier if she hadn't messed up so much with Meg. If their mother-daughter relationship weren't so strained. If she weren't coming home a failure instead of the rich doctor's wife and successful veterinarian she'd secretly dreamed of being. She didn't even have custody of her children. There wasn't one thing in her life her parents could hold up and say, "You did good, honey. Boy, we underestimated you."

Jill cast her a sideways glance. "It'll work out. I think they're so relieved to finally get you back, they don't care why you're coming home."

"You told them about rehab, didn't you?"

"Yes."

"Jill! Why?"

Jill shrugged but kept her attention focused on the steep decline in the road. "Because they're our parents and I didn't see any reason to keep it from them."

"It wasn't your secret to tell."

"You didn't tell me not to." Jill's smug voice acted on Nina's nerves like an emery board on teeth.

"It was implied."

"I'm not very good at reading between the lines." Jill's lips quirked up. "Remember that next time you want me to keep a secret. In the meantime, you need to prepare yourself to answer a bunch of annoying questions."

The sound of squeaking leather from the backseat signaled that Meg had awakened. Nina turned.

Meg sat up, her hair all over the place, eyes squinting in the afternoon sun. "Can we stop soon? I have to pee. Plus I'm starving to death."

"We just passed Branson. We'll be in Abbey Hills in ten minutes." Even as she said the words, Nina's mind had trouble connecting with the reality. Panic slammed into her gut. A glass of wine would definitely calm her frazzled nerves about now. Not that she wasn't glad she'd quit drinking, but at moments like this, she could kick herself for being one of those people who couldn't drink without drinking too much.

The Ozark Mountains framed rolling Highway 65 and rose up ominously all around her. Suffocating her.

Nina's breath came fast and hard. "I need a bag."

Jill kicked at the brake, releasing the cruise control. "Should I pull over? You going to be sick?"

Nina shook her head and pressed a hand against her chest.

"She's having a panic attack." Meggie's voice sounded bored. "She gets this way when she feels out of control."

"What do you do for it?" Jill asked, still slowing the car.

"She usually slams back a shot or two of tequila."

"Meg!" Nina found enough air to raise her voice for one word.

"Nice, Meagan," Jill said, the irritation in her tone making up for Nina's inability to muster her own attitude. "What should we do for her since alcohol is off the table?"

Meg shoved an empty fast-food bag into Nina's hands. "She just needs to breathe into this for a while, and she'll be okay."

Nina felt the relief slip through her with each intake of paper-filtered air, even if it smelled like french fries. By the time the wooden sign welcoming one and all to Abbey Hills came into view, she was able to sit up straight, fold her hands in her lap, and calmly ride into town.

Not much had changed. They drove past Sonic, the Lutheran church, the town park.

"You seriously grew up in this crap hole of a town?" Meg's voice had an edge of disdain only a teenage girl could muster with any degree of believability.

Even though she had felt the same disdain all her life, Nina's stomach tightened with resentment. She watched the Price Cutter grocery store pass by. "Yeah, so?"

"I'd suffocate."

"It's only a week. I think you'll survive."

Meg mumbled something unintelligible and sat back, folding her arms across her chest.

Jill turned down a side street. Nina frowned. "Hey, I thought you bought the old Hanson house. I know I've been gone awhile, but aren't we going the wrong way?"

"Meg's hungry. I thought we'd go to Barney's and eat something before heading home."

"Thank *you,* Aunt Jill," Meg said from the backseat.

Barney's Café loomed ahead, just past the only traffic light in town. Except for a new roof and a fresh coat of paint, it looked exactly the same. A one-hundred-year-old wooden house with a screen door in the front and the back. Walking inside was like going back fifty years. Three generations of Barneys—first name, not last—had owned and operated the restaurant that was more a catfish and southern barbeque house than a café—at least after the morning coffee and oatmeal crowd cleared out. Nina hated the idea of giving folks something to stare at and gossip about, but the thought of southern-fried catfish and fried okra made her mouth water.

"I don't know, Jill. I'm not really ready . . ."

"Don't worry," Jill said. "Barney promised me he'd give us the table in the back and won't let anyone stare at you and Meggie."

"I'm impressed. I guess being the sheriff has its perks. Do you get free coffee too?"

A red glow settled over Jill's features.

Nina's jaw dropped. "No way. Are you dating Barney the Third? Seriously?"

"Shut up. And don't you dare embarrass me."

"Barney? Jill, you've hated Barney ever since he peeked at you through the fence when you were sunbathing in tenth grade."

She shrugged. "So? I don't hate him anymore. Just wait. You'll see."

The screen door complained loudly as they opened it and walked inside. The smell of pulled pork nearly bowled Nina over, it smelled so good.

"Where's the bathroom?" Meg whispered. Nina pointed and watched her daughter make a bee-line for the door.

Barney Jenkins had changed in the past seventeen years. He'd gone from pudgy to muscled, pimply to chiseled. Nina could easily understand why Jill had finally seen the light and fallen captive to the big Peeping Tom's charms.

At the sight of Jill, Barney's entire face lit up. Apparently he had no shame when it came to showing his feelings, because he left the grill and came around the counter, gathering her into his beefy arms. He kissed her forehead, her cheeks, finally settling on her lips and lingering until Nina looked away.

Jill pushed at his arms. "You remember my little sister?"

Barney offered his hand. "Sure, I remember Nina. Been a long time. Good to see you again."

"Thanks, Barney." Nina shifted, nerves suddenly getting the better of her. "The place looks the same. You've done a great job here."

He grinned, boyish and manly at the same time. Nina could definitely see why Jill had given Barney the benefit of the doubt. Somehow, in a town that never changed, Barney had managed to be different. Maybe there was hope for her too.

"What'll you have, Nina?" he asked.

Her stomach rumbled at the suggestion of

food. "I'd kill for fried catfish. And fried okra."

"A girl after my own heart." He nodded toward the end of the room. "Your table is all set up and waiting for you."

Jill smiled at him, one of those private smiles reserved for couples who had something real. Nina headed toward the table, shaking her head. *Good grief. You're jealous of Jill and Barney?*

She slipped her purse from her shoulder and slid into the red vinyl booth. A pretty African American girl about Meg's age appeared carrying an order pad. "Hi. I'm Carrie. What can I get you to drink?"

Nina hoped the surprise didn't show on her face. When she'd left town, there were no African American families in Abbey Hills. Ever, as far as she knew. "Uh—iced tea, I guess."

"Sweet or unsweet?"

"Sweet. No wait. Unsweet. I'll use Sweet'N Low."

The girl made a face. "Gross."

Nina laughed. "Yeah, well, when I was your age, I didn't have to worry about calories. Not the case these days."

"The pink stuff it is." The girl stepped aside for Jill to take the other side of the booth. "Hey, Sheriff. Diet Coke?"

"Thanks, Carrie. My niece will be here in a minute, but you can go ahead and get our drinks if you want."

"You mean the girl who went to the bathroom? She wants water." Carrie grinned. "From a bottle. Says she doesn't like the taste of Missouri water."

Nina rolled her eyes. "Like she'd know."

Carrie tapped the table. "I'll be right back with your drinks."

Jill chuckled as Nina watched the girl walk away. "She's a hot shot. Barney hired her last summer and brags on her like she's his own daughter." Her face softened.

Nina examined her sister's face. Of the two sisters, Jill had always favored their mother with light hair, hazel eyes, and thin lips.

"So what's the story with you and Barney? You getting married?"

Jill nodded.

Nina gasped. "Really? That's incredible, Jill! Congratulations! When's the big day?"

"We're not sure. He just proposed last weekend." Jill held up her left hand. "Didn't you see this?"

How could she have missed it? "I'm so sorry for not noticing. That's gorgeous." The diamond was at least a carat; otherwise, the ring was plain. Understated, but beautiful. Like Jill. "It's perfect, actually. Did he pick it out?"

Jill's face shone. She nodded.

Nina turned to stare at her soon-to-be brother-in-law through the order-up window. "I'm impressed. Who would ever have guessed Barney would turn out to be such a keeper." Jill laughed and followed Nina's gaze. "Cute and responsible—a winning combination." Barney's brow creased in concentration as he studied the orders and slid three plates onto the warm counter. "Carrie!"

The young waitress set their drinks down and grabbed the plates. She said something to Barney, and he grinned and nodded.

Carrie walked past their table. "I'll be back with your drinks after I drop this off at another table." An impish grin slid across her lips. "Barney has this thing about always serving hot food."

Jill smiled back at her. "How unreasonable of him."

"I see what you mean about Barney making a good dad," Nina said, suddenly missing Hunt. "The server seems just as taken with him."

"Poor Carrie. Her dad is the principal at the high school. With all the other kids he's responsible for, he doesn't seem to have a lot of time for his own daughter. Even when she's not working, she's here a lot."

"What about her mom?"

"Died of cancer before they moved here. That was four years ago." Jill's gaze shifted to a spot over Nina's shoulder. "There's Meg."

Nina scooted over, and Meg slipped in next to her.

"I can't believe what a dump this place is," Meg said.

Nina felt Jill bristle.

"This dump, as you call it," Nina told her daughter, "has been part of this town since it became a town. So show a little respect. Besides, your aunt is probably going to be part owner soon."

"You're buying a dumpy café, Aunt Jill?"

Jill scowled. "No. Shut up, Nina."

Nina grinned. "Oh, look who can't remember to tell a person to keep a secret."

"Touché."

Carrie arrived with a tray of drinks. "Tea, Diet Coke, and water—in a bottle."

"Thanks," Jill said. "Carrie, this is my sister, Nina, and her daughter, Meg."

Carrie's smile swept over them both. "Nice to meet you." She focused on Meg. "You here for spring break? Or for good?"

"My mom is moving here. I'm just here for spring break." Meg squared her shoulders. "I live with my dad in Dallas."

"Well, if you get bored this week, give me a call. The sheriff has my number. I'm on spring break too, but my dad is planning to spend the whole week getting caught up on paperwork, so I'm stuck here while most of my friends are away. Let me know if you want to hang out."

"Thanks," Meg mumbled, sipping her water. "I might."

Nina smiled at Carrie. "That's nice of you. Thank you for offering."

"Carrie!" Barney hollered before she had a chance to respond.

"That's probably your food," Carrie said. "I'll be right back."

Jill's phone rang and she answered. Her eyes grew large. "Dear God," she breathed. Concern built up in Nina as Jill's face drained of color.

"What's wrong?" Nina asked when she ended the call.

"I have to go." She tossed Nina her keys. "Drive to my house when you're done. I left some things on the counter I thought you might like. Chips, fruit, cookies, and a can of coffee. I didn't know what kind you like."

"Anything with caffeine. Don't worry about us. I'm worried about you. What was that call about?"

Jill grimaced. "There's been a murder."

"In Abbey Hills?"

Jill gave a nod. "Yes. I think it's bad, Nina. It's"—she cast a quick glance at Meg—"odd. That's all I can say."

Nina watched her stop and speak to Barney, saw the blood drain from his face, and realized Jill wasn't exaggerating. Murder in Abbey Hills? Nina could remember one twenty years ago, but it had involved domestic violence. Jill seemed shaken by this news.

Meg slipped out of the seat and moved to the other side of the booth. She stared at Nina. "Looks like you picked a great time to come back."

"Yep. Looks like it."

Carrie returned and set a plate in front of each of them.

Meg stared at the pile of fried fish on her plate. "I didn't order anything."

"Barney said to give you Jill's." Carrie frowned, concerned. "Do you want me to take it back?"

Meg shook her head. "This is fine. I'll eat it; I just didn't order it. That's all I was saying."

"Barney cooks the best fish. Even with all the great seafood places in Branson, we still get people who drive over just to eat here."

Nina listened halfheartedly to the conversation. She glanced around the restaurant, scoping out familiar faces. Some she recognized; some she didn't.

Barney called for Carrie again, and the girl sighed. "Duty calls. Nice meeting you, Meg."

"You too."

"She was nice," Nina commented.

Meg shrugged. "Seemed a little needy to me."

Nina sighed and examined her daughter. "We're all needy in our own way, I guess."

They ate in silence. This was her first meal out since she'd entered rehab. She ate a piece of catfish. The only thing missing from the meal was a glass of wine. The last time she'd gone to a restaurant, she'd downed half a bottle of white Merlot before the appetizers arrived.

Without warning, memories slammed into her so hard that she could feel the glass in her hand, taste the alcohol. She closed her eyes, savoring the phantom taste. Weakness washed over her.

Even with her daughter present, she felt very alone in this familiar-yet-alien place.

Markus knew the moment the air changed that Nina Parker had come home. The spring breeze had lifted her scent and brought it to him, part offering and part beckoning. It carried the memory of her breath on his neck, the softness of her skin. The tears on her cheeks.

He made his way through town. Ignoring the smells of grease, meat, and humanity, he focused on Nina's sweet signature. He stepped inside Barney's, his heart pounding in his ears, drowning out the café din. The sheriff nearly ran him over as she hurried past him.

"Sorry, neighbor!" she called over her shoulder. "Police business."

"It's all right."

She was easy to spot, sitting in the corner with a teenage girl, talking to Carrie, the waitress. He fought the urge to go right up to her and initiate a conversation. He needed time to temper his raw emotions and form a plan. After all, she had no idea how long he'd been waiting for her, how he'd longed to see her again.

Barney hollered for Carrie, and she turned and spotted Markus. "Hi, Mr. Chisom. You can sit in that booth over there." She motioned toward the wall. "I'll bring you a menu in a sec."

It would be easy to watch Nina from that spot, so Markus nodded. "Take your time. I'm in no hurry."

He slid into the booth, his eyes never straying from Nina's face. The lovely girl he remembered had grown into a beautiful woman. Her once round face had slimmed and matured. Her brown eyes were sad. In the darkness, he hadn't seen much of her eyes that night seventeen years earlier, and when he had, they'd been clouded and confused. She'd been angry then; he could feel the long simmer in her blood. When had the sadness happened?

He'd learned much about human nature through the years. His studies in trial and error had taught him which personality types were more susceptible to his influence. Sadness almost always meant loneliness, and the lonely came willingly. Lonely females in particular. Markus didn't imagine Nina to be weak, but maybe he just wanted her to be like his Kimana.

Carrie approached his table and set a menu in front of him. "Here you go, Mr. Chisom. Know what you want to drink?"

He ordered green tea. He'd never acquired a taste for coffee or soda. "I won't need the menu, Carrie. The tea will be sufficient."

"Coming right up."

Nina turned then and caught his eye. She gave him a quick, tentative smile, then turned back to the sullen girl seated across from her.

Now seemed as good a time as any to introduce himself. Nina glanced up as he approached. Her eyes widened in curiosity, and then a shield slid across her face.

"Excuse me for intruding," he said carefully. "I hope you don't mind, but I wanted to introduce myself since we're going to be neighbors. I'm Markus Chisom. I live next to the sheriff. Jill mentioned you were coming to stay for a while."

Her expression relaxed, and she held out her hand. "Nina Parker. This is my daughter, Meagan."

Daughter? He scrutinized the scowling teenage face, surprised he hadn't sensed the relationship between Nina and the girl. "Nice to meet both of you."

For seventeen years he'd imagined how this day would unfold. Seeing Nina again, feeling her close to him, drinking in uniqueness in this bland place. Now that it was here, he was at a loss for words, which was unlike him. He'd long ago perfected small talk. It was the way he drew people in and gained their confidence. But now he felt like an awkward young man again.

"So what do you do, Markus?" Nina's polite question accompanied a pull of her hand from his.

He cleared his throat as he realized he still clutched her fingers. What was wrong with him? "Actually, Miss Parker . . ."

"Nina, please." She smiled.

"Nina then. Actually, I moved to Abbey Hills to retire."

Her eyebrows arched upward. "You seem a little young for retirement."

"That's kind of you." He chuckled. If she only knew his true age. "I own several businesses in St. Louis, and they caused me no shortage of stress. It was time to turn them over to trusted managers. Take the money and run, as they say."

True enough, although every fifty years or so he sold and bought new businesses. Right now, he held the titles to many plots of commercial real estate in St. Louis.

The daughter gave a short laugh. "Must be nice to be that rich."

"Meg!"

"It's all right." He forced an indulgent smile. It wouldn't do to make an enemy of Nina's daughter. "It's nice to be in a position to retire comfortably in such a friendly town."

The girl rolled her eyes and sipped her water.

"I apologize for my daughter's rudeness, Mr. Chisom."

"Call me Markus, please." He made a show of waving away her concerns and decided an easy lie would be prudent. "I have teenage nieces."

The girl's lip curled. "Then you must know all about girls my age."

Nina glowered at her daughter. "Meg, that's enough. I apologize again for my daughter."

The girl looked at her mother and then at Markus with the same expression of disdain. "I have to go wash my hands." She wrinkled her nose. "They're greasy. I never eat fried food at home."

Nina gave her a tight smile. "Try to come back in a better mood."

Awkward silence settled over Markus and Nina as Meagan walked away.

"Would you like to join us?" Nina asked, motioning to the seat across from her.

Not wanting to overplay his hand, Markus smiled but shook his head. "I don't want to interrupt your dinner. But I look forward to seeing you again soon."

"Oh, that's right. Next-door neighbor."

Her smile slid over him, and he almost changed his mind, but he could tell that, despite her invitation, she'd spoken out of politeness. He sensed the need to go slowly. Nina had grown into a beautiful woman—and one with very high, guarded walls.

Swallowing his impatience, he smiled again and said good-bye.

~

The first time I saw Nina drunk—really drunk—was on our honeymoon. I'd certainly seen her have a few drinks or a glass of wine on occasion, but I hadn't seen her drunk. I didn't know any better than to be amused by her funny antics and aroused by her complete lack of inhibition in bed. After our first night of wedded bliss, she nursed a hangover while I fed her dry crackers, warm 7UP, and Tylenol.

I hated that she was too sick to enjoy our first full day in paradise. She'd never been to Hawaii, this woman I adored. She was so excited when I presented her with the idea that I felt like Superman, Bono, and Merlin all rolled into one.

She'd never flown before, and the morning of our flight she was so panicked she insisted on canceling the tickets and honeymooning somewhere we could drive to. The Grand Canyon, or maybe Carlsbad Caverns. Even Houston. But the tickets were nonrefundable, the reservations in Hawaii set in stone, and I really wanted to show my wife the islands.

She gave in but begged me for Valium. I've never been crazy about calming drugs—too addictive. Instead, I suggested a stiff drink in one of the airport lounges before we boarded.

Now I get the irony of refusing her drugs and introducing the drink. But no one needs LASIK in hindsight, do they?

The cocktail worked, and she relaxed almost instantly. Once we were at altitude, she ordered another from the flight attendant and had downed two more before we landed. I had to carry her into the hotel, which was okay, since I was supposed to carry her over the threshold anyway.

In the years that followed, I carried Nina through a lot of doors. Eventually I became disgusted with her sloppy sexual advances, and I stopped being amused by her antics.

It was years before I was able to forgive myself for suggesting that one calming drink in the airport lounge.

CHAPTER FIVE

Childhood marks our lives. There's no getting around that. The thing that's always puzzled me is how two children can be raised in the same environment and yet become completely different people. It boils down to the old study of nature versus nurture, right? Take Jill and me, for instance. Growing up in picturesque Abbey Hills didn't mean to me what it meant to my sister.

Jill had talent. She had beauty, and she had brains. Straight As and the kind of singing voice and leadership skills that made it impossible for teachers to ignore her the way they ignored me and the rest of the kids without talent and money. We didn't stand a chance in Abbey Hills.

No wonder Jill's memories of our childhood are so different from mine. She was my mother's girl. Dad always said I was just like him.

How's that for irony?

Nina pulled the Camry to a stop in front of the old Hanson house—a white, two-story, country Victorian that looked like it should be a bed-and-breakfast. Nina had always wished she lived in this sort of house when she was a kid. She considered sharing this feeling and turned toward her daughter, but Meg's tight jaw discouraged Nina's honesty.

They must pay the sheriff a pretty good salary in sleepy little Abbey Hills if Jill could afford to buy this place and keep it up all by herself. And no wonder Jill wasn't concerned about the extra company—the house was massive. Even bigger than Nina remembered from her childhood. Things like houses and people usually got smaller as a person got bigger, not the other way around.

Meg slung her backpack over her shoulder, staring in appreciation at her aunt's home. "Nice place. Aunt Jill has taste."

Nina heard the "even if you don't" in her voice but didn't feel like responding to her daughter's bait. She walked around to the back of the car and lifted the hatch. "What did you expect, a ratty apartment and empty pizza boxes on the front porch?"

Meg shrugged. "I didn't really think about it."

Nina grabbed a couple of bags. "Let's go."

"Did Aunt Jill leave the key?"

Nina smiled and tossed Meagan a "watch this" look. Living in a town like Abbey Hills, there was never much reason to lock up. She set down one of her bags and reached around Meg to twist the knob. Predictably, they easily let themselves into the house.

"Amazing," Meg said. "Hick Town, America, where nothing bad ever happens."

"I imagine your Aunt Jill probably wishes you were right about that."

Meg had the good grace to blush. "Oh, yeah. She said someone was murdered."

"Right."

Once word of the tragedy spread, folks might be a lot more likely to lock their doors, but the fifty-year-old locks on most houses in town probably wouldn't keep a mischievous kid out, let alone someone bent on doing harm.

They stepped inside. The house smelled of lemon polish and potpourri, and the wood floors shone as if they'd just been cleaned. Nina glanced about, appreciating the lovely, old-fashioned ambiance. Jill had worked hard to get this massive home ready for her arrival. The thought warmed Nina. When was the last time anyone had gone out of their way for her? Hunt's face appeared in her mind, and she shuddered. She had ruined them, so would she always ache for him?

"Where do I crash?"

Nina shrugged. "Jill didn't tell me which rooms are ours, so I guess we should just leave our things here in the foyer until she gets home."

"Fine." Meagan's pack slid off her shoulder, down her arm, and thudded to the floor. "Can I watch TV?"

"I don't see why not."

"Which way?"

"Your guess is as good as mine." Nina looked around and nodded toward a room to the left of the dark wooden staircase. "That looks like it might be a living room. Why don't you check in there?"

Meagan sighed as only a sixteen-year-old can and started toward the other room.

Nina watched her go. Her chest tightened. What if she couldn't handle everyday motherhood again? Especially with a moody teenager bent on making her pay?

She sank onto the third step of the staircase and rested her feet on the next one down. Burying her face in her hands, she gathered two deep breaths, in through the nose, out through the mouth, and tried to push away the phantom taste of wine at the back of her throat.

Would the day ever come when every little pressure didn't bring on the desire to ease it with a drink? Failure couldn't be an option. It just couldn't.

She had to believe she could do this. One day at a time.

• • •

Meg flipped through the channels, half watching one thing for thirty seconds before turning to something else. She stretched out on the fluffy beige couch, sighed, and flipped the channel again. Her phone buzzed. Finally! Izzy was texting.

We're finally here. Crazy rain. Slow driving. French Quarter tomorrow.

Murder here.

☹ Bored?

Meg grinned and thumbed the letters on the tiny slide-out keyboard.

Real murder. Not bored.

The phone buzzed again.

Huh??

Meg didn't know why she'd said it, except that she was angry. Now that Izzy had made it to New Orleans, the whole situation was more real. After all the weeks of planning—crabbing at the Gulf, lying on the beach, visiting the French Quarter, eating barbeque and gumbo, and drinking coffee so strong you could stand a spoon straight up in it—she was in Podunk, Missouri, with her mother. All she'd wanted was a few days of not having to think about home and all the crazy stress that accompanied being the daughter of a drunk.

At least now that there was a murder in town she had something exciting to talk about.

She ignored the little voice in her head reminding her that someone had lost a loved one tonight. She shoved it so far away that all she could see in her mind's eye was the excitement of a dead body found in this little nothing of a town.

Murder. A real one, she texted.

Izzy wrote, **Wow. You scared?**

Nah. I'm staying with the sheriff.

I'd still be scared. Hey, maybe you can help her solve it.

LOL sure. Meagan PI

Cheesy grin. Mom's calling. Gotta go.

K. TTYL

Meg slid her phone onto the coffee table. Closing her eyes, she listened to the sounds of MTV and thought for the millionth time how unfair it was that she was stuck in this retarded town. Murder or no murder, New Orleans was a lot more exciting.

Nina glanced at the antique chime clock on the wall. Almost eleven. Jill had been gone for four hours with no word.

Nina squeezed out her tea bag, dumped the contents of a pink packet of sugar substitute into the cup, stirred, and tapped the spoon against the side of the cup before placing it in the stainless steel sink. Wrapping her fingers around the mug handle, she walked through the kitchen into the foyer and opened the front door.

The lovely thing about Victorian homes, the old painted ladies as they were called, was the large porch most of them had. This one stretched along the front of the house and around the east side, where, Nina supposed, Jill's room opened through french doors to a view of the historic brick street.

A set of wicker furniture sat invitingly in the cool spring night. Sinking onto the green cushion of a loveseat, Nina rested her socked feet on the wicker table and her head against the back of the chair. She gathered in a deep, rain-scented breath of humid air.

In the west, distant lightning lit the sky, signaling an impending storm. Nina settled into the atmosphere and allowed her emotions to calm. She closed her eyes, savoring the peace.

The peace fled, and her skin prickled as if the tiny feet of a thousand ants were crawling up and down her body. She sat up. Searching the darkness, she shivered, thoroughly spooked by nothing in particular. She saw nothing but open air and house lights up and down the street. A rumble of thunder accompanied the flashes of lightning. She'd be so glad when spring storms gave way to summer heat. She didn't mind the rain so much, but lightning and thunder always made her stomach quiver.

"Hello again, neighbor."

Nina jumped, then felt foolish as Markus

Chisom emerged from behind a holly bush at the corner of the porch.

"You scared me half to death," she said.

"I apologize. I should have been more obvious in my approach. I saw you turn on the porch light and figured you were out here."

She smiled. "It's okay. You a night owl like I am?"

"You could say that. It's a bad habit, but I do my best sleeping during the day."

"I don't sleep day or night." Nina heard the complaint in her tone and felt her face warm. "Well, I do sleep some. Obviously."

He stopped at the bottom of the steps and looked up.

"Sheriff Parker hasn't returned, I take it?"

Nina shook her head. "Public service. I suppose overwork is what she signed on for."

"During certain times, for sure."

Silence pervaded the night air between them, and Nina realized she hadn't asked him to sit or even invited him onto the porch. She scooted to the other side of the loveseat so he wouldn't have to step over or around her. "Would you like to join me?"

"Sure."

As he climbed the steps, Nina studied his face in the soft glow of the porch light. She hadn't noticed earlier how good-looking he was. Tall, really tall. He actually looked a little bit like

Clive Owen. She tilted her head, studying him. Her heart rate picked up as he dropped onto the loveseat next to her. She averted her gaze as she realized she'd been staring.

"Spring is beautiful in the Ozarks, isn't it?" he said.

"I suppose. I grew up here, so there's not much thrill in it for me."

He cocked his head and looked at her. "Beauty is beauty."

She smiled. "I've only been back a few hours though. Maybe things will look better in the morning."

He chuckled. "I wouldn't bet on it. Storms are supposed to blow through tonight with a chance for tornados."

"Welcome to spring. It's the same in Texas. Spring storms and hot summers."

"You came from Texas?"

Nina nodded. "Dallas."

"So your daughter's father is still there?"

"Yes. And my seven-year-old son, Adam." She stared at the distant flash of lightning.

He stretched his long legs in front of him and folded his thick arms across his chest. "Ah, you have two children then. You must miss your son."

"Yeah." Nina didn't trust herself to say any more without a rush of unwanted tears.

"It must help some that your daughter is with you."

Nina couldn't hold back a sigh. "Meg's dad

will pick her up at the end of the week. She's only with me for spring break."

He remained silent, and Nina was grateful he didn't offer platitudes or false comfort. She kept her gaze on the coming storm. A gust of wind blew up the scent of honeysuckle. "I suppose it is beautiful here."

"You should have seen it many years ago, before the cities were built and industry thickened the air."

Nina laughed. "I guess we should all have been so lucky."

Markus cleared his throat. "Did you know that at one time all the Ozarks belonged to the Osage Indians?"

Nina nodded. "Dad and I used to look for arrowheads during our fishing trips."

He smiled. "Did you ever find any?"

"Once or twice."

"Did you keep any of them? I'm something of a history buff, so I could probably verify the authenticity for you."

She shook her head. "Thanks, but I don't have the arrowheads anymore. I packed pretty light when I left town. I'm sure my folks cleaned out my room and tossed them years ago."

A clap of thunder, much louder and closer than before, made her jump.

"Looks like the storm is tired of playing around," she said.

Markus nodded. "I think so."

Lightning struck the ground, too close for Nina to feel safe on the porch any longer. She stood. "Sorry, neighbor, but that's my cue to go inside."

He chuckled and stood next to her. "Mine as well."

Nina hesitated. Did he expect her to invite him in?

As if sensing her discomfort, Markus held out his hand. "Thank you for a nice conversation, Nina Parker. I'm sure I'll see you again soon."

Nina took the proffered hand, relieved. "I'm sure you will. Good night."

She waited while he descended the steps, turned and waved, then walked toward the house across the side street. Once again she felt the sense of unease that had surrounded her earlier, and she hurriedly opened the door. Inside, she turned the lock, then hesitated and unlocked it. Jill might not have a house key.

On stormy nights, Nina's routine was typically a bottle or two of wine, candles, and a good mystery. A sense of longing stirred inside her.

She shoved aside the thought. It was time to start developing some new habits. The effort would be worth it. She was sure of it.

Creaking hinges woke Nina from a restless sleep in a prettier-than-it-was-comfortable wingback chair. She stood and met Jill in the foyer. Her sister's face was pale, and she seemed shaky as she looked at Nina.

"Nina. Why are you still up? It's after midnight."

"We weren't sure where you wanted us."

"What? Oh . . . sorry. I didn't think. I should have called you and checked in. Either of the rooms at the top of the stairs. Take your pick, and give Meggie the other. The rest of the bedrooms don't have beds yet."

Nina nodded. "I'll just let Meg sleep on the couch tonight if you don't mind. She can move into a room tomorrow."

Jill gave a distracted wave and nodded. "Yeah. Don't wake her. You could have gone upstairs and explored, you know. You're smart enough to figure out which rooms have beds and which don't."

Nina grinned. "You never liked me snooping in your stuff. I remember what happened when I borrowed your Whitney Houston tapes."

"Only because you took them out of the case and replaced them all with heavy metal the night of my fifteenth birthday sleepover."

"Oh, yeah." Nina grinned. "I forgot about that. It was sort of funny watching the horrified expressions of your goody two-shoes friends when Mötley Crüe blasted your room."

"They didn't think it was very funny. And those sorts of stunts were exactly why you never got invited to join us in anything we did."

Nina gave a nonchalant wave. "Your friends were way too tame for me back then. Anyway. Back to the present. I didn't want to snoop. Mötley Crüe notwithstanding, you never liked me in your stuff."

"I don't mind so much now." Jill sighed. "Guess I'm growing up." Her tone seemed detached, far away.

"Hey. Everything okay?"

Jill shook her head. "I never thought I'd see anything like this in Abbey Hills." She blew out a long, slow breath. "It was pretty gruesome."

Nina grabbed her arm. "Come into the kitchen. I'll make you some chamomile tea. I couldn't find the coffeepot."

Jill motioned to the cabinet over the refrigerator as she dropped into one of the six wooden chairs around the table. "It's old, but I guess it works. I don't do coffee."

"That's just weird."

Jill shrugged. "Weird seems to be following me lately."

"Try to relax, Jilly."

Jill's attempt at a smile was painful. "You haven't called me Jilly since we were kids."

"I haven't seen you this freaked out since we were kids and Mr. Michaels followed us home from school. Remember that?"

Jill nodded, unlacing a pair of black military-style boots. "Speaking of weird, he was a real weirdo. I remember we hid at Barney's a couple of times until we saw him go by."

"Barney the Second." Nina grinned. "You have Barney the Third wrapped around your little finger, don't you? I was watching you two."

Jill smiled. "Works both ways."

Nina set the kettle on the stove and sat across from Jill while she waited for the whistle. "Can you talk about the murder? Or do you have to wait until the family is notified?"

"I've seen the family already." Jill's face had begun to regain its color during the course of the conversation but once more turned white. Her eyes took on a hollow, haunted look. She met Nina's gaze. "Nina, it was Amanda Rollings. She was Amanda Baylor during high school. She graduated with you."

Nina nodded. "She was pregnant with Pete Rollings's baby at graduation. Did he have anything to do with her death?"

"Pete says no, of course. Claims he was home all night with their two younger kids, but we still have to investigate him. There was weird bruising on her neck."

"You mean like she was strangled?"

Jill shook her head. "More like tiny stab marks."

"Strange."

Jill bit her lip, her eyes almost glazed, as though picturing the scene too clearly for comfort. "She was stabbed. Repeatedly. And then her torso was carved up, ritualistically." She traced the path of the knife on her own body with her index finger. "A slash across the throat, and then a long cut between her breasts, like a T or a cross."

Nina shuddered. "Stop it. That's awful."

"Sorry. It's just so vivid. Anyway, the bruising makes no sense. She was hanging upside down. The killer took her heart out. Three animals cut the same way have been discovered in the last few weeks."

"Wild animals or domestic?"

"A deer, one stray dog, and a possum."

Nina swallowed hard. "So was it Satanists or witches or something?"

"I don't know. The coroner will do an autopsy, and we'll send our evidence to the crime lab in Springfield. We won't know anything for a couple of weeks, probably."

The kettle whistled and they both jumped. "Should folks be worried, or do you think Amanda was a specific target?" Nina stood and walked to the stove.

"We just don't know, Nina. I don't want to alarm people. It wouldn't take much to cause a panic in a town the size of Abbey Hills." Jill's eyes narrowed with concern. Her shoulders seemed to slump as the weight of responsibility bore down upon her. "What if we find out it was a domestic situation after all? Pete and Amanda got into a fight and things took a violent turn? He got laid off recently. Maybe the financial pressure was too much, and he just snapped. If that's the case, no one else is in danger. I'm sure he knew about the animals. That isn't information a town like Abbey Hills can keep secret. Maybe he cut Amanda the same way to throw us off his trail."

Nina took out a tea bag and set it in a mug. Steam rose to her face as she tilted the kettle and poured the water for Jill's tea. "That's possible, I suppose. On the other hand, if there's a serial-killing Satanist out there carving up sacrifices to his dark god and you *don't* warn people to use the buddy system, you might have more deaths to investigate. And then you can kiss reelection good-bye."

Jill rolled her trademark brown eyes, so dark they could have been black. "Reelection is the least of my worries. But the rest of what you said . . . that's my dilemma. Mass panic or more deaths?"

"Or neither."

"Right. Or neither."

Jill retreated into silence, staring into her tea-cup as if it were a crystal ball. Nina knew better than to try further conversation. In a city the size of Dallas, murders were fairly common. A couple hundred a year, more or less. A random killing might make the news one day, but by the following day, local media outlets had moved on to the next big thing.

But in a town like Abbey Hills, with just over a thousand residents, one grisly murder would be felt like a freight train charging down the center of Main Street. Jill wouldn't be able to keep the news from spreading. By morning, Pete Rollings's neighbors would be sending condolences and baking casseroles. And by evening, every household in town would know there was a killer among them.

CHAPTER SIX

I only had one friend growing up, a boy named Stephan. He was a grade behind me and a head shorter, until he reached tenth grade, when he shot up over the summer, surprising us both. He lost most of his pimples that year too. The newly acquired clear skin gave him the confidence he needed, and he started working out, filling out in all the right places.

We used to sneak out after our parents were in bed. Stephan would walk a mile to get to my house, and we'd lie side by side on the picnic table in my backyard, staring at the stars and dreaming of the day we would be old enough to leave Abbey Hills.

He tried to kiss me once. I threatened his life, and he didn't try again for a long, long time. Things went back to normal after that . . . almost.

Stephan tried out for the football team and turned into a hot shot. He got a cheerleader girlfriend after his first touchdown, and we barely spoke until the end of senior year.

Nina lay motionless, listening to the rain beat against the roof.

Still storming. The kind of storm that sent nervous types to the basement with a flashlight, protein bars, and a couple gallon jugs of bottled water in case the house crashed down around them and it took rescue teams several days to dig through the rubble.

Nina's internal alarm always went off after four hours of sleep, no matter what time she finally dozed off, which in this case was around 2 a.m. She'd long ago resigned herself to making do with half the sleep the average person needed and had learned to function just as well as the next guy—even with a hangover.

Another earsplitting clap of thunder shook the house, rattling the windows. Nina sat up with a start and stared at the double windows only two feet from her bed. The thin white curtain billowed in the wind, and a light spray blew through the screened window.

Nina shivered. Maybe it hadn't been such a good idea to leave the window open, but the smell of rain called to her, and she'd had one of those unexplainable sensations of longing deep in her gut. Nothing smelled like rain, and nothing ached like the desire to be young again—at least before cynicism set in around the age of ten. There was something about the way rain could wash away the old and leave everything pure and fresh, plump with the possibility of a do-over, so she'd given in and opened the window. But while she slept, the wind had shifted and was driving the rain inside, onto Jill's wood floors.

A streak of lightning split the sky, so close that if she'd pushed her hand out the window, it would have struck her. Thunder clapped on its heels, and she shuddered.

Pushing back the covers, Nina swung her legs to the side of the bed. Her feet landed on the damp wood floor. She took a couple of steps on her tiptoes and lowered the window.

The bathroom light glowed through the crack she'd left for a night-light, and she followed it to the door. She snatched the hand towel from the rack on the wall and went back to the window to wipe up the rain.

Nina stayed by the window until an invisible hand brushed the storm eastward, the dark clouds surrendering to impending daybreak. She leaned against the windowsill and let her gaze wander to the street below. The streetlights shimmered on the wet pavement.

Across the street, a light snapped on in Markus Chisom's house, and a figure appeared in the upstairs window. Nina's heart raced at the thought of Markus. He seemed to stare straight at her, and Nina slid back from the window. Then she chided herself for being paranoid. There was no way he could see her. His light was on. Hers was off. So why did it feel like he was watching her?

A creepy shudder slipped down her spine. She dropped the sheer curtain and stepped back.

Coffee called her name. Her bare arms felt like ice, so she grabbed a St. Louis Rams sweatshirt and slipped it on over her T-shirt.

In the kitchen she pulled the coffeepot from the cabinet above the refrigerator and looked inside the decanter. It was coated with brown residue, as if the last person who used it hadn't bothered to wash it out, and a few dead spiders lay in the bottom. She wrinkled her nose and began cleaning it out. After scrubbing the pot, she ran some plain water through the machine to clean the insides.

She'd never been a morning person, but when you only slept a few hours a night, morning became inevitable. Besides, she needed to plan her day. Barney didn't expect her to start work for a couple of days, so she decided to explore the town and check out anything that might be new since she'd left. Maybe Meg would enjoy taking the fifty-cent tour with her.

The machine took forever to brew a crappy cup of coffee. Nina mentally calculated how much cash she had in her purse. Definitely not enough to justify buying a coffeepot. She'd just pick up some vinegar and try to dislodge the lime buildup in this one. Maybe that would improve the burnt, muddy taste. Either way, caffeine was caffeine.

She was on her second cup, doctored with two tablespoons of lite nondairy creamer and three packets of sugar substitute when Meg stumbled into the kitchen. She yawned, grabbed a cup from the cabinet, and pulled the pot from the machine.

"Since when do you drink coffee?"

Meg shrugged and dropped into a chair. She spooned sugar and dumped creamer without measuring. "Awhile."

"Well, drink that at your own risk. It's awful."

"You're not going to hassle me about it?" Meg's eyebrows rose.

Nina shook her head. "Why should I? It's not much different from all the soda you drink."

She wasn't thrilled with Meg drinking coffee, but picking her battles was part of recovery, and getting into an argument that she was a hypocrite for drinking coffee by the gallon while denying her daughter the same right didn't seem like the smart choice.

There was just one thing. "It'll stunt your growth."

"I knew you couldn't let it go."

"Just saying, shorty."

"Whatever."

Jill picked that moment to shuffle into the kitchen. "Morning, family. Arguing already?"

Nina frowned. "How can you sound so chipper at six-thirty? It's not natural."

"I got a gene that skipped you, I guess." Jill wrinkled her nose. "Smells like burnt coffee."

"I wonder why. How old is that pot?"

Jill shrugged. "It came with the house."

"That explains the brown goo and all the dead spiders I had to wash out."

Meg pushed her cup away and leaned her chair back on two legs. "Gross."

Nina took another sip. She ignored Meg's look of disdain and stared at the back of Jill's head as her sister opened the tap and filled the teakettle.

"So, Meggie. How about having breakfast with your grandparents today. They're dying to meet you." Jill tossed the words over her shoulder.

"Great! I'm dying to meet them too."

"Oh?" Dread hit Nina, full and without mercy.

Meg stared hard without blinking, her dark eyebrows slightly arched, challenging. "If I'm going to be stuck in this town for a week, I think I have the right to at least meet them, don't you?"

Right was such a complicated word. The girl's sense of entitlement was warranted, but it made Nina feel as though she'd done something wrong in keeping Meg away. And she honestly didn't think she had. She'd stayed away for her own reasons. She had a right to live her life, didn't she?

Meagan gave a huff. "Well?"

"I don't care, Meg," Nina said. "Meet them if you want. You're old enough to choose."

Jill pulled a teacup from the cabinet and set it on the counter next to the stove. "You should come too, Nina. Mom is fixing breakfast for us this morning."

"Now isn't the time, Jill."

Annoyance crossed Jill's features. Nina prepared for a confrontation, but it didn't come. Instead, Jill turned her gaze to Meg. "We leave in half an hour. Better get ready if you want to go."

"I'm going." Meg dropped the legs of her chair to the floor with a thud and stood up. Nina watched her leave the room.

Jill tucked a leg beneath her and sat catty-corner from Nina. "What about you?" Jill asked. "It's been awhile, you know."

"Tell them I said hi," Nina offered.

"Maybe you should tell them yourself." Jill's tone was sharp and short.

"Okay. Forget it then." The teakettle whistled.

Jill rolled her eyes and stood up. "I'll tell them. Do you have any idea when you might go see them?"

"What difference does it make? I'm going to be here awhile, Jill. We've got time."

Jill poured her water and set the teakettle back on the stove. She lifted her cup. "I know, but . . . never mind. Do what makes you happy."

"Look, I can't be around Dad right now. I'm

119

only ninety days sober. All I have to do is smell it on his breath, and I could ruin everything."

Jill's eyes narrowed. "Seriously?"

"Don't you think it's a valid enough reason?"

"It would be if he still drank."

Nina's gut tightened. "What are you saying?"

"He hasn't had a drop in eight years."

"Dad's sober?"

"Stone-cold sober."

The news shattered over Nina like broken crystal. She sat unmoving as the strength left her body, starting at her head and sliding downward.

"You're saying Dad quit drinking?"

"Yes. Eight years ago."

"And you never told me?"

Jill frowned. "I guess by the time we reconnected, I was used to the new dad. And you changed the subject every time I brought up our parents."

"True." Nina shook her head. Dad not drinking was a foreign concept. It would take a while to stop picturing him with a drink in his hand. "What made him decide to stop, finally?"

"You sure you want the answer?"

Nina nodded. "I wouldn't have asked if I didn't."

A flicker of annoyance passed over Jill's face. "When Reverend Fuller retired about ten years ago, we got a new, young preacher with a wife and two kids. Landon Bradley. One night he found Dad staggering home and offered him a ride. He asked Dad to call him if he needed a ride. No questions asked."

"And Dad did?"

Jill grinned and shrugged. "I know it sounds strange, but for some reason Dad trusted him, and they struck up an odd sort of friendship. Like something out of a movie."

"The preacher and the drunk."

"Something like that."

"Sounds like a sitcom."

"That friendship saved Dad's life. One night, he called the reverend and then started walking home anyway. Reverend Bradley caught up to him just as he was passing out from vomiting up blood. He has cirrhosis of the liver."

Nina's heartbeat increased with alarm, which surprised her. She'd thought her heart had closed off to him so long ago that all she had was this cold, dark place where her love for him used to sit.

"He had a partial transplant a few years ago," Jill continued.

"They did a transplant on an alcoholic?"

Jill nodded. "Reverend Bradley went to bat for him. Dad had been doing odd jobs around the church as his strength held out. He sat with Dad through three nights of shakes and hallucinations while he detoxed. Dad has been devoted to the church, and specifically the reverend, ever since."

The town drunk found religion. Nina found it

interesting, if slightly unbelievable. "So I guess Dad's just a sweet old man now, all Jesus-fied and waiting for glory."

Jill scowled. "Not even close. And you don't have to be so sarcastic. Does anything make you happy?"

"Nothing about this town, Jill."

"Maybe you shouldn't have come back."

Nina glared back. "Maybe I shouldn't have."

After a moment, a slow grin spread over Jill's face. "Know what this reminds me of?"

"What?"

"Old times." Jill walked over to her, bent, and gave her a hug. "I've missed you. Let's find something in Abbey Hills to be happy about."

Nina sat at the table staring at her empty coffee cup long after Jill and Meg pulled out of the driveway in Barney's truck. What would make her happy?

How about going back in time and never taking that first drink. Not alienating her family. Getting her husband back. Those things would make her happy.

She didn't know what she had expected, but it wasn't the pretty sixtyish Grammy—as her grandma insisted upon being called—with kind, twinkling eyes and a busty embrace. For some reason, Meg felt the urge to cry, but she held it back.

Grammy ushered Meg and Jill inside the two-story brick home. It was a simple but well-kept home, sitting on a simple, well-kept lot. Inside, it smelled of pine and brilliant cooking.

Grammy smoothed a veiny hand over Meg's head. "You have your mother's hair. Except curlier."

"Exact same eyes," Meg's grandpa said, taking her into his arms for an embrace. A really tight hug Meg wasn't sure she'd recover from.

"Don't squeeze the breath out of her," Grammy scolded.

"You just hush. I finally get to hug my only granddaughter, and I'll do it however I want," he said, but he loosened his death grip.

Meg grinned. "Thanks for letting me breathe again. What should I call you?" She called her dad's dad Grandpa.

He winked again and gave her an understanding nod. "I've always been partial to Poppy. Does that seem too corny?"

Meg shook her head. "I think it fits."

She loved him already. What was Nina's problem?

His face was bony and pale, and his pants were belted tight, like they were too big. "You like fishing?"

"As long as you don't use live bait." Meg grinned to show him she didn't want to hurt his feelings. "It's cruel." She had only been fishing once and hated every second of it, but for her newfound "Poppy," she'd give it another go.

He nodded. "Okay, then. I won't get worms. We'll go this week, you and me. Then we can have a fish fry. Maybe your mom will come." He pulled out a mug. "You drink coffee?"

"Only when Mom's around." She lifted her eyebrows and grinned. "It bugs her."

He chuckled. "You really are like her."

Her grin faded. She was nothing like Nina. Her grandparents would find that out soon enough. Her insides shook a little. If they hoped to have Nina back through her, they were going to be disappointed. Really disappointed.

"So you like to fish, huh?" she said to change the subject.

"Your mom and I used to go."

So much for diversion. Did everything have to come back to Nina? What would these folks do if they knew what their precious daughter was really like? On the other hand, Nina had blown them off for seventeen years, so they probably already knew she wasn't that great.

"Yeah, that's what Nina said."

"She told you about those days, huh?" Poppy looked pleased, and Meg didn't have the heart to tell him there hadn't been any flattery involved in the revelation. He jerked his thumb toward Aunt Jill, who had followed them into the kitchen and stood at the stove, stirring gravy.

"Her sister never was much for outdoor stuff. She liked to read and sing and all that."

Aunt Jill turned from the stove and stared hard at Poppy. "I don't remember ever being invited to go fishing."

A look passed between them, something Meg didn't understand and felt uncomfortable watching. She pulled out a chair and plopped down. "So, Grammy, Aunt Jill says you make the best biscuits and gravy ever."

Grammy pulled her attention away from the thick resentment passing from Aunt Jill to Poppy. She smiled at Meagan, the kind of approving smile that said she understood and would have changed the subject herself if Meg hadn't. "Aunt Jill is right." She forced a laugh. "They're not too bad, if I do say so."

Poppy slung his arm around Grammy's shoulders and gave her a quick squeeze. "Been a long time since you had a kid to cook for." He winked at Meg. "She made enough for a football team, so you'd best be hungry."

Meg grinned. "I'm always hungry."

"Just like your mama always was at your age."

Disappointment surged through her. Meg knew the tenderness in his eyes was for a memory, not for her.

There was no point pretending that being back in Abbey Hills didn't affect her. She slipped on a pair of sunglasses to fend off the brightness of a sun that shone down on wet streets. The rain had stopped three hours ago, and the clouds gave way to a brilliant, blinding sun. Nina was glad for the opportunity to hide behind the glasses.

She sipped on a diet cherry limeade from Sonic and pulled over at Maise Park, where she'd fished and had many Easter egg hunts. Softball practices were held in the ball field on the other side of the pond, as were all the football games until the town finally built a football field behind the combination junior high and high school.

Nina grabbed her brown bag special and headed for a picnic table next to the pond. The wet grass tickled her toes in her cheap Wal-Mart brand flip-flops.

A dozen ducks headed toward her. So much for the "Don't Feed the Ducks" sign. These fat birds had been human fed forever. Every generation of the semiwild birds relied on the kindness of strangers. They waddled around her feet, following her like they'd imprinted on the Sonic bag.

She slid onto the tabletop and looked out over the pond. "Listen, little guys," she said to the quacking beggars. "Let me at least eat what I want before you take my lunch."

"Not exactly peaceful is it?"

Nina started and almost screamed as she

126

whipped around. Her pent-up breath whooshed out of her. "Markus! Warn me next time."

His brown eyes took her in, and he lifted his hand, palm forward. "I've startled you. Again. Does twice make it a habit?"

"It's okay. Again. What are you doing here?" Her face warmed as she realized he was dressed in Nike shorts, a T-shirt, and running shoes.

"I come here to jog around the track."

"When did they build a track at the park?"

He shrugged and smiled. "I'm the new guy in town. It was already here when I arrived. It's only a fourth of a mile though, so it gets a little monotonous if I run more than a couple miles."

"In high school, I used to run at the animal sanctuary outside town."

"I never thought about that." His eyes brightened. "There are great trails out there."

"You've walked them?"

He nodded. "I go out there from time to time to visit the General. I usually walk the grounds with him. He'd never admit it, but I think he enjoys the company. I know I do."

Nina couldn't help but flash her dimple at the image of this refined man taking time to relieve an old man's loneliness. Maybe he had a sixth sense about the lonely.

"Do you want to sit?" she asked.

"Sure you don't mind?"

"Not at all." Nina smiled again, realizing it was

the first time in a long while that she'd felt relaxed around a stranger. Since her marriage had fallen apart and with her history in rehab, she just never wanted to have to tell her story.

Markus scooted onto the top of the table and rested his feet on the seat the way Nina did. He seemed out of place in such a casual position. Perhaps because she knew he had been in business, but more likely because he seemed too regal to be comfortable in a pair of running shorts, sitting on a dirty picnic table.

"How are you adjusting to life back in Abbey Hills?" he asked.

Nina shrugged. "It's been less than twenty-four hours, so I haven't really wrapped my brain around being back yet. It's hard to think about the idea of permanent residence right now." She tossed some bread to the ducks.

"Do you think it's safe to be alone with a killer on the loose?"

Nina frowned. "What do you know about that?"

"I was at Barney's this morning. Mrs. Rollings's death was all everyone talked about."

"I don't think I'm in much danger. I'd say the killer is either someone she knew and fought with . . ."

"Pete, for instance?"

"Maybe. I never would have thought Pete a killer. He was a decent guy in high school. But people change, I guess." She shrugged. "Or

Amanda truly was a random act of violence, and the killer has moved on."

Although the way Jill described the body didn't seem to fit a random killer just passing through. It was cultish.

Markus smiled. "Do you know that when you frown you get two lines right there?"

He reached out with his index finger. Nina pulled back before he could touch her.

"I'm sorry," he said, dropping his hand. "That was inappropriate. I said what I was thinking instead of thinking before I spoke and acted."

Nina willed her heart to stop racing. "I'm sorry. I guess I'm a little jumpier than I thought. The murder was pretty gruesome from what Jill said."

"Would you feel more comfortable if I left you alone?"

"Actually, I think I'm going to take off and explore a little more, see what's changed. What's still the same. All that."

"I understand." He hopped off the table and offered her his hand.

Nina took it and allowed herself to be helped down because she was too surprised not to. "That's very gentlemanly of you. You don't see gallantry every day. Where'd you learn it?"

"I attended Harvard." He smiled and a glint appeared in his eyes. "We were taught to be gentlemen."

Nina laughed. "Harvard, huh? That's pretty impressive. No wonder you're smart enough to retire at such a young age."

He smiled. "I'm flattered."

"You should be."

As she walked away, Nina wondered, with a tiny jolt of shock, if Markus was really watching her or if maybe that was nothing more than wishful thinking on her part.

CHAPTER SEVEN

Coffee has been my drink of choice since I turned ten. That's also the year I stopped sleeping. When Stephan and I decided to watch all the Nightmare on Elm Street movies back to back, fear of sleep robbed me of my formative years.

"You sleep, you die."

I'm convinced that lack of sleep combined with a serious caffeine addiction deprived me of several inches of height, thus my five-foot-three compared to Jill's five-eight.

I eventually got over my fear of the dark—for the most part—but they'll bury me with my coffee cup in my cold, stiff hands. That year, Stephan moved on to freakier things like Ouija boards and séances. I went along because he was my only friend and no one can afford to be without at least one friend. Stephan never took any of it seriously, but I couldn't get over that skin-crawly feeling every time a candle flickered without wind or a door closed by itself.

N ina stood by her bedroom window at 6 a.m. and watched the old 1974 pickup chug to a halt outside Jill's house. The same rusty blue pickup she'd driven home from fishing more often than she could count from the time she was ten years old and had to sit all the way at the edge of the seat to reach the pedals.

Her gut squeezed as she watched Meagan jog from the porch to the pickup and get in. Smoke puffed from the tailpipe as her father pulled out, neither knowing nor caring that Nina watched, terrified that her baby seemed to adore her father the way she had until she realized what he truly was. She couldn't help worrying that Meg was in for the same letdown. He didn't drink anymore, but was he any better at keeping his promises?

Meg had spent most of yesterday with them, and all she could talk about during dinner was "Grammy and Poppy" and how awesome they were.

Nina turned at a tap on the door. "Hey, Jill."

"I had a feeling you'd be watching them leave. You okay?"

Nina shrugged. "I guess I don't have any choice in the matter."

"You didn't have to let her go."

"What could I have said? I'm trying to fix things with my daughter, not push her away. But I'm not sure she cares."

"Oh, Nina, stop. She's sixteen. How about

having breakfast with me at Barney's?"

"I was actually thinking of going for a run."

A grin tugged at Jill's mouth. "Ambitious for your second day in town."

Nina smiled back. "Might as well get started on the right foot."

Jill sat on the end of the bed and pulled her legs up to her chest. "You know, Nina, seeing Meggie with Mom and Dad was sweet. She adores them, and the feeling is mutual. Are you sure you want to miss out on all that?"

The thought of squaring off with her parents filled Nina with a tension she couldn't face. Not yet.

After a few minutes of silence, Jill must have gotten the hint. She padded to the door. "I still have Barney's truck, so feel free to use my car again today."

"Thanks, Jill."

"I'm sorry coming home has been so hard for you."

"It'll get better. Just not overnight."

Nina threw on a pair of running shorts, running shoes, and a tank top and headed to Jill's car. Her conversation with Markus the day before had reminded her about the General's perfect running trails.

The General's reserve had once been a public display of exotic animals, but sometime in the eighties, a tiger had gotten hold of a teenage kid full of taunts and pokes, and that was the end of that. A concerted effort had been made to close it down for good, but the General had federal approval and state backing and had the right to keep the sanctuary running as long as he didn't profit from it. People steered clear, and within a year, the General had given all the animals to other reserves or zoos and started concentrating on abused horses.

Nina had loved the atmosphere, the horses, and the General.

She'd taken up running when she was sixteen, about the time Stephan had moved on to football, but running in town meant nothing but strange looks and catcalls. Even the school track got her unwanted attention. Football players hollered lewd comments from the field inside the track, and the track coach tried to get her to join the team. She never was much of a joiner, so she'd talked the General into letting her run the trails at the reserve. Those runs with the horses were the only times she felt truly happy.

Nina drove through town, the lovely picturesque homes reminding her of the dreams she'd had during her childhood of a normal family and a nice home. She wanted to live in those houses. Like Hunt's house. Well-kept lawns and clipped bushes were the norm until she got closer to the edge of town. Then the older, less-kept homes came into view.

The road ahead rose and dipped, twisted and straightened. A natural roller coaster, these Ozarks back roads. Seventeen years in Texas had left her with only a distant memory of the beauty of the winding road.

The reserve seemed pretty deserted as she pulled into the long drive. The General lived in a small log cabin centered between another log building and a barn. The log building had been a conservation center with brochures and a small museum but had become a storage area when the reserve closed to the public. The barn looked in need of repair. The roof sagged, and some of the fencing looked broken. Didn't he have any help?

Nina slipped the gearshift into park and cast a nervous glance at the Great Dane barreling toward her car. He placed his massive paws on the window and pressed his wet nose to the glass. Her tension eased, and she laughed as he licked the glass, trying to say hello.

The General showed up a second later. He looked older. He'd been kind of old seventeen years ago, but now he stooped a little and seemed to have shrunk. Nina sat for a second while he called off his dog, then opened the door. The hand that held on to the dog's collar was knobby and arthritic. Sympathy and maybe a little disappointment squeezed at her heart. He was one of two strong men she'd known in her life and the only one from her childhood. Now he stood before her, weakened with age.

She pasted on a smile and opened the car door.

The General scrunched his bushy gray eyebrows. "Thought you was the sheriff. That's her car."

"She let me borrow it. I'm Nina, her sister." She was a little embarrassed that he didn't seem to recognize her.

"You skittish about dogs, or can I let Harvey go? He's about to break my fingers off."

Crusty as ever. The familiarity lifted her spirits.

"Oh, he'll be okay."

"He'll likely jump on you. Don't be scared. He wouldn't hurt a fly. Just likes attention." The General let go of the dog's collar and scratched Harvey's big square head. A contented moan left the dog's throat, and he pressed himself against the General, who obliged with a vigorous scratch behind the ear.

Nina laughed. The sound reminded the dog he was no longer being held by the collar. In one leap, he moved from the General's loving attention to Nina's personal space. She didn't have time to brace herself for the impact before his full weight, which she figured was around one hundred fifty pounds, slammed into her. She lost her balance and landed hard on her backside with Harvey in her lap, slobbering all over her face.

She grinned, feeling light and loved as his long tongue unrolled from his mouth and made a fast lick from her chin to her forehead. She put her hands on either side of his head and scratched behind his ears. He rewarded her with another warm lick.

"Okay, bud, you're going to have to move now," she said. "I have no feeling in my legs."

The General stepped forward and looped his fingers through the dog's collar. "Harvey, get off the lady. Where are your manners?"

Nina pushed, the General pulled, and finally Harvey moved off her. Nina hopped up before he could change his mind.

She brushed off her bare legs and kept a wary eye on Harvey while she held out her hand to the General. "You don't remember me, do you?"

He squinted, as though trying to place her.

Her face felt feverish. So much for thinking she was memorable. No wonder no one had bothered calling or coming by to say hi. Not that she'd have expected anyone to care whether she showed up or not. But she'd grown up in Abbey Hills. Her sister was the sheriff. Wasn't anyone at least curious?

"Try to picture me seventeen years ago," she said.

His dull eyes went wide. "Oh, the little girl who used to run my trails. You were the sheriff's sister?"

"She wasn't the sheriff back then."

He gave a hoarse chuckle. "Guess not. You stopped coming around. Didn't even say good-bye."

"I know. I left town pretty suddenly." Nina leaned against Jill's car.

The General squinted against the sun behind her. "I missed ya. Thought something bad mighta happened. Even asked around."

"I'm sorry, General. I didn't know it mattered."

"Well, don't beat yourself up about it." He stood awkwardly, as if he wasn't quite sure what to do next.

"I came out to see if you'd mind letting me run the trails like I used to."

"Still a runner, huh?"

He folded his arms. Any other man between the age of fifteen and seventy would have looked at her bare legs, but not the General. He looked her square in the eye and asked it like he wanted to know the answer.

She shrugged. "Not in a long time. I'd like to take it up again. It's good for clearing the mind."

He seemed to consider this, then nodded. "You run all you want. Just don't upset my family."

Nina frowned. In all the years she'd known the General, she'd never known him to have family in the area. "Family?"

"The horses. And keep Harvey away from the fences. A couple of the stallions have been known to jump over to get a crack at him."

"Can't you tie him up or something?"

"No." He shook his head. "Don't believe in tying up an animal. He's as free to run those trails as you are."

"Okay. Sorry I suggested it." She would never condone tying up an animal for long, but this one would likely be all over her the entire run. "If I'm not back in an hour, call 911."

"Abbey Hills ain't got 911."

She'd meant it as a joke but decided it wasn't worth explaining.

She set off walking down the trail, Harvey darting ahead and barreling back toward her, forcing her to sidestep each time he tried to jump on her. By the time she broke into a jog, he had settled into the same easy rhythm next to her. Nina's breathing sped up, then evened out as she found her pace. Slow but steady.

A smile spread across her face as a slight breeze blew over her.

There were a lot of reasons to dread her home-coming, but for the moment she felt content.

Meg let her legs hang over the side of the boat. Cold river water grazed the tips of her bare toes. She felt like a regular Tom Sawyer or Huck Finn. "When do you think we'll catch a fish?"

Poppy stared out across the water as though summoning the fish. He almost strained in his telepathy. "Directly, I reckon."

She tried not to be impatient, but that's what he'd been saying for the past two hours. She was glad she'd had the foresight to bring a pair of sunglasses, because the eastern glare sliding across the water had begun to hurt the back of her eyes.

"So you and Nina used to come out here, huh?" She pointed at the empty bucket. "Were there any actual fish in the river back then?"

He turned a frown on her. His gray eyebrows, scraggly and wild, shoved together. "How come you call your mom Nina?"

Anxiety beat a slightly higher than normal rhythm in her ears. "I don't know. She's not really the motherly type." Maybe at one time. Meg had flashes of spending time with Nina at the park, days at the zoo, dress-up, tea parties. Early days when Nina smiled and seemed to mean it.

Poppy flinched as though she'd struck him. "Your aunt says she's here to stay for a while."

Not the direction Meagan had planned. She'd hoped to learn about her Poppy, not put out a full-page exposé on Nina's plans. Not that she had any idea what those plans were.

"So she says. But don't get your hopes up. She changes her mind a lot."

"I take it the two of you don't get along?"

If anyone else had asked that, Meg would have come back with something witty, but she couldn't bring herself to show him her sharp side.

"She's been gone a lot," she said.

"Gone where? Working?"

"Just gone. Doing her own thing. Dad has custody."

"But gone where? Doing what?"

Meg shrugged. She'd said too much, but what could she do about that now? "She drank a lot the last few years. She just got out of rehab, so she's sober. For now, anyway."

The edge of his pole jerked. He seemed not to notice, though he stared right at it. His pole jerked again, and Meagan knew he had something else on his mind.

Markus left his car in the woods behind the reserve and carefully pulled apart the barbed fencing he'd cut last time he'd come this way. He tried not to hunt on the General's land, but sometimes there was no other choice.

He froze at the sound of barking in the near distance. Harvey never ventured this far from the house unless he was with the General. How would Markus explain his presence? The old man was suspicious by nature.

The barking grew steadily closer. Markus turned toward the fence, but the dog had already spotted him. Harvey's jogging companion came to an abrupt halt. Obviously she'd seen him too. He chided himself. If he'd been paying closer attention, he would have caught their scent much sooner and might've been able to get away. Maybe. His instincts, speed, and strength were duller, slower, and weaker than normal. He was thirsty.

He watched Nina approach. His heartbeat thudded in his ears. As Harvey broke into a run, Markus braced for the impact.

"Harvey! No!"

Her voice, husky with just a hint of sweetness, floated on the air, distracting Markus long enough for the Great Dane to get the upper hand. He felt the air leave his lungs as the ground rose up to meet him. Harvey's long tongue soaked his face. The close proximity to warm flesh slammed into Markus. He could hear the runaway beating of the dog's large heart.

"Harvey, you're such a pain." Nina grabbed the dog by the collar. "Come on, move it." Amazingly, the dog obeyed. "Good boy!" She rubbed his head, then turned to Markus and reached down.

Markus took her warm hand and let her haul him to his feet.

"Thanks." He couldn't bring himself to pull his hand free, and she didn't seem in any hurry to do so either. "That dog is a menace."

"Tell me about it," she said wryly. "I just met him, and I'm already convinced that obedience school is his only chance at a future."

Her hands were damp, warm, so human. Willing

himself to proceed carefully, he summoned his strength.

Then she smiled, tilting her head against the glint of the sun. The animal rose up inside him, taunting him and prodding him to cast aside common sense and act on instinct.

She pulled her slick hand from his. The jerky movement drew him back to reality and common sense.

"You seem to be making a habit of showing up wherever I am," she said. "Should I be worried?"

Despite her laugh, Markus sensed a bit of tension in the question.

"Just a nice coincidence. For me, anyway." He smiled as he dusted off his jeans. "Although, I have to admit it seems a little strange the way we keep meeting. Are you sure you're not the stalker in this scenario?"

She smiled. "I was here first."

"True." Markus laughed.

"Now that we've established that, what are you doing on the backside of the General's reserve?"

"Turkey hunting in the woods." The lie rolled easily off his tongue.

"Without a gun?" she asked.

"Hmm?"

She nodded to his hands. "You're hunting without a gun?" Her eyebrows went up and she laughed, a short, dubious sound.

"Not exactly." He humored her with a smile. "When I was putting my gun back in my car, I noticed someone had cut the fence over there. I thought I'd look around and make sure everything was okay. Especially after the killing Sunday night."

"That was thoughtful." Her tone softened. "I'm sure the General would be pleased to know someone is looking out for his family of horses."

"That's one of the things that drew me to Abbey Hills. The way small-town folk seem to care for each other."

Nina gave a short laugh. "There's a thin line between caring and just being nosy. But I guess either way, it's nice to have people watching your back."

A dimple flashed as she smiled, and he found himself staring. When her face reddened and she averted her gaze, he took a step back and cleared his throat.

"I'll let you and Harvey get back to your run."

"Yeah, I guess we'd better. It was nice bumping into you again, Markus. I'll see you later, I'm sure."

She was right about that.

She turned to go. He couldn't take his eyes from her. Dark hair, eyes the color of maple bark, skin that glistened with a thin layer of perspiration.

"Nina," he called after her.

She turned.

"Don't forget there's a murderer loose in Abbey Hills."

Her face clouded.

"You have to be careful if you're going to be alone."

She nodded. "I won't forget. Thanks." She gave him a wave and took off running, Harvey trotting along beside her.

His stomach tightened. Nina had no idea the danger she and this town faced. He needed to keep her safe. He couldn't lose her again.

Nina dripped with sweat by the time she got back to Jill's car. She grabbed her towel from the backseat and dried her skin, then laid the towel across the seat to sit on during her drive back to town.

She reached forward and pulled the keys from under the seat, where she'd stashed them while she ran. As she started the engine, her thoughts went back to Markus and finding him out on the trail. Why would he be hunting this time of year? Turkeys were in season, she supposed. Still, he didn't have any gear on him and even his Italian leather shoes were wrong. Not the sort of shoes one would expect from a hunter.

Shaking aside the thoughts, she shifted into reverse. Right now she had a bigger situation on her hands than Markus Chisom's shoes. Namely, whether or not to tell Hunt about the strange occurrences happening in Abbey Hills. She hated to take a chance he'd come and get Meg. But then maybe it wasn't such a bad idea if he did.

As if by providence, her cell phone rang.

Hunt.

"Hi," she said. "I was just thinking about calling you."

"Oh? Is everything okay?"

Now why would he automatically assume that something was wrong just because she was going to call him? "I guess it depends on what way you look at things."

"And that would mean . . . ?" His tone was cautious. And Nina realized why.

"Oh, Hunt. I'm still sober."

His breath released in a rush through the phone. "That's good, babe."

Nina's heart jumped. "You haven't called me that in a long time."

"Slipped out. Sorry."

Truth be told, she sort of enjoyed hearing it come from Hunt. Enjoyed it a lot actually. But he seemed a little embarrassed, so she let it go.

The rural highway rolled and turned, forcing Nina to drive slowly, concentrating.

Hunt cleared his throat. "Still there?"

"Yeah. I'm driving on a curvy road."

"I should let you go then."

Nina frowned, not wanting to let him go. "Wait, Hunt. Why did you call?"

"I just wanted to make sure everything was

going okay. I talked to Meg. She's pretty excited about your parents."

"I know. According to Jill, they're eating up grandparenting. I'm happy for them."

"You still haven't gone to visit?"

Nina sighed. "I'm getting there."

"That's good." He hesitated. "Meg told me there was a murder in town."

She should have known Meg would tell him. Why shouldn't she? A girl would be a little frightened and need to get reassurance from her dad. "I was going to talk to you about it. Do you want to come get her? I would understand."

"I've been considering it. But it sounds like they think it could be domestic."

"Well, maybe, maybe not."

"You sound concerned." Hunt's voice sounded like a frown. "Do *you* think I should come get her?"

"I don't want you to. I think we can keep her safe. But I wanted you to be aware that Jill isn't convinced that the murder was domestic. As a matter of fact, she's leaning away from the husband."

"Listen, I have to go. I just got a page. I'll think about this some more and get back with you."

Nina released a relieved sigh that he wasn't picking up and hurrying to Abbey Hills. At least that showed he had developed a little bit of confidence in her.

"Bye, Hunt."

He remained silent for a minute and Nina waited, breath held. "Bye."

Nina's heart hurt with disappointment.

The call was disconnected from his end.

CHAPTER EIGHT

In all honesty, not every memory of my home life is horrible. My mother loved old musicals. Those crazy, unrealistic shows with Judy Garland, Fred Astaire, Gene Kelly, Bing Crosby.

As much as Jill was into music, she never could stay awake the nights those movies were on late, and Dad was always passed out by ten-thirty.

So Mom and I would sit in the dark, popcorn popped, breath held, hearts beating with excitement as the music swelled. Meet Me in St. Louis. Singin' in the Rain. Easter Parade.

To this day, when I watch the DVDs of these old favorites, my mom's face smiles in my mind's eye. I feel her hand brush mine in the humongous Tupperware bowl as we both reach for popcorn.

I sometimes wish those movies had played more often than two or three times a year.

Sweat beaded Nina's forehead as she hurried through Barney's from one table to the next, taking orders, delivering drinks and food, cleaning tables, and setting up for the next customers. How on earth could a town the size of Abbey Hills keep a restaurant so busy that a waitress couldn't find five minutes in five hours to sit down?

"For Pete's sake, Nina," Barney growled, tossing a barbeque plate in the window. "Get the lead out. I thought you had experience waiting tables."

"Give me a break, Barney. I haven't done it for ten years, and you know it."

He scowled and waved her away. "Take that out. And get the order for table six before he gets fed up and goes to Sonic for lunch."

She sighed. "I'm going as fast as I can."

On the way to the table, plate in hand, she glanced at the clock. Thirty minutes until her shift ended. It would be a miracle if she survived that long considering her bruised, swollen feet. A raw spot on the back of her heel had been a hot spot at eleven o'clock, a blister at one o'clock, and she could only imagine the mess she would find when she took off her sock in twenty-seven minutes.

She delivered the food as pleasantly as she could muster, given the pain in her feet, and moved toward table six, pulling her order pad from her pocket. A lone man sat in the booth, faced away from her, his cropped hair leaving a long, tanned neck above a T-shirt collar. His head stayed down, eyes fixed on the menu as she approached. Hopefully, he wouldn't be the sort that made her wait for five minutes while he tried to decide between catfish and barbeque.

"Hi," she said in her friendly server tone. "What can I get you to drink while you're deciding on lunch?" She scribbled the table number on her pad and looked back at the customer. Familiar blue eyes stared back at her.

"Stephan." She swallowed hard.

He smiled, his teeth as white and straight as she remembered. Still the all-American boy. "I heard you were back in town."

"Yeah. For a little while." Her hands shook, and she looked at the order pad. "Do you know what you want yet?"

"A cheeseburger and onion rings."

"Drink?"

"Coke."

"Okay."

She turned, breathing a sigh of relief. Maybe it would be okay after all. She just had to deliver his order when it came up, get him a refill or two, and that was that.

As she turned in his order, the bell above the door chimed. Nina released a frustrated breath. Would the lunch rush ever end? It was almost three o'clock.

Nina forced a plastic smile and turned to find Jill stepping inside. Relief filled Nina until she saw who followed her sister inside. They were definitely older, but she would recognize her parents anywhere.

Shyly, she met them halfway.

Her mother's face glowed, her eyes shining with joy. "It's so good to see you," she said barely above a whisper.

"You too, Mom." The word seemed foreign on her tongue. It had been a long time since she'd used it. Her mom seemed unsure, but held out her arms anyway. Nina allowed a quick hug.

Dad had changed the most. He seemed more frail, definitely skinnier. No beer belly. His eyes took her in. "Good to see you're still alive."

Nina tensed at the accusation in his tone and tried not to reciprocate it. "Good to see you're alive too, Dad." She turned to Jill. "If you'll find a seat, I'll be there in a sec. I need to get a drink for a customer."

For the moment, she was glad to have Stephan's—anyone's—Coke to deliver. She just needed time. First Stephan, now her parents? *Seriously, if a person ever had a reason for needing a drink,* Nina thought sardonically.

She set the Coke in front of Stephan, planning to retreat as quickly as possible, but he seemed to have a different agenda.

"How've you been, Nina?"

"Fine. Living my life. Just like you and everyone else."

"I hear you have a daughter." His eyes grew hard. "They say she looks a lot like you."

"Yes, she does." Nina tried to keep her expression stoic. "She's only here for the week. She's going back to her father's on Saturday."

"Her father's, huh?" His nostrils flared a little. "How old is she?" He seemed to hold his breath.

"Why?" Nina clenched her jaw, wishing she'd thought to just lie. Meg would be gone in days.

"Why do you think?"

Thankfully, Barney bellowed at her from the kitchen.

"Looks like your order is up," she said. She made her way to the window, grabbed Stephan's order, and set his plate in front of him. The brief trip gave her time to gather her wits and bolster her courage. She looked Stephan square in the eyes. "The subject of my daughter is off limits to you."

Anger flashed in his eyes. "That tells me everything I need to know . . . for now, anyway. See you soon, Nina." He jerked his chair back and stood, then tossed a wad of money on the table to cover his ticket and stomped out. His plate lay untouched.

"Aren't you two a little old to be carrying on that way?" Jill's voice whispered close behind her.

Nina turned, scowling. "You'd think." She walked through the restaurant, eyeing her tables as she made her way to the galley area.

Jill followed her. They stopped next to the soda machine. "Listen, Nina. I just got a call. One of the General's horses was murdered and carved up like . . . well, like Amanda Rollings. I have to go."

Alarm squeezed Nina's stomach. "Is the General okay?"

Jill nodded. "Physically. He's the one who called it in. But you know how crazy he is about his animals. I'm sure he's broken up about it."

Nina grabbed a cloth and wiped down the soda machine. "I'll stop by and see him tomorrow."

"He'd appreciate that." Jill glanced back toward the window. Barney was hard at work. "I hate to bother him; I have to go. Will you fill Barney in on what's going on?"

Nina nodded. "Be careful."

"I will." She nodded toward the table where their parents sat. "Be nice to Mom and Dad, okay?"

Something in Nina softened at the picture of the two of them trying not to be obvious as they darted glances toward Jill and Nina. She nodded. "I will."

She watched her sister walk away and turned to face sixteen more minutes in her shoes and the parents she'd ignored for nearly two decades.

Meg's day had been about the most boring in her life. Nina was at work, Grammy and Poppy had a doctor's appointment or something, and Aunt Jill had driven them. They'd invited Meg, but vegging in front of the TV seemed more appealing.

That had been a few hours ago, and she'd had about all she could stand. Aunt Jill didn't have a computer at home. How was that even possible?

When the phone rang, she was actually relieved. "Sheriff Parker's residence."

"Meg?"

Meg frowned. She didn't recognize the voice on the other end of the line. "Who's this?"

"Carrie. I waited on you and your mom Sunday? At Barney's?"

"Oh, yeah."

"I invited you to hang out if you got bored?"

"I remember. Thanks."

"I'm about to go to a yoga class. Want to go with me?"

"Abbey Hills has a gym?"

"No. It's in a house outside of town. One of those huge old Victorians like your aunt's. The instructor moves all the furniture on class day."

It wasn't a tough decision. Yoga actually seemed like a nice distraction, and she hadn't worked out in a few days.

"Okay. I'll go."

"Great. I have my dad's car. I'll pick you up in thirty minutes."

~

Not long after our marriage, I realized Nina had no intention of ever opening up about her family

155

or her past, as though her life began when she moved to Dallas the year she graduated high school.

Two months after our marriage, I rented a cabin in the woods, and we took Meggie camping. I rested my back against a tree, and we stared at the fire as I held Nina tightly to my chest. Meg slept in her arms, and we were content.

Until I asked about Meggie's biological father.

"He's not in the picture," was all Nina said.

Maybe I should have let it go, but I wanted so much to be Meg's father, and the thought that another man might have a claim to her gnawed at me. So I pressed her for information.

"But, honey, why isn't he in the picture?"

I expected her to continue to be evasive, but it was as if by pressing I had punctured that secret place she'd held close. Everything came spilling out.

She'd been raped the night of graduation. That's why she'd left home. She refused to say more. The pain wouldn't allow her to. I held her as she wept silently, not wanting to wake Meg.

The following Monday we started proceedings for me to adopt Meg. The court granted the adoption without hesitation and with very few questions asked. I understood Nina not wanting to share the details, but everything in me roared to be her hero. To find the rapist and make him pay for every second of pain he'd caused this woman I loved with all my heart.

Even as I raged inside, Nina dried her tears and composed herself, stuffing the memory deep into a pool of hurt I suddenly knew I'd never be allowed to dive into.

That realization began an eleven-year gnawing inside me. It bit and burned with painful, rat-like teeth, sharp and relentless, reminding me that I had no choice but to live her pain with her. She'd never let it go. And though her pain cut me too, it was hers alone, and she'd never share it.

To this day, my prediction holds true. As much as I loved her, I couldn't fix what had taken a lifetime to break.

CHAPTER NINE

I went to church camp the summer before my seventh-grade year. I don't know why I went, except that I didn't have anything else to do and the Baptist church youth pastor knocked on my parents' door and offered to let Jill and me go for free.

Jill got sick and couldn't go, but I did. Something tugged at my insides all week, and by the last night, I could no longer sit still when the minister asked, "Do you know where you'd go if you died tonight?" On an emotional high and pushed by a strong fear of consequences, I prayed the prayer.

Throughout the rest of the summer, I was determined to be different. I didn't steal any of my dad's beer and stayed away from parties. I even read the New Testament my camp counselor gave me because I didn't have a Bible of my own. I never quite made it to Sunday school. I couldn't get up early enough, although I always had the best of intentions on Saturday.

Then school started. With only a few hundred students in the whole town of Abbey Hills, the junior high and high school students were all in one building. I knew from rumor that seventh graders caught a lot of garbage from the upper grades, so I entered junior high with little excitement and plenty of trepidation. I prayed that this year would be different. That somehow I wouldn't be the girl everyone loved to pick on.

My prayer went unheard.

After a full day of every grade, including my own, calling me "Puke" and knocking my books out of my hands, I figured if God existed, it wasn't for kids like me.

At home that afternoon, I snuck into Dad's vodka.

And I felt better.

Nina carried her shoes as she walked along the wet sidewalk toward Jill's house. Drizzle fell, sprinkling her hair, her neck, her arms, but she didn't mind. It felt too good to be out of that hot restaurant.

Home wasn't far away. All she wanted to do was soak in a hot bath of healing salts, dress in warm pajamas, and curl up in front of the TV. Maybe she and Meg could watch a movie together.

As much as she'd dreaded the encounter, Nina was relieved to have the first meeting with her parents out of the way. They'd mainly discussed Meg. Meggie was a safe subject, something they could agree on, and before she knew what happened, Nina had agreed to a farewell dinner for Meg on Friday night. The lunch encounter hadn't been nearly as bad as she'd feared.

Stephan . . . He was another matter altogether. She had no idea what he would do.

Her stomach tightened at the memory of his cold eyes and red, angry face. *That tells me everything I need to know.*

Instinct told her to call Hunt immediately and beg him to drive down tonight and get their daughter out of town before Stephan made some sort of move. The thought of Meagan encountering Stephan terrified Nina.

Reason took over, and she shook her head, arguing with herself. What could Stephan possibly do? Even if he suspected that Meg was his biological daughter, did he really want the whole town, including his parents, to know what he'd done that night after graduation?

No, he wouldn't push the matter. Surely.

Her blistered feet screamed in pain, demanding her attention. She'd forgotten how badly she hated waiting tables. Insistent customers, grouchy boss—even the nice ones were impatient during a rush—the incessant service with a smile. After she'd gotten her veterinary license and opened her own clinic, she'd thought her days in food service were over. But drinking during the day led to mistakes, missed appointments, and one or two lawsuits, and business at her animal hospital dropped off to the point that she was losing too much money to keep her doors open.

She was still a few blocks from home when the rain picked up. It wasn't a violent, stormy kind of rain, merely a spring shower, greening up the grass and urging the flowers to bloom. Still, wet was wet, and Nina was getting sick of the way her hair stuck to her neck and face.

Blisters or no blisters, she was about to break into a run when a car pulled up beside her and honked its horn. She turned and looked into the darkened windows, her heart lurching as she wondered if it was Stephan. The passenger side window lowered.

She smiled. "Markus."

"Hi, again, neighbor."

"Can I give you a ride?"

"Oh, no. I'm soaked. I don't want to mess up your seats." She eyed the interior of his very expensive Lexus.

He smiled. "They're only seats. I can't drive away and leave you walking in the rain. The sheriff might arrest me for obvious neglect of her sister."

He leaned over and opened her door.

"All right. But I warned you." She slid onto the leather seat, her muscles relaxing into the soft warmth. She set her shoes in her lap and stretched out her legs. "Thank you for stopping. Most people wouldn't."

He didn't answer. Instead, when she glanced up, she found him staring at her feet. His face had drained of blood, and he looked white.

"Do you get queasy?" she asked.

"Hmm?"

"At the sight of blood. My feet are pretty beat up."

His eyes found hers, and something in them startled her.

She reached for the door handle. "Are you okay?"

Her words seemed to snap him out of his stupor. His face relaxed, and he gave her a weak grin. "Sorry. Now you know my shame."

Loosening her grip on the handle, she willed her heart rate to ease. "Shame?"

"Weak stomach."

"Sorry. Want me to put my shoes on?"

"No. Of course not. Sorry for staring, but that's a lot of blisters. It looks very painful."

Nina released a sigh. "I borrowed Jill's white shoes instead of springing for my own. She still wears a seven, and I've graduated to a seven and a half."

"Thus the blisters." Markus checked his rear-

162

view mirror, then turned the wheel and maneuvered the Lexus back onto the wet street.

"Yep. So, Markus," she said, eager to turn his attention away from her feet, "where did you come from? Why settle in Abbey Hills of all places? I know you said you enjoy the small-town atmosphere, but there are a lot of small towns in the United States."

He pulled into Jill's driveway and slid the gearshift into park. Leaving the engine running, he turned in the seat.

Nina looked at the dashboard. "What I mean," she said with effort, "is that if I could retire, I'd go anyplace but here."

"Why is that?"

"Let's just say all my demons converge in this place." She grimaced and rolled her eyes. "That sounded a little melodramatic, didn't it?"

"A little." He grinned. "But it's okay. Sometimes our truth feels that way."

"Hmm. You Harvard guys really are quite the philosophers."

"Are you flirting with me, neighbor?" His eyes perused her face and settled on her eyes, inquisitive. She didn't blame him.

"Probably. But I didn't mean to. I'm sorry." Embarrassment heated her cheeks.

His expression moved from teasing but definitely interested to bewildered. "Should I be insulted?"

Nina shook her head. "No. I'm ninetyish days sober and still hung up on my ex-husband. Flirting with you or anyone else is just stupid."

"Still hung up on your ex?" His eyes narrowed.

"I'm afraid so. And believe me, the feeling isn't mutual."

"Then he's crazy."

She gave a short laugh. "Yeah, because I drove him there."

He chuckled. "Okay, so you are still in love with your crazy ex-husband who doesn't know what he gave up." He peered closer. "He is the one who gave you up, I assume? Not the other way around, since you still have feelings for him?"

"Yeah, he's the dumper. I'm the dumpee." Nina's face warmed. "For good reason."

"For things that happened pre-ninetyish days ago, I'm guessing."

"Very insightful of you." She tossed him a dubious smile. "And I don't blame Hunt at all. I wasn't a fun drunk. Well, unless you happened to be one of the other drunks in the bar."

His smile faded, and his eyes grew serious as they searched hers. "Sounds like you're still pretty mad at yourself."

"I have a lot to be mad at myself for, believe me. Addiction isn't pretty."

He turned away and stared out his window toward his house. "I can imagine."

An uncomfortable silence fell between them.

Nina took that as her cue to get out of the car. "Thanks for the ride, Markus. My feet are forever in your debt."

Her words freed him from his deep thoughts. He turned. "Anytime your feet need me, I'm just four wheels away." His face gentled into a smile.

"Thanks, Markus. And that thing I told you about ninety days of sobriety? I'm not really proud of having been in rehab, so maybe we could just keep it in the car for now?"

"Your secret is safe with me, Nina." He touched her shoulder. An uncomfortable tingle crawled over her skin, and she shivered.

He frowned. "Sorry. You're wet from the rain. I should have turned off the air conditioner."

"Don't worry about it. Thanks again for the ride." She slipped out of the car, carrying her shoes, and waved as she headed up the sidewalk.

"Nina?" Markus called.

She stopped and turned. "Yeah?"

"For what it's worth, I'm glad you're in Abbey Hills."

She smiled. "Thanks."

Nina entered the house, and a smile slid across her face. It was nice to have a friend.

Incense nearly choked Meg as she stepped inside the house with Carrie. Yoga had seemed like a great idea twenty minutes ago, but she'd never taken a class in this kind of atmosphere.

"The incense and low lighting are for relaxation, I take it?" she asked.

Carrie shrugged. "I guess. I've never asked."

Meg followed her into the foyer. "Are you sure it's okay to just walk in without knocking?"

"Positive. I come three times a week."

A shudder went through Meg. "I have a weird feeling about this. I think maybe we should go."

Carrie shrugged. "You don't have to take the class if you don't want. Stay in the car until I'm done. Or walk the seven miles back to town. I don't mean to be rude, but I'm taking the class."

Meg sighed. "All right, fine. I'll stay." She still had a bad feeling, but she wasn't sitting in the car for an hour like a loser, and walking seven miles was out of the question.

They walked down a short hallway and into what was probably the dining room, where twenty people waited to bend themselves into a series of downward-facing dogs.

Carrie's back straightened as she stepped over the threshold, as though she gained confidence just joining the group. Her eyes searched the room, and she smiled as they landed on a middle-aged woman whose dark hair was pulled into a braid that wrapped around her head.

As though summoned by the depth of admiration glowing in Carrie's face, the woman turned away from the group surrounding her. Her face brightened, and she broke into a smile and glided toward them. She wore yoga pants, her feet were bare, and she had a dancer's body. Meg felt herself responding to the woman's smile, the glow of health on her face.

"Hello, girls," the woman said. "Class is just about to start."

Meg dug into her bag for the twelve dollars Carrie had told her to bring.

The woman held up her hand. "First class is free. I'm Eden."

"Meg Hunter. I'm just here for spring break."

"I'm glad you've come, Meg Hunter. You are welcome to join any of the classes while you're here. My treat."

"Wish I could, but I'll only be here a couple more days."

"I'm sorry to hear that."

Polite words anyone could speak, but coming from Eden's mouth, Meg believed she truly was sorry. And for that second, Meg wished she never had to leave Abbey Hills.

Eden's eyes were an odd combination: one blue, one brown. Meg found it difficult to look away. The compelling woman reached out and touched her arm. "Let's get started."

Meg watched her walk to the head of the room where a cold stone fireplace stood like a king holding court.

Carrie nudged her. "Told you you'd like Eden."

Like was an odd choice of word. *Intrigued*

suited the situation better. Still, Meg couldn't take her eyes off the tall, muscular African American woman.

She raised her arms in a stretch, breathed in the incense-filled air, and let peace take over.

CHAPTER TEN

I played softball the summer before I entered sixth grade. I walked to each practice, determined to excel. And I did. I played first base and played it very well. I think I surprised the coaches. Small-town parents of my classmates who knew I was the underachieving Parker sister.

I never asked my mom to come to a game. I figured if she wanted to come, she would. She never did. Dad came once with Jill. He staggered into the stands and yelled, "That's my baby!" every time I made a move. Jill looked like she wanted to die as much as I did. We lost the game because I couldn't catch a ball, couldn't get anyone out at first.

Jill apologized later. Going to the game had been her idea.

I turned in my uniform the next day and never played sports again.

Nina's thoughts returned to the ride home as she went about her evening alone. With Jill still working on the ritual-like murders and Meg's phone call explaining she was going to be out with Carrie, Nina had plenty of time to think about the events of the day.

First thing on the agenda: hot bubble bath. She soaked for an hour and a half, easing her raw feet into the water an inch at a time, gradually feeling the stinging subside.

Even though it was early, she pulled on comfy pajamas and a fluffy robe. She padded barefoot into the kitchen just as the phone rang.

She reached for the receiver. "Sheriff Parker's residence."

"Nina?"

"Who is this?" It wasn't Hunt, and she couldn't imagine what other man might call her at Jill's.

"It's Stephan."

"What do you want?"

He hesitated. "It's about your daughter."

"Off limits, Stephan. Seriously."

"She's mine, right?"

Nina closed her eyes and gathered in a breath. "Come on, Stephan. You know she's never going to be yours."

"But that night by the river. We made her?"

Nina bit her lip. What was the point of denying it anymore?

The front door slammed. "Nina! I'm home."

Relief flooded her at the interruption. "Look, Stephan, Jill just got home. I have to go."

170

"All right. But I want to talk about this."

Nina's heart pounded in her ears. "We will. Soon." She hated the tension in her voice, but she couldn't help but plead with him. "Please don't approach my daughter without my permission." The thought terrified her. She would never win Meg back if Stephan ruined things by introducing himself before Nina had the chance to run interference.

"You know I wouldn't."

She hung up just as Jill entered the kitchen, slid her gun belt onto the table, and plopped into a kitchen chair. "What a day."

Nina sat across from her. "Yeah."

"How was your first day at work?" Jill asked.

"Fine."

"Fine? Barney told me to look at your feet. Said you could barely walk by the time you clocked off." She glanced down and her eyes went wide. "Ouch! At least you won't have to work tomorrow."

"I don't really have a choice."

"Barney's is closed because of Amanda Rollings's funeral." Jill bent over and began unlacing her boots. "But more about that later. Who was on the phone when I came in?"

Nina opened her mouth to say "wrong number" but changed her mind. She needed to talk to someone and might need the added support in the days ahead.

"Stephan Bailey."

Jill nodded and her eyebrows rose. "Really? He still asks about you. Every time I see him, as a matter of fact, which is a lot."

Nina grabbed her arm. "What have you told him?"

"Nothing. Just that you were married but divorced. Two kids. The usual casual stuff. You're rattled about this, aren't you?" She grinned knowingly. "I hear he's separated from Jodi. Maybe it's fate. Childhood sweethearts reunited."

Nina went to the fridge and pulled out sliced deli ham, tomato, mayo, and mustard. "First of all, if I were interested in anyone in Abbey Hills, it would be the guy next door."

"Oh really?" Jill's singsong voice and chuckle followed Nina around the kitchen. Annoying but manageable.

Nina carried the sandwich items to the table and set them down. Then she grabbed the bread from the breadbox and a couple of butter knives from the drawer.

"You hungry?"

Jill shrugged. "Might as well eat. But let's expound on this topic of your interest in my cute neighbor."

"I said *if* I were interested, which I'm not. And FYI, Stephan and I weren't childhood sweethearts. We were friends for a while as kids. That's it."

"Defensive." Jill frowned. "Are you sure you don't still have a crush on him?" She took out two slices of bread and opened the mayo.

"I never had a crush on him." Nina blew out a breath. "We share some history, that's all. So, how's the General holding up?"

All the amusement slid from Jill's face. "Not well. The state patrol came and took the horse." She slid a couple of slices of ham onto one mayo-slathered slice of bread and topped the meat with the other slice. No tomato, no mustard.

"The horse had the same markings?" Nina slashed across her throat and between her breasts.

Jill winced and pushed away the sandwich she'd just put together. "Exactly like the others, including Amanda. I have to get to the bottom of this before anyone or anything else is killed."

"What about the crime lab in Springfield? Have they come up with anything about Amanda's death?"

Jill shook her head and released a sigh. "They've collected all the evidence they can from her body and completed the autopsy, so the funeral is tomorrow."

"How long before they know something?"

Jill shrugged. "We're just another case to them. Especially since Springfield is the only crime lab within a hundred miles."

"You going to Amanda's funeral tomorrow?"

"Of course. You should go too. It wouldn't be

good for your reentry into town to miss the funeral. Especially since you graduated with her."

Nina groaned. "I haven't seen Amanda in nearly twenty years. I hate funerals. Maybe I should help Barney with the food. That way at least I'm visible after the funeral. Folks will know I care, but I don't have to actually be near the body." She had only been to one funeral—her baby daughter's. The memory of that terrible time flooded over her. Her head swam as she tried not to allow the rush of pain to swell into a break-down.

"It's closed casket. The church ladies take care of setting things up and serving. The food's done buffet style. Barney just offers the restaurant as a place for everyone to gather. One thing about our community, everyone comes out in support of each other during times of tragedy or disaster."

"I'll remember that." Nina's entire childhood had been a tragedy. No one had been there to support her.

"I just meant that no one household has enough room to hold everyone who wants to show their support. At Barney's, everyone can come and go as they please without getting too crowded."

"Okay, stop pitching me. I'll go to support a townsperson—you."

"Well, no pressure." Jill grinned.

"Right. No pressure."

"Stephan will probably be there," Jill teased.

A chill ran down Nina's spine. Jill didn't have a clue. The thought of Stephan made her skin crawl and turned her stomach.

She needed to call her sponsor. Now.

Excusing herself, she grabbed her cell, headed toward the stairs, dialing the number as she climbed.

Markus sat on his porch as twilight hovered on the horizon. The day's rain had ended, but the scent of wet, freshly cut grass lingered in the air, nearly overloading his senses. He watched with great interest as a car pulled into the sheriff's driveway.

The passenger door opened, and Nina's daughter got out.

The wind lifted, drawing her scent toward him. There was something familiar mixed with the smell of warm skin.

Eden.

He swallowed hard, then stood and closed the distance between them before the girl could enter the house. In his haste, he moved too quickly. She jumped, gave a little screech, and vaulted onto the porch.

Markus held up his hands. "I'm sorry. I'm not going to hurt you."

She frowned but thankfully didn't scream. "Who are you? You look familiar."

"I met you at Barney's the day you arrived. I

live next door." He jerked his thumb in the direction of his house.

"Oh. That's right." She watched him with suspicion, her eyes narrowed, stance wide. "What do you want?"

He could smell the incense clinging to her. "Where have you been?"

She frowned. "What's it to you?"

Annoyance stung him. Kids had no respect for their elders any longer. If he'd spoken that way to an adult when he was a child, he would have been severely punished. So severely, in fact, that by today's standards he'd have been taken away from his family and his parents imprisoned.

Unfortunately, he didn't have time to revise the question into something the strong-willed girl might actually answer. The porch light switched on, and the door opened.

Nina stepped outside. "What's going on? Meg?"

Markus sucked in a breath. She'd changed into a pair of yellow lounge pants and a light blue tank top. He allowed a quick look and then averted his gaze.

Meg threw her arms around Nina. "You came out just in the nick of time. I was afraid for my life."

Markus chuckled at the audacity of the little twerp.

"Meggie," Nina's tone rang with censure. "Don't be impossible."

"Sorry." She tossed out a cheeky grin and slipped inside.

"Were you looking for me?" Nina asked.

There was no way he could admit to seeking out her teenage daughter. He pulled his mouth into a smile. "Of course."

"What do you need?"

"It's a pretty evening. I thought you might like to go for a walk with me."

Nina looked at the western horizon, and her eyes lit with gentle wonder. "Wow, you're right. It is pretty. Not raining for a change."

"Can I take that as a yes?"

She smiled, and he was suddenly glad for the misunderstanding.

"I'll go grab a sweatshirt and some shoes." She paused. "Do you want to come in and wait?"

Markus shook his head. "I'll wait out here."

She smiled and opened the door. "Be right back."

He slid his hands into the pockets of his jeans and stared into the night. The smell of incense and Eden still lingered. What was Nina's daughter doing mixed up with Eden? The answers would lead to nothing good and might keep him from making Nina his.

Meagan grinned as she replayed the look on the neighbor guy's face. She slipped off her shoes and walked into the kitchen, her mind on the fantastic yoga workout and healthy tea and fruit afterward with the class. Eden had insisted they stay, and neither Carrie nor Meg had the desire to refuse.

Aunt Jill sat at the table, reading a law enforcement magazine and slurping at a bowl of soup. Next to her bowl was a dessert plate piled with saltine crackers. She glanced up. "Oh, hey, Meggie. Where've you been? Mom and Dad's?"

"No. I thought they were with you."

"They were earlier, but not since about three."

Meg had been with Carrie since three-thirty. A sudden disappointment slithered through her. "I wish I'd known. I went to a yoga class with Carrie."

"Yoga? I didn't realize we had a yoga instructor in town." Jill sat back and gave Meg her full attention. "Why didn't I know we had yoga in Abbey Hills?"

"How would I know?" The words flew from Meg's mouth without thought.

Aunt Jill looked askance at her, her brow raised.

"Sorry," Meg muttered. "Reflex."

"Maybe you should work on that attitude."

"You've been talking to Nina."

Aunt Jill glared.

Meg shrugged. "Sorry again."

The front door closed.

"Who's that?" Aunt Jill frowned and stood. She eyed her gun belt, which lay on the table.

"Nina was still out there talking to your neighbor when I left her," Meg said.

Relief crawled over Aunt Jill's face.

Meg frowned. "Is there something wrong?"

"Nothing you need to worry about tonight. Just be careful about going off without letting us know, okay?"

"Sure."

Nina's footsteps clunked on the stairs as she ran up. Aunt Jill met Meg's gaze.

"What do you think that's all about?" Aunt Jill asked.

"My guess is your neighbor."

Something inside Meg rebelled against the idea. She was old enough to understand that parents got divorced and moved on, but her dad hadn't once looked at another woman like that. At least not that Meg had noticed. And more than a few of the single women at church had made it clear they'd welcome some attention.

Poor Dad. He'd never said anything about it, but Meg knew he still loved Nina. She'd caught him looking at their wedding picture one night, and he'd been crying.

Who knew how Nina felt about Dad? But obviously she liked the guy next door.

Nina's steps thumped back down the stairs. Aunt Jill met Meg's gaze again, and by unspoken consent they met Nina in the foyer.

"Where are you going?" Meg asked.

Nina held a sweatshirt in her hand. "For a walk with Markus. It's gorgeous out."

Aunt Jill gave a short laugh. "Oh, really? Kinda late, isn't it?" The amusement in her voice annoyed Meg.

"I already told him I'm not interested in anything but friendship."

"Well, if you told him . . ."

Nina scowled at Aunt Jill. "He understood. If he had any ideas to begin with, he doesn't anymore."

"And yet you're going for a walk together on a pretty spring evening."

Meg glared at Nina. "In your pajamas."

Nina rolled her eyes and walked toward the door, sliding on her sweatshirt. "I'll be back in less than an hour. Do you want to pick out a movie? We could order pizza and make it a girls' night in."

Meg shrugged. "I ate with Carrie."

"I'll order pizza anyway. And get a movie. Maybe you'll change your mind."

Meg headed to the stairs and forced herself to climb them without looking back at Nina. She felt cheated somehow. Eden had invited them to an evening poetry reading, and she'd turned it down. She thought Nina might actually care if she was home or not, but apparently Nina would rather go off with a guy. Whatever.

The front door closed before Meg reached the

top of the steps. She checked her phone. She hadn't had a text from Izzy all day and was starting to feel ignored. She flopped onto her bed and stretched out, staring up at the ceiling and fingering her phone. Maybe Izzy was waiting for her to text. Maybe she was feeling just as blown off as Meg. The thought made her feel better. She lifted her phone and punched in the letters.

Hey, what's up?

She waited for a reply. And waited. Finally, after what seemed like forever, she gave up and tossed her phone onto her bed. She padded over to the chest of drawers and pulled her pajamas and a clean pair of underwear from the bottom drawer, one of two drawers Aunt Jill had cleaned out for her. The yoga workout had been intense, and she needed to soak her muscles.

She'd finally done something interesting today. Something she'd love to share with Izzy, and her so-called best friend was totally blowing her off.

Guilt bit at her because, actually, she'd had a great time so far. No thanks to Nina, of course, but her grandparents were cool and Aunt Jill was a lot of fun. And yoga had been great. She regretted not knowing about the class sooner. She would have gone Monday. Eden had invited her to come back, and if she could work it out she would.

Her stomach growled. Nina's suggestion of pizza wasn't a bad idea. The fruit table at Eden's house hadn't done much for her hunger. She hated the thought of giving Nina the satisfaction of pizza and a movie, but it actually did appeal to her.

If Nina came back when she said she would, anyway. Meg wasn't going to hold her breath. When it came to her mom, it usually proved a waste of time.

The cool, fragrant breeze caught Nina's hair, lifting it, tickling her neck. She shivered.

"Are you cold?" Markus asked.

She shook her head. "The temperature is perfect. I'm glad you suggested this walk. Spring nights are my favorite time to be outside. Everything is so crisp and fresh. The air feels clean."

"If you think this is clean, you would have loved the air two hundred years ago, before industry dirtied things up." He looked down at her from his height of well over six feet, and she couldn't help but notice how good looking he was. Full mouth, piercing brown eyes. He had movie star looks, and as she looked into his eyes, her brain started to muddle.

"Something wrong?" he asked.

Nina pulled herself together. "No, nothing. I was just thinking about what you said about the air. In Dallas, I often wonder what the city sky would look like without the hazy air."

"Everything was nicer back then." He glanced around as though trying to picture it.

Nina laughed. "I wouldn't say everything. Electricity, for instance, is better than none. And indoor plumbing—I like that too."

He nodded but didn't even crack a smile. "But you don't miss those things when you've never known them." They stepped off the curb onto the brick street and walked past Markus's house. Nina's gaze moved to the driveway. His Lexus was parked there. Along with a black Lincoln MKS.

Nina motioned to the cars. "Do you have company?"

"No. Why do you ask?"

"You have two cars in your driveway. Are they both yours?"

He nodded. "I like nice cars."

"Wow."

"Would you think I'm bragging if I admitted that I have two more in the garage?"

"Yes." He angled his gaze to her, and she grinned. "Kidding. If these are the cars you leave out of the garage, I have to ask what you're hiding in there."

"I have a restored 1903 Ford Model A and a 1932 Ford Roadster."

"Ford man?"

"I like beautiful old cars. I'm in the process of buying a 1925 Studebaker. We're still searching for the original seats."

"What if you can't find them?"

His eyes scanned her face, resting when they

met her gaze. "Then I'll take the next best thing. Would you like to go to the garage and see the other cars?" His voice hummed in her ears, and she was about to agree when a car drove by and the peripheral movement broke the spell. She stepped back.

"How about another time?"

His eyebrows drew together. "I understand. But I hope you'll take the time to come by soon. They truly are things of beauty."

Nina stepped forward and resumed their walk along the residential block. The houses on either side of the brick street were old, almost picturesque in their timeless qualities. Markus fell into step alongside her.

"Where were we?" he asked.

"You were talking about smog, I think." She smiled, enjoying the fresh scent of rain-sprinkled, freshly cut grass.

He heaved a sigh. "Yes. Most of the time I wish society had never progressed to where it is. The Indian way of life was the best. Hunt and eat and make war only when necessary."

"You really are a history buff, aren't you?" Nina stuffed her hands into the front pocket of her sweatshirt.

He nodded. "This area fascinates me."

"You mentioned once that the Osage Indians used to occupy all this land. Do you study the Indians or the area?"

He cast a cursory glance toward a flowering dogwood as they passed the fragrant tree. "You can't study one without the other. The Indians were magnificent. Respectful of the land, taking only what they needed. The land was beautiful —the river clean and filled with varieties of fish, the woods full of deer and squirrels and rabbits, even bears." He released a breath, and it almost seemed like a sigh. "And the buffalo. Their pelts made blankets that warmed us against the winter winds. Buffalo hunts were always exciting. The meat from one full-grown bull could feed several families for days. What wasn't eaten immediately, we dried to preserve it."

"We?" Nina laughed. "Are you channeling an ancient Indian? Or are you just really into it?" They stopped at a curb and waited as one of Jill's deputies pulled up to the stop sign, held up his hand to wave, and then drove on.

Markus stood tall and unapologetic as he looked down and grinned at her. "I guess so. I've spent hours reading up on the Indians. History, legends, and lore. When I look around, I don't see all the streets and houses. I see an Indian village with long lodges."

"No tepees?"

He shook his head. "Long houses. Two or three families lived in each one."

"Interesting."

"I'm sorry. I'm a bore, aren't I?"

"Not at all. This is what getting to know a person is all about. Listening to what they're interested in."

"True. So what are you interested in?"

"Uh . . . good question. My kids, of course. Animals. I'm a vet."

"Will you practice in Abbey Hills?"

"I hadn't planned to. I don't think the town could support a vet of its own. Do you?"

He shrugged. "Maybe. You wouldn't get rich, but you could probably make an okay living."

"I'd have to get a Missouri license before I could practice."

"So you think you might stay in Abbey Hills?"

Nina shook her head. "I doubt it. My plan is to stay long enough to save for a few months' living expenses back in Dallas. I want to reestablish my own animal hospital and sort of reinvent myself."

"Why would you want to do that? I like you just the way you are."

Nina gave a short laugh. "Did you already forget our conversation in the car? I ruined a lot of things while I was drinking, and one of those things was my career." She chose not to remind him about the other topic. The one where she couldn't be interested in him because she was still in love with Hunt and always would be. Hunt. She wondered if he was sitting on the porch, looking at the same sky.

"Are you sure you're not too hard on your-self? Because I think you've paid enough."

Nina's cheeks warmed. Part of her wanted to continue this line of conversation since it felt good to be the subject of approval for a change. But that was the old Nina, the one who needed approval from men. This Nina, the one working to stay sober, knew she had a lot to prove to the people she'd hurt in the past.

"I only wish I were being too hard on myself." She gathered a breath of sweet, fresh air and gave in to the need to change the subject. "Did you hear about the General's horse?"

"I take it we're moving on."

"Yeah. Do you mind?"

He smiled. "Not at all. What about the General's horse?"

"He found one dead, drained and sliced across the neck and torso like the other animals and Amanda."

Markus jerked, and his feet stopped moving forward. "A horse?"

Nina halted and turned back to face him. "Yes. According to Jill, the General is pretty shaken. He loves those animals."

"Yes, he does. Maybe we should go check on him."

Nina hesitated. She'd promised Meg pizza and a movie. Of course, Meg had been under-whelmed with the offer, so she'd probably wilt in relief if the "girls' night" was rescinded.

"I think it's a great idea," Nina said. "Let's go check on him. We could stop and pick up some pie or something."

"Pie?"

"I don't know. I hate to go to someone's house after a loss like this and not bring something."

He grinned. "All right then. Pie it is."

Nina felt herself responding to his grin. His eyes. And once more she got a dizzy rush. Warmth crawled up her neck like the cozy feeling of peace that followed a glass of wine.

Nina blew her off. Meg wished she hadn't ordered the pizza. It would be obvious when Nina got home that she'd been interested in the whole girls' movie night.

A tap on her door pulled her attention away from the phone in her hand. She forced her face to show something other than the anger brewing below the surface. "Come in."

Aunt Jill poked her head in the room. "Hey, I was going to drive over to Ruby's and pick out a DVD. Wanna come with?"

"Pizza should be here any sec."

"Oh, it's on the table. The guy just came." Aunt Jill grinned. "I know I ate soup, but it's girls' night. I'll force down a couple slices of pepperoni. What movie do you think your mom wants to watch?"

Meg shrugged. "She's going somewhere with that guy next door."

"A walk. She should be back soon. She said less than an hour."

"Apparently she got a better offer than girls' night in."

Aunt Jill frowned. "What are you saying?"

"She called me and asked if I really wanted to do the movie and pizza thing."

"And of course you said no."

Meg shrugged.

"You two are such pains." Aunt Jill motioned with her hand. "Come on. You and I are going to get a movie. Then we'll pig out on pizza while we watch it. And we'll give your mom a break because she probably really thought she was doing you a favor by letting you off the hook."

"Whatever." Meg glanced at her phone. Still no answer from Izzy. "Let's go get the movie."

They walked out of the video store twenty minutes later with three movies, all horror flicks with no friendship or mother-daughter themes.

"Are you sure your mom isn't going to be upset about the rating on these?" Jill asked.

"Please. As if she notices."

"Okay, but if she gets mad, I'm throwing you under a bus."

Meg grinned. "Sounds fair."

As they walked toward the car, Meg stopped

short. Eden stood next to the car parked beside Aunt Jill's Camry.

"Hi, Meg." Eden smiled a perfect smile that, even under the lamplight, seemed too white to be real.

"Hi." Meg's heart gave a little skip that Eden remembered her name. "Are you getting a movie?"

Eden pushed a strand of hair from her eyes. "No. My friend is picking us up some food at Barney's. Fruit didn't fill us up."

Meg laughed. "Same here. We ordered pizza."

Aunt Jill cleared her throat and stepped forward, shifting the bag of movies into her left hand. She reached out to Eden. "I'm Jill Parker."

Eden's eyebrows rose. "Sheriff Parker?"

"Yes."

"Aunt Jill, this is the instructor of the yoga class I took today."

"I've never seen you around," Aunt Jill said, a confused frown creasing her brow. "How long have you been in town?"

Meg grimaced. Why did it sound like Aunt Jill was interrogating Eden, as if she were a suspect in a crime?

Eden didn't seem to mind. She turned her smile on Aunt Jill. "A few weeks."

"How is it that you've been running a yoga class without my knowledge?"

Eden shrugged. "I haven't advertised. It's just

been word of mouth. I instruct yoga and host poetry readings. As a matter of fact, we're having a poetry reading this evening." She slid her attention back to Meg. "I'm sorry you couldn't stay, but if you change your mind, you're still most welcome."

"Thank you." Meg grinned. She'd give anything to be able to attend that poetry reading, and she didn't even like poetry.

Aunt Jill tilted her head. "But if you didn't advertise, how did anyone know there was a yoga class? Meg said you're a few miles from town."

"Word of mouth is a powerful tool, Sheriff. I mentioned the class to Carrie when I stopped at Barney's the first day I arrived in town, and before I knew it, I had twenty-five students. I like to think I'm gifted to teach the classes, but Carrie's a great recruiter."

Carrie was Eden's friend in Barney's? Betrayal bit deep inside Meg. Carrie must have gone back after dropping Meg at home.

As if on cue, Carrie sauntered toward them, a bright smile on her face. A weird jealousy slammed into Meg as Eden's expression softened with obvious affection for Carrie.

"Hi, Meg!" Carrie said.

Eden turned to Meg with a sudden movement. "I hope you'll join me for another class before you leave town, Meg. I enjoyed getting to know you today."

191

Aunt Jill stepped forward. "We'll see. She's leaving in a couple days, and I'm sure her mom will want to keep her pretty close until then."

Meg glared at her aunt and might have spoken up, but Eden broke in first. "Is your mother waiting for you at home?"

"No," Meg said.

"Oh?" Eden's tone spoke volumes. She clearly saw how close Meg's mother kept her.

Meg sniffed. "She's on a date."

Compassion softened Eden's expression as her gaze perused Meg's face. Meg felt instantly that Eden truly understood, as though without saying a word, Meg had conveyed all her hurt and disappointment in Nina, and Eden completely got it and was on her side. Meg couldn't count on Nina to be there, ever.

"Eden," Jill said, "it was nice to meet you. Welcome to Abbey Hills." She turned to Meg. "Well, kiddo, we'd better go."

Eden stepped closer.

"So long, Meg," Carrie broke in, annoying Meg. She'd interrupted just as Eden was about to speak.

The serenity seemed to wash from Eden's face for a split second but returned just as quickly. She held out her hand, and Meg placed hers inside. In that one warm bit of contact, Meg felt accepted, understood. She felt like she fit.

CHAPTER ELEVEN

The year I turned ten, I left my childhood behind. I didn't become a woman in the physical sense of the word, but in the same way that happiness is a state of mind, in my mind I was no longer a child by the end of that year.

After the incident with my dad's half-full vodka bottle, I realized there was a good chance I'd get another opportunity. And I did. A few nights later. I started sneaking drinks from Dad's open bottles and discovered I enjoyed the numbing sensation that accompanied the few sips it took to buzz the mind of a seventy-pound girl. It took a few more sips for the eighty-five pound eleven-year-old, and by the time I hit my early teens, I could drink any of the football players under the table. By keeping up with the boys, I was able to shed my "Puke" identity and enjoy a new reputation as the girl no one could trick into bed by giving her a little too much to drink. I had my own group of secret admirers, though no one invited me to slumber parties or out to the movies. God forbid the girls should socialize with me or the guys date me— though the latter probably would have happened if I'd been the kind to put out.

My tenth year is when I realized who I was and began to act accordingly. I was the daughter of the town drunk, a chip off the old block. That was who I was, and I really didn't care.

As it turned out, the General was already in bed and wouldn't open his door. Nina slipped back into Markus's car and waited for him to fold his large body into the driver's seat and close his door.

His eyes lit with amusement as he turned to her. "Well, so much for doing the right thing."

Nina laughed. "I can't believe he yelled at us for waking him up. At eight-thirty." She sobered. "You don't think he's in bed early because he's depressed, do you?"

Markus started the engine. He shook his head as he slid the gearshift into place. "I don't think so. He didn't sound depressed, just really, really irritated."

Nina sat quietly for a moment while Markus drove down the General's gravel drive. "These killings are so strange," she said. "The blood draining especially. Don't think I'm crazy, but it almost seems like something is draining the blood to drink it." Nina shuddered.

Markus's lips twitched. "You mean something like a vampire?"

She shrugged and felt stupid. "Not the kind with stakes and crosses and holy water, but maybe a vampire-wannabe cult or something. Or maybe black magic that uses blood sacrifice."

"You could be more right than you imagine."

"Stop teasing me. I'm just trying to look at all the possibilities. I know the police are considering witchcraft or Satanism. They'd have to be."

He eyed her silently, then turned back to the road. "There have been rumors of vampires in these parts before."

Nina laughed. She hadn't honestly been talking about vampires in the mythical sense. And even though she'd been raised here, she'd never heard anything about vampires. On the other hand, there were all sorts of ghost stories and other oddities in the Ozarks, so why not vampires too? "More of your research?"

"Something like that." His tone didn't hold a hint of amusement as his gaze stayed on the dark, winding road.

"You mean it?"

He nodded. "Do you want to hear the lore?"

She shivered. "I suppose."

"It started in the 1700s, not many years before

the American Revolution. Of course this area wasn't under British control. The French owned all of this land until the Louisiana Purchase in 1803."

He gathered in a deep breath. "The story goes that a young trapper named Alexander Lafitte lived somewhere in the woods above the river. He and his bride ran a trading post for the other trappers and Indians in the area. He maintained a good relationship with the Osage and other Sioux tribes."

"Let me guess," Nina said, forcing humor into her voice. "He was bitten by a bat or an ancient vampire and became the undead?"

"No. Vampires aren't turned that way. Vampirism comes through the bloodline like any family curse."

Nina stared at him. He acted as though he truly believed what he was saying.

Markus tilted his head and grinned. "Or so the Ozark legend goes."

A breath of relief pulsed through her throat. "So no undead vampires making other vampires with their poisonous bite?"

"Not that I'm aware of." He gave her an indulgent smile.

She settled into the seat and tried to relax. "Tell me the story, then. I promise I won't interrupt."

"The trapper Lafitte began to feel the urge for blood when he reached full manhood, but he was able to keep it at bay. He enjoyed his meat bloody and rare, but many men did, and his wife never suspected anything was amiss. They had a good marriage in the beginning, and for several years everything was fine."

"Where did they meet?" Nina asked. "I mean, I thought most trappers took Indian wives."

"I thought you weren't going to interrupt." Markus smiled.

"Sorry, but all good vampire stories have a strong romance."

His dark eyebrows rose, and he took his eyes from the road long enough to send her a questioning glance. "Do you think so?"

"I know so. I'm an expert on the genre. I've watched every episode of *Buffy the Vampire Slayer*."

He chortled.

"Fine, mock me, but I need to hear how Lafitte won his wife. It's the romantic in me."

"Her name was Madeline." His voice softened as he spoke her name, and Nina wondered if he was a bit of a romantic as well. "She came from Virginia. Her father outfitted Lafitte to come to Osage territory and open the trading post. Madeline and Alexander fell in love before he finished his preparations for the journey. He proposed, and she agreed to be his bride. Unfortunately, her parents had other ideas about whom she should marry. She cried and pleaded, but her father refused to bless the marriage, so they ran away and were married anyway. Her parents never considered her marriage binding because a Protestant minister performed the ceremony. She tried to go home when their child was born so she could raise him in society and get him schooling, but her parents wanted nothing to do with her."

"She wanted to leave Lafitte?"

He gave a solemn nod. "For their first two years of marriage, Madeline couldn't have asked for a kinder, more loving husband, but not long after their son was born, Lafitte began to change. He grew violent and often slapped her or even hit her with a fist. He never went all out and beat her, but the small bursts of violence were enough to slowly bruise much more than her body."

"Her heart."

He angled his gaze toward Nina, and she was surprised to find sadness there. As though he truly felt the weight of the story. Madeline's sadness. His voice softened. "She lost her passion for him and began to pour her love into raising their son."

For some reason, disappointment slid through Nina. She wanted love to matter, to last. These two lovers alone in the wild with a son should have leaned on each other. Cared for each other, been each other's strength. "Why did Lafitte turn on his bride? Do you think he went a little crazy because of cabin fever or something?"

"I think as the vampiric tendency grew inside him, the demon started overtaking his humanity."

Vampire. She'd forgotten. Nina laughed. "I forgot this was a story. I was treating it like history."

"Perhaps it is history."

"Vampire history?" She laughed again.

"Humor me."

"Okay. You're the one telling the story. I'll suspend disbelief."

"Thank you. You're a good sport." He slowed to take a sharp curve and picked the story back up. "Legend says that by now Lafitte was beginning to crave blood. By the time the boy was five or six years old, Lafitte would leave for days at a time and come back with blood caked in his beard. His eyes would be wild, but his manner more sedate. He would be kinder to his wife, for a while."

"What was the boy's name? You haven't said."

Markus hesitated, frowning. "Madeline wanted to name him Alexander, after Lafitte, but Lafitte wouldn't hear of it. He insisted his son wouldn't bear his father's name or his grandfather's."

"Because the vampiric tendency came from his father's side?"

"Yes." His expression remained grim. He took his Ozark legends seriously. "They named him

Pierre, after Lafitte's maternal grandfather, who was a strong man of Christian faith. A very poor Protestant minister, in fact."

The lights of Abbey Hills came into view. "So when little Pierre Lafitte was five or six, his dad would come home with blood on his beard," Nina prodded.

"Those were the only times he seemed to have any peace. Within a few days he'd inevitably grow restless, and the violent episodes would erupt. He always left before doing any real damage. Until one night." He slowed the Lexus as they passed the Welcome to Abbey Hills sign.

"One night?"

"Pierre was sleeping in his corner of the cabin under a pile of buffalo robes when a loud crash woke him up. He watched while Lafitte roared through the house, grabbed Madeline, and tore open her throat with his teeth. She didn't even have time to scream, it happened so fast."

Nina swallowed hard. "What happened to Pierre?"

"Lafitte stared down at his dead wife, still half-crazed, until Pierre started screaming. Then his eyes widened in horror as he realized what he'd done to the woman he loved. The mother of his son.

"He turned to Pierre, but the boy couldn't stop screaming. It was all he could do. He'd lost the ability to reason, to speak. He screamed and screamed until Lafitte ran out of the cabin. Only then did Pierre stop screaming, terrified his father might return and kill him as well. He hid under the buffalo robes for three days until a hunting party of Osage warriors stopped by. They took Pierre and burned the cabin with Madeline inside. They felt the only way to purge the area of evil was to burn everything."

"So Pierre was raised by the Indians?" Nina asked.

"More or less, yes." He turned onto their street.

"Is that all there is to the story?" Nina pressed. "One act of vampirism?"

"Isn't that enough?"

"It's enough to be disturbing and tragic, but not enough to be a legend that could connect with Amanda's death or the animals."

As Markus maneuvered the car into Jill's driveway, Nina noticed the glow of the TV through the living room window.

"There's quite a bit more to the story," Markus said. "Do you want to hear it tonight?"

"I'll have to take a rain check. It looks like Jill and Meggie rented movies after all."

Nina felt a little left out. If she'd known they'd actually go through with the girls' night plan, she never would have left.

Markus touched her shoulder. "We haven't been gone that long. You haven't missed much."

He was sensitive; she had to give him that.

"Thanks for the walk and the ride out to the General's." She smiled. "And the story. You tell it so well. I hope I can sleep at least a little tonight."

"I should be thanking you."

She opened the car door. "Good night, Markus."

"Good night."

He watched until she slipped inside the house. Something about that comforted her, as though she were being watched over. And the idea brought Hunt's image to her mind's eye.

~

I've never regretted my relationship with Nina. Not even when the drinking became dangerous and I had to choose between my love for her and my need to protect my children.

The truth is, things weren't all bad. Nina had spurts of sobriety. Once she even went two years without a drink. I thought we had endured the worst, but we lost a baby one year after Adam was born. The pregnancy surprised us both, coming so soon after Adam's birth.

She carried our baby to term and gave birth to a beautiful daughter who lived only three hours and slipped away, cuddled in Nina's arms. Nina wouldn't be consoled. She was convinced her drinking had caused our little girl's heart defect, but she hadn't taken a drop for months before becoming pregnant with Adam, let alone this baby.

The day of the funeral, she drank herself into a stupor and begged me to give her another baby. She was in no shape physically or emotionally for me to make love to her, so I convinced her to let me hold her instead. She passed out in my arms and stayed drunk for the better part of the next four years.

We discovered later that I had a brother who had died in infancy from the same heart defect. Nina stopped blaming herself and started blaming me. Either way, she drank to numb the pain.

And I was left to grieve alone.

Meg hated to admit that she was glad when Nina walked in during the opening credits of *A Nightmare on Elm Street*.

"Oh wow. Great choice," Nina said as she set a pie on the coffee table. "From Barney's." She grabbed a slice of pizza and a napkin and sat next to Meg on the couch.

"Retro girls' night in," Aunt Jill said, grinning. "Great idea to get a pie."

"It was supposed to be for the General, but he wouldn't let us in."

Aunt Jill's face registered concern. "Is that where you went? That's a nice thought, Nina. He's not holing up in that cabin, is he?"

Nina shook her head. "We woke him up. Boy, was he mad. We tried to give him the pie even if he didn't want us to come in, but he said he has diabetes and asked if we were trying to make him go blind."

A throaty chuckle left Aunt Jill as she relaxed. "His loss; our gain. I'll get plates. You want to pause the DVD, Meggie?"

She did. Nina's gaze pulled on her like a magnet until Meg looked up.

"Thanks for texting me that you were going to do yoga with Carrie," Nina said.

"I didn't want to get yelled at."

"Smart move. So how was it?"

Meg felt her spirits perk up. "Great. The instructor is fantastic."

"I'm glad to hear that. Who knows, I might start going to yoga classes too now that I'm running again."

In the kitchen, Aunt Jill's house phone rang.

Meg tuned out her aunt's quiet voice answering the phone, as the image of Nina in Eden's house doing the peaceful incense and tea thing just didn't sit right with her. "I don't think you'd like it."

Nina's eyebrows went up, but Jill called from the kitchen before she could respond.

"Nina, you have a phone call."

Meg frowned. "Who would be calling you on Aunt Jill's land line?"

Nina's face had gone white, but she shrugged. "I'm not sure." She sounded worried.

Aunt Jill came back into the living room with a knife, a pie server, and plates and forks. "You're going to love the peach pie from Barney's. Mrs. Mackey makes them for him and sells them on consignment. She could probably open her own shop, but Barney would have a cow if she did."

Meg wanted her to be quiet so she could hear Nina's words. She could tell by the muted rise and fall of her voice that her mother wasn't happy.

Aunt Jill cut a generous slice of pie, put it on a plate, and handed it to Meg. Meg hesitated as she looked at the slice, which was more like a third of the pie.

Aunt Jill gave her a look. "No girly calorie stuff tonight. It's our night to pig out and scream together."

"Okay. If Mom ever gets back in here. Who's she talking to anyway?"

"Mom?"

"Nina. She's my mother, remember?"

"Yeah, I remember. I just wasn't sure you did."

Meg felt herself blushing. "Whatever."

Nina came back before Meg had taken more than three bites.

Aunt Jill glanced up with a grin. "Twice in one day. Stephan must be the one still carrying the torch of love."

"No, he isn't." Nina's abrupt tone took Meg by surprise.

And apparently Aunt Jill as well. "Sorry to touch a nerve. I just always thought you two had a secret thing going on when we were kids."

"We had friendship. Then he wanted more and I didn't, so we stopped being friends. Period."

Meg rolled her eyes. "Can we please watch the movie?"

Aunt Jill grabbed the afghan from the edge of the couch. "Okay, but we all have to sit together on the couch and share the afghan so we can protect each other from Freddy Krueger."

Nina laughed. "For a tough cop, you're a big sissy."

"Don't tell anyone."

"Stop bugging me about Stephan, and I'll keep my mouth shut about your cowardice."

Aunt Jill gave a girly giggle. "Deal. Now scoot to the middle so I can snuggle up close."

Meg looked at Nina. Despite the quick comebacks, her face had paled a shade or two since she'd walked in the door a few minutes ago. Meg suspected that loss of color had something to do with the phone call.

Who was this Stephan really, and what had he said to Nina that had so upset her?

PART TWO

Death may be the greatest
of all human blessings.

SOCRATES

CHAPTER TWELVE

High school was a nightmare. By the time I was fourteen and began my freshman year, I already had a bad reputation, most of it deserved.

I drank anything I could get my hands on, and I had plenty of opportunity. Dad was never without a bottle in grabbing distance, no matter what room of the house he happened to be in. They were everywhere, and he never noticed when a bottle emptied out a little faster than it should. I never stole anything until he was too wasted to notice.

Jill and I couldn't have been more different as sisters. Mom and Jill were gone almost every weekend for one of my sister's extracurricular events. Jill sang, she played basketball, and she had a firm place on the cheerleading squad all four years of high school.

I asked my mother once why they never invited me, and she said, "Be serious, Nina. You know you'd be bored stiff. You hate that sort of thing."

How would my mother possibly know what sort of thing I hated?

Looking back, I can't blame my reputation on Dad. I did it all myself. Jill was the good sister; I was the party girl. And that was the way I liked it. I didn't care about the pain I saw in my mother's eyes when the principal called to say I'd been caught with a flask or when I stumbled home at five in the morning, drunk out of my mind.

I knew she hated me, and I didn't care. By the time I reached high school, I'd stopped trying to gain her approval, much less her love. She only had room for Jill.

Dad liked me fine, and he left me alone, which was all I wanted. To be left alone.

At three o'clock in the morning, headlights pulling into Markus's driveway and shining into her window was the last straw of a disturbingly sleepless night. Between the nightmare mix of Freddy Krueger, trapper vampires, and Stephan's phone call, she had barely slept at all.

During his call, Stephan claimed he didn't want to upset Meg's life. How laughable.

Nina had tossed and turned in bed as long as she could stand. She snatched her robe from the chair next to her bed and slid her arms into the fuzzy depths as she padded from the room in her socks.

Making her way to the kitchen, she was glad Jill used nightlights to mark the way through the house. She set up the coffeepot and brewed a pot. After cleaning the pot several times with vinegar, the coffee tasted much better, though it still left a lot to be desired. Coffee was coffee, and if she was going to wake up at three in the morning, she had to have caffeine.

On a whim, she rifled through the cabinets as quietly as possible and pulled out the ingredients to make cinnamon rolls. Meggie had always loved her homemade cinnamon rolls. Back when it was just the two of them and the ingredients were much cheaper than buying treats, Nina would freeze most of the recipe and bring out one roll per day for each of them and microwave it to gooey warmth. Then they would drink milk and watch a Disney movie together. Those were the days before Hunt walked into the bar and took Nina's breath away.

She had stopped drinking while pregnant with Meg and never drank one drop while raising her little girl alone, even though some days she had to fight the urge. The responsibility of caring for her young daughter had weighed heavily on her shoulders, sobering her up and keeping her that way until her honeymoon. She had eased into daily drinking after that until within a few months she couldn't sleep at night without a bottle of wine. Eventually, she needed a bottle to get through the day and another bottle at night.

Her thoughts swirled as she prepared the dough recipe from memory. She had shoved that night seventeen years ago from her mind, forcing the memory deep into a place where she never had to deal with it. She knew coming home meant she would have to face it again, but for some reason, she'd believed Stephan would assume Meggie had been conceived after Nina left Abbey Hills. The fact that he'd connected the dots within a couple of days came as a shock. She'd most likely been in denial, but then, addicts were good at denial.

By 5 a.m. the dough had been rolled, cut into cinnamon rolls, and sat rising to be baked. While she waited for the rolls to rise, Nina ventured into the living room and turned on the first news of the day.

A pretty, thirty-something brunette appeared somber as she read from her teleprompter. "We have breaking news to report. The body of a homeless man was found an hour ago in downtown Springfield, in the alley outside Flannigan's. The body had been . . ." The anchorwoman's face blanched, and she swallowed hard, frowning. "The, um, body appeared to have been drained of blood, but authorities say cause of death will not be confirmed for several days. The body has been taken to the Springfield crime lab to be autopsied and examined."

The newswoman tried to force a professional smile as she turned to her male co-anchor. He seemed just as confused as she did. "Have they said whether or not they believe this to be a homicide?"

His partner stared back at him, as though she thought him a proper idiot. Nina had to give her that one.

Her silence appeared to unnerve him. He cleared his throat. "I mean, could an animal of some sort have gotten hold of the poor man?"

The anchorwoman's face twisted in horror. "Let's hope not. I'd hate to think of such an animal roaming downtown Springfield."

He nodded. "Or a murderer, for that matter."

Nina shook her head at the discourse between these two talking heads. The channel should fire them both and hire a couple of anchors with some brains. Speculating on a poor, dead homeless man as if he were lost in the Serengeti instead of Springfield, Missouri. It sounded like a murder to her.

The stairs creaked in the other room. Nina turned to see Jill, dressed in a terry-cloth robe and a pair of wool socks. She moved silently through the room.

"Sounds like the same thing that happened to

Amanda." Jill sat on the couch and stared at the TV. "Did they mention how the victim died?"

"Just that his body had been drained of blood."

"No cuts or anything? Amanda's throat and chest had a T-shaped cut, and her heart had been cut out. Same with the General's horse yesterday and the other animals we've found."

"I remember." Nina shuddered. "They didn't mention anything like that, but I doubt they'd be that graphic on the morning news, anyway."

"Good point."

Nina pushed herself up from the couch. "I'm going to put the cinnamon rolls in the oven and make some frosting." It seemed odd to go from murder victims to cinnamon rolls, but the need to remove herself from the topic sent her to the first thing she could think of.

"Homemade cinnamon rolls and homemade frosting? What's gotten into you?"

"I like to bake when I can't sleep. Which is most of the time."

Jill moaned. "I'm going to get fat while you're living here."

A smile slipped across Nina's lips. "You'll just have to use some discipline."

"Discipline when there are cinnamon rolls? Don't make me laugh."

"Want me to put the kettle on so you can have your tea?"

Jill nodded. "Thanks. I'm going to watch for a

few more minutes in case they say anything else. Otherwise I'll have to call and ask for a copy of the police report."

"You can do that?" Impressed, Nina stood in the doorway between the living room and the foyer.

"Well, sometimes they're reluctant to share, but professional courtesy usually gets me what I want." Jill sighed as the anchors introduced the weather girl. "Might as well get my own tea. They're not going to say anything else about the body."

"Probably better to get it straight from the source anyway."

When they reached the kitchen, Nina saw that the rolls had risen to an enormous size. Just the way she and Meg loved them. Nina lifted the pan of rolls and carefully slid them into the pre-heated oven.

She pulled out the ingredients for icing, then fished a mixing bowl from the cabinet and mixed up a creamy, sugary concoction.

Jill came up behind her and scooped a finger-ful of buttery icing from the bowl. "My mouth is watering. This is going to set my diet back a week."

Nina nudged her away with her elbow. "You shouldn't be on a diet anyway."

"Yeah, right."

Jill had always lamented her curves, but she'd

grown from a slightly chubby teenager into a lovely, curvy woman. Her figure was nothing to be ashamed of.

"So," Jill said, and Nina tensed. She knew what was coming. She poured herself a cup of coffee and headed to the table to sit and wait for the rolls to finish baking. Jill filled the teakettle with water and sat across from her. "All right. The truth."

"What about?" Nina asked.

"Stephan." Jill's eyes were intense, as though willing the truth out of Nina. "He wouldn't keep calling you just because he misses you or wants a date. It's not his nature to be insistent."

Nina gave a short, mirthless laugh. "Right."

"What? Nina, what aren't you telling me?"

The secret was so well preserved that the thought of opening up the jar of truth seemed foolish, dangerous even, as though the release of pressure might cause an explosion. Nina wasn't sure she was strong enough to let it out.

"Can I ask if Stephan is the reason you ran away the day after graduation?" Jill pressed.

Nina nodded.

"What happened?"

Nina mustered as much courage as she possessed, which wasn't much, and stared Jill down. "If I tell you, you have to promise you won't tell anyone. This is my secret to tell or to keep as I choose."

"You have my word." Jill's tone was stoic, her face grave.

"I mean it. You can't tell Mom, Dad, or Barney. Or anyone else."

"Well, if I can't tell those three, it's not likely I'd tell anyone else."

Nina released a breath. With the tip of her index finger, she traced a ring around the top of her coffee cup. "Graduation night, there was a party at the river."

"I know. I was really hurt that you didn't invite me."

That was news Nina didn't expect. The thought that Jill might want to go to that sort of party seemed beyond foreign to her.

"Believe me, Jill, I wish you had been there." Nina shook her head and sipped her coffee.

"What happened?"

Nina looked into Jill's earnest eyes and was just about to recount that night when the buzzer went off. She gave a shaky laugh. "Saved by the buzz."

She pulled the pan from the oven and set it on top of the stove to cool. Then she took the coffee-pot to the table to warm up the half cup she'd left untouched.

"You're stalling," Jill said softly. "You don't have to tell me anything you don't want me to know. We can stop right now."

Nina considered it, but Stephan wasn't going

away. She needed someone on her side, and Jill would understand. At least Nina hoped she would. "I'm not sure if you ever deduced it since I've never answered your questions about Meg's father, but it was that night. It was my first time. I had been drinking, but not that much. I would have drunk a lot more, but I never got the chance. I think my beer was spiked because everything was so strange and surreal in my head."

Anger flashed in Jill's dark eyes. "You think Stephan spiked your drink?"

"I don't know what to believe anymore."

"What does he say about it?" Her indignant attitude and support made Nina wonder why she hadn't confided in her sister years ago. She wished she had.

"We haven't talked about it since that night, Jill. I haven't had any contact with him."

"And?"

"My memory is fuzzy, but he acted as though I came on to him. Like I asked him to be my first."

"If you were drugged, that would make sense." She scowled. "And that was probably his plan all along. What a creep."

"I'm not sure if Stephan is the one who did the drugging. I think he would have broken down and confessed by now instead of continuing to act like the other half of Victims-R-Us." Nina stopped talking and met Jill's gaze. "Right?"

Jill shrugged. "I would think so. He always

seemed crazy about you. It's hard for me to imagine him slipping you a drug and taking advantage. But then bad guys hardly ever look like bad guys until they do something bad."

Nina laughed, grateful for the momentary levity.

"You mean like maybe he's a sociopath and no one knows it?"

"You never know. That's all I'm saying."

Nina sipped her coffee. Her mind didn't want to give up the thought of Stephan being the bad guy. But she couldn't help but rethink things. "If he didn't rape me, then where does that leave Meg?"

Jill's cheeks puffed out as she exhaled. "That's a tough question."

"Stephan wants to meet her."

"Oh." Jill cleared her throat and raised the tea to her lips. "That could create a problem. For you, anyway."

"And for Hunt. But especially for Meg." Nina glared into her cup. "I mean, how is she going to feel about the circumstances of her conception? She already loathes me."

"What does she believe now?"

"Honestly? She's never asked. She might have, if we'd been closer the last few years and she wasn't so angry at me."

"Looks like you'll have to open up and be honest with her now. You might not have a choice." Jill's eyes held compassion. "Don't sell your daughter short. She's stronger than you imagine. If Stephan presses this, and he might, I don't see that you have many options."

Nina propped her feet up on an empty chair and stared at the half-empty cup resting between her palms. Why did this have to happen now? Just when she thought she might have a chance to reach Meg?

A vibrating pillow woke Meg from a deep sleep and a weird dream about the lotus position. She fought her way through the fuzzy haze to consciousness.

Her phone. She'd laid it on the pillow last night, hoping Izzy might get her messages and call or text. She felt until her fingers found her phone. With great effort she opened her eyes and glanced at the screen.

Sorry I missed u ystrday. Crazy. Going crabbing in a few.

Crabbing was like fishing. Maybe Izzy's vacation wasn't that much better than hers, though Meg's had turned out a lot better than she thought it would. Between meeting her grandparents and meeting Eden, it was going pretty well.

Oh it's okay. Took a sweet yoga class.

Yoga? You must be bored! Ha-ha

No. It was great.

Ok I'll take ur word for it.

Meg wanted to throw the phone across the room. Izzy had no idea how awesome Eden was or how bad Meg wished she could stay another week just to take more classes. And she definitely wished she could see more of her grandparents. She couldn't help but feel a little let down at Izzy's tone.

Got 2 go. I smell breakfast.

K. TTYL.

Meg slid out of bed and headed downstairs toward the kitchen. She could hear the soft tones of conversation between Nina and Aunt Jill, but mostly she could hear breakfast, which smelled like cinnamon, calling her name.

She ventured closer and heard, "Meggie."

Listening in on a conversation about her was more than Meg could resist. She tiptoed to the doorway and hung back out of sight.

"How do you think Meg would handle it?" Aunt Jill asked.

"I don't know," Nina said. "But what if you're right and I don't have any choice but to introduce them?"

Meg frowned. This sounded more serious than just a little Meg bashing or whining about her lack of interest in bonding.

"Maybe you don't have to do anything you don't want to do," Aunt Jill said. "Meggie's sixteen years old. It would be stupid and costly to pursue anything legal at this point in her life.

All he has to do is wait a year and a half, until she's of age."

Trying to wrap her head around the conversation in progress was like fitting together pieces of half a puzzle. There were just enough pieces to see part of a picture, but not enough to see everything.

It sounded like Nina might be talking about her biological father. Could that even be possible? Meg didn't know anything about him. There had always been an unspoken understanding that she hadn't had a father before Hunt adopted her when she was six. She'd barely had time to miss a male role model. Thoughts of her biological father came only with fleeting curiosity. She knew Nina hadn't been married before Hunt. And Hunt was her father. Meg had always felt that way.

She pressed her back against the wall as the two women continued their conversation.

Nina's voice trembled. "I need to talk to Stephan and ask him to wait until Meggie is grown. Then if he wants to approach her, he can."

"That might be the best choice for her sake," Aunt Jill said. "She's been through so much lately."

A heavy sigh drifted across the kitchen, but Meg wasn't sure if it had come from Nina or Aunt Jill.

"The next time Stephan calls," Nina continued,

"I'll appeal to his sense of decency. Meg has a right to finish her childhood without more pain caused by me."

And once again, it was all about Nina. That was all Meg could take. She stepped into view. "Don't you think you should ask me what I want?"

The look of guilty surprise on their faces was exactly what Meg had hoped for. She fought to keep tears of betrayal at bay.

"I'm sorry you heard that, Meggie."

"I bet." Meg flounced into the kitchen, her head high. She had nothing to be ashamed of.

Aunt Jill shoved back her chair and stood. "I'm going to get dressed. You taking my car today?"

Nina nodded. "Thanks."

"Going somewhere?" Meg asked, grabbing a warm cinnamon roll. She plopped into a kitchen chair and raised an eyebrow at Nina.

"Running. Unless you want to impale me with something instead. Your sharp tongue, perhaps?"

Meg gave a short laugh, her bottom lip trembling a she fought to hold off tears, "I'd be within my right, don't you think?"

"I don't know. Maybe you could ask why before you start accusing me of something."

"Oh, that's right. I forgot it's all about you. Always has been. Always will be." *Rats!* Tears poured into her eyes, clouding her vision.

"Come on, Meggie." Nina's calm, controlled voice set Meg's teeth on edge. "I gave you a wonderful father."

A twinge of guilt pricked Meg. Her dad was the envy of all her friends. He was patient, available, giving, all the things her biological mother never had been. She gulped back the tears as anger rushed back in. "You gave him to me? Funny, I thought you married him because you loved him. Or did you have ulterior motives in marrying him?"

Nina set her cup down, and not softly. Coffee sloshed onto the table, but she seemed not to notice. "Hate me for all the things you've got bottled up—the drinking, the neglect, not showing up at important games and concerts. I deserve it. But don't cheapen what I feel for your dad. Got it?"

Feel? Meg's stomach quivered. That one-word admission from Nina took all the fire from Meg.

She flung herself back in the chair. "Fine. Whatever. What about this guy claiming to be my sperm donor?"

Nina shrugged. She stood and grabbed a paper towel from the counter. "If you hadn't overheard Aunt Jill and me, I wouldn't have done anything about him except try to avoid him until your dad picks you up on Saturday." She wiped up the spilled coffee and tossed the towel in the garbage. "But I guess it's your choice."

"I'm going over to Grammy and Poppy's today. I'll ask Aunt Jill to drop me off on her way to the station." She couldn't think. Her head hurt with the thought of this Stephan.

"Okay. If Stephan calls me again, do you want me to tell him that you know about him and I'm leaving the choice up to you?"

Meg stood, taking her roll with her. "Tell him whatever you want. I doubt I'm going to meet him anyway. I have a dad."

"Hey, we can talk more about this if you want. I'll tell you everything you want to know."

"Just one thing—did you love him?"

"No." Nina drew a long, slow breath. "We were at my graduation party down by the river. We were drinking. Do you want me to go on?"

"No."

Meg left Nina alone in the kitchen. She blinked away tears. She wouldn't even be here if Nina hadn't been drunk. Figures. What was the point to her life? She wasn't even supposed to be alive.

Nothing but a waste.

CHAPTER THIRTEEN

The first time I felt actual shame over my drinking, I was sixteen. The General had asked me to keep an eye on the horses while he visited his son in Arkansas overnight.

I lied and promised that my parents were okay with me staying overnight to look after his place.

But seeing the disgust in the General's eyes the next morning when he found ten hungover teenagers in his living room, two naked teens in his bed, and several twelve-packs worth of empty cans littering his floor left me empty inside and feeling anything but proud.

"The apple doesn't fall far from the tree, does it?"

"Guess not," I mumbled, sick, embarrassed, defiant.

"Get these kids out of here."

In fifteen minutes, all dozen teens had stumbled away, leaving me to face the General. He kicked cans out of his way, pulled a glass from the cabinet, juice from the fridge, and motioned for me to sit. I watched the orange juice fill the glass.

"You sorry?" he asked.

I nodded. If he only knew how sorry.

"Took care of my animals before your little friends got here?"

"Yes, sir."

"Then drink your juice, and we'll get this place cleaned up."

"You're not mad?"

"Aw, not too much. I shoulda known better than to ask a kid to look after things." He speared me with the intensity of his gaze. "This a one-time thing? Or you got the same problem as your dad?"

"I—I don't have a problem."

"Hmm."

I could see his opinion in his eyes, and it cut me. I would never drink again, never risk the General's disappointment.

Too bad Mom and Dad showed up. They burst into the house, accused the General of all kinds of perverted things, from getting me drunk to threatening to have him arrested for statutory rape. The General accused them right back. Of neglecting me. Of raising me to be an alcoholic by ignoring me and *being bad examples. And if anyone was violating me, it was them. Violating my heart by not loving me the way a kid deserved to be loved. They stood speechless as he ordered them off his land.*

When we walked in the door of our house, my parents sent me to my room, grounded indefinitely. As soon as it got dark, I snuck out and went to a party at the river.

Harvey barked a welcome and sprang from the porch as Nina drove up to the General's home in Jill's car. Nina could have sworn he was actually grinning as he barreled toward her, his long tongue waving in the wind. She knew now to brace herself for his attack of joy, so when he leaped, placing his paws on her shoulders and bathing her face with kisses, she was ready. She accepted the affection and laughingly shoved him off with one arm, holding a plate of cinnamon rolls high above her head with the other.

The General, on the other hand, barely gave her a nod in response to her enthusiastic greeting. He brushed by her, distracted and mumbling something about a foal in the barn.

"Need some help?" she called after him.

"I got it." He waved her away. Nina smiled. Most horses delivered with thirty minutes or so of hard labor. The General just needed to stand back and be ready to offer assistance if the mare needed him. Usually the mares didn't.

She opened the car door and set the plate of treats on the seat. The temperature was just right. They'd be fine for a little while.

She raked her nails across the top of Harvey's head. "Ready to go, bud?"

His tail moved back and forth so fast, Nina thought the dog might achieve liftoff. He knew they were about to go running, and every inch of his body vibrated in anticipation. Nina couldn't help but laugh. Despite the Great Dane's bad manners and tendency to knock her off her feet, she felt a sense of comfort in his presence as she ventured out across the acres of lonesome field. Though she doubted seriously that he'd be much protection if they confronted a blood-draining monster.

She felt yesterday's blisters through her Band-Aids as she jogged down the trail that wound between disabled electric fences. She had the eerie feeling she was being watched. She thought of Markus's story and imagined the wild eyes of a bloodthirsty trapper peering at her from the trees. But that was crazy. The only things out here were deer, horses, and the occasional coyote, according to the General. Worse than her fear of any outside threat was the memory of Meg's face when she'd walked into the kitchen that morning.

A knot formed in her gut and seemed to grow as the minutes ticked by. What if she'd lost Meggie for good? But how could she have possibly told her about Stephan? She still wasn't sure he hadn't drugged her that night. But if not Stephan, then who? And why would anyone else have done it, since he seemed to be the only one to benefit from the incident? Or was there more she couldn't remember?

Her mind raced over and over the events of the evening, beginning at the moment the group of teens had descended upon the gravel at the river's edge. The beach, they called it. Dane Williamson had brought a keg. Someone handed her a plastic cup of foaming beer, but her mind wouldn't produce an image of the face. A guy for sure. Stephan? Dane? Why couldn't she remember?

Frustration propelled her feet forward, as she ran faster along the path. Her legs felt heavy. The exertion of forcing her body out of its comfort zone and fighting against the unhealthy habits she'd inflicted upon herself over the last few years took a toll. Her labored breathing reminded her that it hadn't been that many months since she'd given up smoking and that it had been more than a year since she'd attempted any kind of cardio workout.

After only a mile, she dropped from barely a jog to a walk, pinching the stitch in her side to ease the spasm.

Harvey kept running, then realized she had stopped. He skidded to a halt and trotted back to her, pressing his enormous head into her hip and pushing her off balance. He whined.

"Sorry, bub," Nina said. "You might have the energy of six generators, but I'm wiped out. Besides, my blisters are starting to hurt."

Nina rubbed his head absently as they walked. She lifted her gaze to the horizon beyond the boundaries of the reserve. The river wasn't far. Just a short walk through the woods, a mile maybe. If she revisited the location of the party, would she remember what had happened?

Her breathing evened out within a couple minutes. Just as she was about to kick it back into a jog, she noticed a couple of vultures settle a few yards ahead. Harvey noticed at the same time. He leaped forward, barking.

The vultures started and lifted, their odd-shaped bodies flying awkwardly away. Turning, they circled, watching while Harvey barked a warning.

Nina covered her nose and mouth with the collar of her tank top as she approached the dead animal on the trail. It was a deer, barely recognizable.

She knelt next to the decomposing animal. Harvey nosed in close, a whine vibrating his throat. Nina pushed him back. "Go sit down, Harvey."

The deer lay shriveled. Nina realized it had been completely drained of blood.

Invisible fingers traveled up her spine, causing a shudder to move over her entire body. No animal she knew of did this. What was happening in Abbey Hills?

She lifted her cell phone from her pocket and dialed Jill.

"A deer," she said when her sister answered. "It's been drained."

"What are you talking about?" From the background noise, Nina could tell Jill was at Barney's.

"I was running, and I came across a dead deer. It's been drained, like Amanda. Like the General's horse and the other animals. It has your T-shaped cut at the neck and down its torso. Heart is gone."

Jill gasped. "Stay there. I'm calling the state patrol."

Harvey let out a string of warning barks at the vultures as they swooped overhead.

Jill groaned in Nina's ear. "Is that Harvey?"

"Who else?"

"Keep him away from the deer."

"Don't worry. He's more interested in the buzzards."

"Well, keep the buzzards away too."

"I'll do my best. When will you get here?"

"I'm on my way in the squad car. As soon as I get your statement, you can go."

Fifteen minutes later, her arms ached from fighting to keep the dead animal safe from the buzzards and Harvey. She felt like a lunatic, jumping around, waving her arms, and yelling. Harvey loved the fun and knocked her down twice in his enthusiasm.

Thankfully, Jill arrived with the General riding shotgun in the squad car. He took over Harvey's discipline and got the dog to hush and sit still.

"Thought you was a fancy animal doctor," he said. "You can't keep a puppy in line?"

"Yeah, well, I'm not a dog trainer," Nina replied, wiping sweat off her forehead. "Besides, that so-called puppy's the size of a VW bus."

"Bah."

Jill slipped on a pair of surgical-looking gloves and squatted next to the deer. Her face blanched, though whether at the sight or the smell, Nina wasn't sure.

"It's the same?" Nina asked softly.

Jill nodded. "Someone's messing with us. This is too much to be coincidence."

A cloud moved across the sun, bringing a cooling wind. Something about it seemed ominous. Nina shivered.

Jill stood and pulled a small notebook out of her pocket. "I need to get your statement."

Nina recounted how she'd come upon the animal. "Sorry there isn't more to tell."

Jill shrugged. "It's one more lead in Amanda's

death as far as I'm concerned." She glanced up and met Nina's gaze. For the first time, Nina noticed the shadows under her sister's eyes.

"You okay, Jilly?"

"Just desperate to figure out who's behind all this before another resident of Abbey Hills turns up dead—animal or human." Jill took a deep breath and exhaled slowly. "You should head back. The highway patrol will be here soon. We'll get this animal back to the lab. Don't forget the funeral is in a few hours."

"I'll stay with you until they get here," Nina said. What if the killer was hanging around? No way was Nina leaving Jill to fend for herself. And even if the killer was long gone, which was more likely, Nina couldn't leave Jill when she was so obviously distressed.

The General didn't seem to have the same sense of chivalry. "Harvey and me are gonna head back to the barn. I shouldn't have left Tabby alone as it is."

Nina glanced at her watch. She had started her run over an hour ago. "She hasn't delivered?"

The General shook his head. The worry in his eyes told her all she needed to know.

"Is this her first foal?" she asked.

"Yep. She's too young. Was carrying when I took her in. I figured she'd miscarry, but she's a strong little filly."

"Do you want me to stop in after the state

police get here? Maybe I could help. Not that you aren't capable of delivering a foal without me."

His head inclined toward her. "She might need someone with more experience than I got."

"All right then. I'll see you in a few minutes."

He nodded. "You two girls holler if you need me."

Luckily, they didn't have to wait long before two SUVs with Highway Patrol emblazoned across their sides arrived. A squad car followed.

"The Calvary's arrived," Nina said.

"Cavalry," Jill corrected.

"Oh, yeah. I always get those mixed up."

"How can you get a bunch of old horse soldiers mixed up with the place where Jesus died?"

She shrugged. "I don't know."

Jill shook her head, then squinted toward the plume of dust kicked up by the SUV tires. "I'll take it from here. These guys are pretty hard core and condescending. Go on back and help the General deliver the foal. The old softy will be heartbroken if anything happens to mother or baby."

Nina nodded. "Good idea."

"Wait. I forgot."

Nina stopped and waited. "Yeah?"

"I need a ride to the funeral. My deputy will have the squad car parked early at the funeral home for the procession to the grave site. Can you pick me up?"

"Of course. What time?"

"One. That will give us plenty of time to get there by one-thirty."

Jill cast a furtive glance toward the SUVs, her eyes squinting against the sunlight. Nina felt her tension and followed her gaze.

"No problem."

Tires crunched on the gravel path as the SUVs parked twenty feet away. Jill cast a sideways glance at Nina. "Here we go."

Nina could hear the relief in Jill's tone. She might be a leader in a tough job, but she was glad to relinquish this situation to the state patrol. The animal lying there drained could just as easily have been another person.

The thought sobered Nina, and she walked back down the path, wondering what could possibly be causing these horrific deaths. She picked up her pace and broke into a jog, ignoring the heated pain in her feet where her skin had been rubbed raw. She wanted to get to the comfort of the General's presence as quickly as possible.

Markus knew Eden would have created a refuge for herself in some out-of-the-way spot. A one-hundred-year-old house in the woods, for instance, where she could lure young people with her compelling ways, as she'd always done.

As she'd lured him in years ago.

He spent enough time in the woods outside town that it wasn't difficult to discover where the yoga classes were being held. The enthusiastic girls who attended were happy to confirm his suspicion. Markus had a feeling they were encouraged to do so. Eden had always enjoyed the adoration of many. She would want to grow her group of followers quickly.

He'd been one of her admirers once, captured by whatever allure she possessed, but he'd long since escaped. And now she'd followed him. Would he ever be free?

She glided onto the porch as though she knew he was watching, waiting for her to appear. She held a cup of what Markus assumed was an herbal tea. Her fingers curled around the mug, almost seductively. Everything she did seemed seductive, though not always sexual. There were other seductions, and Eden had mastered them all.

Stepping from the protection of the trees, he walked toward her.

She turned and smiled without surprise, as though she had sensed his presence. She probably had. "Markus. I knew you'd come."

"I'm surprised I didn't figure it out sooner."

"I'm a little surprised myself. I've been here for a month."

He walked closer, stopping at the bottom of

the steps. "The killings are your handiwork, I take it?"

Her full lips curved upward into a pouty smile. "I had to get your attention somehow, didn't I?"

"You could have gotten my attention in a less gruesome manner, don't you think? Knocking on my door, for instance."

"But not as intriguing." She glided across the porch and lowered herself onto the porch swing.

He stepped onto the porch. Up close, her presence, her scent, her body clouded his senses. "Your power has grown, I see."

"I'll accept that as a compliment." She patted the seat beside her with a slow, deliberate movement. "I've missed you."

He ignored her invitation and leaned against the porch railing instead. Better to keep a safe distance from her. "Why have you come after me, Eden?"

"I told you I would. I will never stop coming for you." The wind lifted her laughter and seemed to fill the air with song. She was beginning to get to him, and she knew it.

Unable to resist her gaze, he lifted his eyes. "And every time you find me, I'll leave again. I want peace. I loathe the evil. I'm so tired of it."

"Evil?" Her eyes narrowed. Gone was the pretty pout, the sensual beauty. "How can you say such a cruel thing? Could I love you so much if I were full of the evil you seem to think possesses me?"

"Eden, you feel numerous things, I don't doubt, but love isn't among them."

"Fine. You haven't come to see me out of love —at least not yet." She smiled. "So why have you come?"

"As I said. The killings."

"What about them? Surely you of all people aren't judging me?"

"Not judging. Merely suggesting you stop killing around here—particularly humans. This town is not like New Orleans or St. Louis, where you can hide among the masses."

Eden tilted her lovely neck and stared at him. "What about Springfield? Was the death behind Flannigan's your doing? I know it wasn't mine."

Markus narrowed his gaze. He didn't like her veiled threat. He wasn't sure what she was threatening, but her malevolence was obvious. She knew he never killed for sport, and he didn't take anyone who didn't have it coming. Thieves, rapists, the dregs. He certainly didn't kill young wives and mothers. Eden had no qualms about who she killed. And she enjoyed it, the way he once had.

"I'm not going to justify myself to you," he said. "Leave the people of Abbey Hills alone, and don't kill any more horses on the reserve."

Her spellbinding eyes narrowed. He had to look away. "I've waited a long time to see you again, Markus. Why are you being so harsh with me?"

He needed to tread lightly. Eden could be kind and calm, but it didn't take much to make her angry. And when she was angry, she was capable of causing great pain.

"I'm not trying to be harsh." He kept his tone soft, hoping to soothe her. "I just don't want you to ruin what I have here."

His gut clenched, and he sucked in the suddenly cold air. She stood before him before he even registered her movement from the porch swing.

"Ruin what?" she asked. "I assumed you were wooing the mousy neighbor woman merely to feed on her, but perhaps there is more. Are you in love with this human who can never love you back? Not for who you are, anyway." Her long fingers threaded through his hair.

His head grew cloudy, and he closed his eyes against the effect, gathering all the control he could muster. "I'm not in love, Eden. You cured me of that."

She dropped her hand. "You are too cruel."

It took every ounce of will to look away from her. He stepped to the side and moved down the stairs. She looked down upon him. Standing at the top of the steps, she looked like a beautiful African statue. Tall, muscular, but still feminine. He had to resist her. Resist the memory of bedding her. Falling back into her arms would mean more than he wanted to consider.

"Eden, don't make me fight against you, please."

"Fight against me? Why would you do such a thing?" She glided down the steps, her movements achingly beautiful. "Now that I've found you, I win. You'll come back to me."

As though they had been playing a complicated version of hide-and-seek for the past thirty-five years. She was such a child in so many ways.

Her lips curved upward. Reaching out a dark, slender hand, she raked her nails lightly across his cheekbone, trailed down his jaw line, and rubbed the tips of her fingers across his lips. Markus shuddered, closing his eyes.

She leaned forward, pressing lightly against him, and held her lips close to his ear, her breath warm and inviting. "Now, tell me about the woman."

The switch in topic caught Markus off guard. He couldn't stop the images of Nina and Meg floating to his mind. Eden had manipulated him.

"You care for her. I sense it. But I don't understand it. She's so . . . so weak . . . human. Very fragile, this one." The temperature of her voice had dropped. No longer was she warm and pliable, filling him with images of past encounters. Anger snapped in her eyes and her movements quickened. She moved back onto the porch.

"Eden," Markus warned. "Leave her alone."

"All you have to do is come back to me, Markus. It's so simple. I give you my word nothing will happen to her. Or her daughter." His face must have registered his alarm because she smiled a cold, hard smile. "Oh yes. It isn't difficult to surmise that Meagan is this woman's daughter. Her mother is the sheriff's sister. You live next to the sheriff. I'm not blind, you know. It's a small town, and I do pay attention."

A growl began deep inside Markus, rage he had controlled for so many years. He leaped onto the porch, grabbed Eden by the neck, and pressed her against the door. "Don't go near either of them. Is that clear?"

"Of course." Eden's tone remained fixed, her eyes glittering in warning. "As long as you come back to me."

"That's not going to happen."

"It's too bad for them, then."

He dropped his hand from her throat. What was the point? He couldn't kill her without removing her head.

He stood unmoving as Eden slipped inside the two-story, white farmhouse—a home that had been standing for over a century—in various states of remodel.

He wished he'd never told her about his life with the Osage Indians in this place, so long ago.

He had lived with Eden for over a hundred

years and had tried to break free more than once, only to be lured back by her beauty, her black magic, her pure abandon of all consciousness outside her own needs. Eden had come into his life during a time when he roamed, much like his father before him, unkempt, taking what he needed, not caring who knew he was a vampire. He hated himself then and had dared someone to kill him. In many ways, he owed her for finding him, pulling him out of his destructive ways and helping him find a way to accept the life he'd been handed.

Did he still owe her? How much longer would he have to pay his debt?

He knew the answer. Eden would never willingly let him go. If he ran again, she would eventually find him. The cycle wouldn't end until one of them was dead.

Nina arrived at the barn fifteen minutes after breaking into a jog. She paused at the open door, clutching the stitch in her side.

The General's thin body bent over a groaning horse. "There, Tabby baby. Everything's gonna be just fine. The doc's on her way."

"I'm here, General," Nina said through gasps.

The pregnant mare groaned. Nina lifted the bottom of her shirt and wiped the sweat from her brow as her veterinary instincts kicked in. She hesitated, remembering the disastrous last time she'd entered the stall of a horse. But this was no time for self-doubt. Not when Tabby needed her.

"Well? You just standin' there?"

The General's voice shoved her into gear, and she nodded, breathing heavy from exertion and nerves. "What's the problem?"

"I think that's pretty dang obvious."

Nina rolled her eyes as she stepped into the stall. "No kidding. I mean do you have any idea what we're dealing with? Why isn't the foal coming?"

The General's shoulders slumped, and he shook his head. "Your guess is as good as mine."

"Good thing I know what I'm doing. Let me in there so I can have a look."

Reluctantly, the General stepped back, but Nina noted that he didn't leave the stall altogether. Kneeling next to the writhing horse, she ran her hand along its swollen middle and spoke softly. "Hi, girl." A contraction seized the half-ton animal. Her legs kicked as she groaned.

After a careful exam, Nina sat back, helpless. "She's small."

"I was afraid of that." Pain thickened the General's voice. "I'm gonna lose her?"

Normally, Nina would say yes; no way could this poor animal deliver her foal without more help than she could give in this old barn. "All right. I need disinfectant for my hands and arms."

"What do you reckon to do?"

"I'm going to reach inside her and try to get the foal unstuck. If that doesn't work, we can try a C-section, but without the proper facilities and a sterile environment, I'd hate to predict the outcome for either of them."

The General's face blanched at her prognosis. Like an expectant father, his hands trembled.

"Look, General," Nina said, "I know you're worried, but this poor horse has been in labor too long. She's getting weak. Her breathing is slowing down. If we don't deliver her foal in a few minutes, she's going to die and so is the foal. I don't want to be disrespectful, but you need to move it."

That seemed to be the push he needed. He nodded. "Disinfectant. Alcohol work?"

"Yes. That'll be fine."

He turned and headed toward the door.

"Do you have a sink somewhere in the barn?" she called after him.

"Room in the back," he shouted over his shoulder, already breathless from his quick walk across the barn.

She found the bathroom. The sink looked like it hadn't been scrubbed in months. She gave a frustrated sigh and pumped some soap from the dirty container. After she scrubbed up, she left the faucet running rather than touch the dirty tap and negate the cleaning she'd just given her hands and arms.

The General was already kneeling beside the agonized mare when she got back. "Took ya long enough," he said.

"If you cleaned your filthy sink, I'd have been quicker," she snapped back. "Where's the alcohol?"

The General nodded toward a bottle on the ground next to Tabby.

The air left Nina's lungs in a whoosh. "Brandy?"

"I keep it around for medicinal purposes. It's alcohol. You said that'd work."

She was all too aware it was alcohol. Nina's gut tightened. She smelled the alcohol and felt the phantom burn in her throat. Her head rushed with desire.

Oh, God, grant me the . . . the what? What came next?

Weakness slipped into her knees, into her stomach, into her throat. "I—I thought you meant rubbing alcohol." She could barely get the words out. "General . . ."

"What are you waiting for? She's dying!" The old man looked angry, and Nina glimpsed Hunt's anger in the General's face. Would she disappoint another person?

She had no choice. "Okay. Get the bottle. You'll have to pour."

He turned.

She grabbed his hand, oblivious to the germs. "Listen, do not leave one drop in the bottle. Do you hear me?"

He frowned and tried to back away.

She tightened her grip around his bicep, thin with age, and gave him a shake. "I mean it. Promise right now that you'll use every drop and then immediately get that bottle out of here."

He gave an emphatic shake of his head. "I ain't goin' nowhere. I ain't leavin' her."

"Then I'm not lifting a finger to help this animal." Her recovery meant more than the life of a horse and foal. God forgive her, but she hadn't worked as hard as she had to avoid all temptation to risk failure now. "I swear, I'll walk out of here right now and let them both die."

Outrage sparked in the General's eyes, narrowing his gray eyebrows. Then understanding softened his angry frown. "I promise."

With a nod, she released him. "All right."

Weak with effort, she took a deep breath.

Serenity. That was it.

She closed her eyes and held her arms straight out in front of her. "Pour from my shoulders to my fingertips, all around. There shouldn't be anywhere on my hands and arms that isn't covered in the b-brandy."

God, grant me the serenity . . .

He unscrewed the lid, and the seductive aroma sought her out, speaking in soft tones and whispering its promises. All she had to do was surrender to her desire, and pleasures awaited. It drew her near, weakening her resistance.

She exhaled as the General tipped the bottle, and the liquid slid like silk over her skin. One thing was certain. She needed to call her sponsor.

Tabby moaned. Time was slipping away for the horse. Nina had to get it together. Or was she going to harm another animal?

God. A simple cry from her heart to heaven. One word, but it was all she could find.

As the General screwed the lid on the empty bottle and walked away, something happened. The brandy seeped into every scratch Harvey's nails had inflicted on her arms while she guarded the deer. It set her skin on fire.

Okay. This would do it. She burned, the pain taking the edge off her need to toss all of this aside and drive to the nearest liquor store.

The General came back in seconds.

She gave him a tight smile. "Let's help Tabby." She knelt in the bloody hay. "Rub her, General. Speak softly. If I can get the foal loose, I'm going to need her calm enough to push at the right time."

The horse was too weak to put up much of a fight as Nina reached both hands inside her fully-dilated body and felt the foal, wedged firmly inside the birth canal. It was impossible. Nina's heart pounded.

Another contraction hit, and Nina's fingers moved gently between the walls of the birth canal and the foal. The foal moved. Nina's stomach tightened, and she had only a second to move her arms backward as Tabby pushed out the foal.

Tears streamed down Nina's cheeks. She settled back as Tabby sat up and forced herself to stand on trembling legs. She seemed to weep as she found her baby.

Nina stood on her own trembling legs. She knew she was covered in blood, but she couldn't care less. She had done it.

She turned at the sound of the General's loud sniff. He glowed, tears pouring down his lined cheeks. "You did good."

Nina nodded. "I'm not sure how much of it was me."

A chuckle rumbled his chest. "I'm sure the Almighty had plenty to do with it too, but He uses human hands. Yours."

An uncomfortable feeling hit Nina's stomach. Like butterflies, only more achy, almost painful. All she wanted in that moment was a drink. She felt so close to making some excuse for needing another bottle of alcohol for sanitary purposes.

"Thank you for taking care of my girl," the General said.

At first Nina thought he was speaking to her, but she realized his eyes were closed. His face glowed with such joy, Nina had an uncanny sense that something otherworldly must be happening in his head.

She cleared her throat. "I'm going to go clean up. Stay with Tabby, and make sure she delivers all the afterbirth."

"That much I can do."

Practically running, she reached the bathroom and slammed the door shut. She leaned back against it and closed her eyes, waiting for her brain to catch up with the day's events.

Meg finding out about Stephan. Scary dead deer. Massive test of will. Saving two animals. Too much, too much, too much. And she was alone. All alone. The back of her head hurt, and she realized she was beating it against the door.

How would she ever make it back to town without stopping at a liquor store? If she gave in, just this once, wouldn't she be justified? The last few days had been pain upon pain. Even in the moments with glimpses of joy, she felt herself drowning in loss. Lost childhood with her parents. Losing each moment with her so-angry daughter. Lost son. And lost Hunt, her love whom she'd hurt so badly. Couldn't she give in just once? Then she'd jump right back on the recovery wagon.

Nina staggered forward. Oh, God, what was she doing?

Then she was on the floor. She hadn't even felt herself sliding down until she lay on her side on the filthy floor, bloody and broken and sobbing, sure that as soon as she walked out the door, she was going to fail.

And she was powerless to do anything about it.

CHAPTER FOURTEEN

My sixteenth birthday was anything but sweet.

My mother baked a double-layered, heart-shaped, pink cake. I could have suffered the ridiculous cake and heart-shaped balloons if the only witnesses had been my parents and Jill, but I walked into the house, sweat pouring off me after a five-mile run at the reserve, and suddenly the house was filled with the sound of "Surprise!"

Surprise? Who even wanted to come to a party for me? Stephan hadn't been my friend for a while, yet there he was, looking retarded in a cone-shaped party hat. The football team was there, as were all my party buddies.

What had mom been thinking, inviting those guys? A bright, giddy smile spread across her face. She obviously didn't realize she had just made me the butt of a joke.

The plates were pink; the cups were pink; the stupid paper tablecloth was pink. The forks were white plastic, the *only contrast in the entire Pepto-Bismol theme. I could tell by my "friends'" faces that I was going to catch all kinds of crap at our next tailgate party.*

After the initial excitement died down, I slipped away, unnoticed. After all, no one was really there for me. I stepped outside and sat on the picnic table, wishing everyone would just leave.

Dane Williamson came outside a minute later and sat next to me. My fickle heart responded as it had six years earlier when we held hands in the balloon. I sighed as he reached out and drew me close. "Happy Birthday, Puke," he whispered just before he pressed soft, warm lips to mine. They lingered, a perfect kiss, tasting of Hi-C and wintergreen gum. I slipped my arms around his neck and allowed myself to forget who I was. Who he was.

Until the yard filled with football players, all vying for their turn to kiss the birthday girl. I told them where to go, stomped to my bedroom, and left my mom to get rid of them.

Bailey. Stephan Bailey.

Meg felt a little guilty about prodding the name out of Grammy by asking about Nina's old friends. Apparently Nina had been best buds with Stephan throughout their childhood. Grammy had no idea why they stopped hanging out during high school, but she provided Meg with enough information to carry out her plan.

Meg slipped into the kitchen while her grandparents were dressing for the funeral. She didn't have much time. Dad was taking her home Saturday. This might be her only chance. Rummaging around the kitchen drawers, she located a phone book and slipped outside.

She already loved the picnic table in the middle of the yard. Poppy had told her Nina used to love it too. Normally that sort of information would have immediately reversed Meg's opinion on principle, but she liked the spot and tried to imagine the things that had gone through Nina's mind when she ventured out here, just like Meg was doing, then lay on the tabletop and stared at the sky.

It wasn't hard to imagine Nina as a teenager. Grammy had photos all over the place, from Nina's infancy up to her graduation, but nothing beyond. She did have photographs of Meg and Adam. Nina sent school pictures, Grammy told her. She said it with such sadness that Meg had reached out and given her a spontaneous hug, which surprised Meg. She wasn't a spontaneous hugger of anyone, but something about her grandparents swept her with love, and she hated the idea of leaving them again. She intended to speak to her dad about regular visits for her and Adam.

She sat on the picnic table and opened the phone book—which was the size of a magazine for a town so small—to the Bs and skimmed until she found the number she was looking for.

She took a deep breath and punched in the number.

A man's voice answered on the second ring.

"H-hey," she said. "This is Meg . . . Nina's daughter. Is this Stephan?"

He hesitated, and she heard him draw in a breath. "Did Nina tell you my name?"

"I overheard it. Have you talked to her today?"

"No. I was going to try to speak to her at the funeral." He paused. "Does she know you're calling me?"

"No."

"Then maybe you shouldn't have called."

Disappointment nearly overwhelmed her. He didn't think she should have called him? Was he kidding? "Maybe you shouldn't have butted into my life if you didn't want me to call."

Relief shot over her when he chuckled, a deep, rich sound. "That's fair, I guess."

"Anyway, Nina said it was my decision whether to see you or not."

"That's a surprise considering the conversations I've had with Nina this week. She didn't seem so open to it."

"Are you calling me a liar?"

"No." He paused again. "Are you calling because you want to meet me?"

Suddenly Meg wasn't so sure. Her curiosity had definitely reached a new level, but how would her dad feel if she decided to meet this guy? "I'm not sure. I have a dad. You know that, right? I don't need a dad."

"Look, I'm going to the funeral for Amanda Rollings today."

"Yeah. Creepy."

"Well, it starts soon, and I'm a pallbearer, so I have to be there early. I don't want you to feel like I'm not interested in this conversation or in meeting you, but I have to go."

"Okay." Her voice sounded like it came from far away. "I-I'm leaving Abbey Hills Saturday."

"I know. I hope I get to meet you in person before you leave."

"Yeah, we'll see."

She hung up with that after-Christmas-letdown feeling. She'd expected a lot more than she'd gotten from that phone call.

That was an understatement. She'd gotten nothing.

~

The first time Nina went missing, I was so frantic I thought I'd lose my mind. The police wouldn't do anything for twenty-four hours. Dallas is a big city. She could have been anywhere.

I dropped Meggie off at my mom's and searched every inch of the city I thought she might have gone to. I stayed close to home at first, searching the restaurants that sold liquor. After three hours, I changed tactics and started looking in bars. Don't ask me why I didn't start there. I suppose I was in denial, thinking she wouldn't actually walk into a bar. Not alone, like a desperate woman, wearing too much makeup and not enough clothing. That wasn't my Nina.

As I entered each bar, I held my breath, praying I would find her. Praying I wouldn't. At that point, I almost would rather she'd been in a non–alcohol related accident than find her in a seedy, smoke-filled place like the bars where I ended my search.

I left Meg with my mother overnight and made it home by three in the morning, praying Nina would be there. My prayer was answered. Her car was parked so crookedly, I couldn't get mine in the driveway. I knew she'd driven home drunk.

I parked next to the curb in front of the house and headed for the porch. Call it intuition—a voice, a premonition, whatever—but I knew somehow she'd never made it inside. I strode across the grass, and when I reached her car, my heart nearly stopped. Her face was pressed against the driver-side window, her lip split and covered with dried blood. It was growing purple.

I opened the door, my legs weak and shaky. Someone had hurt this woman to whom I'd pledged my life, and I couldn't bear knowing she'd been harmed. I slid one arm behind her back, one under her legs, and lifted her from the seat as though she were a baby.

She moaned. "It hurts."

"What happened, baby?" I asked.

"Dancing," she mumbled.

Pain gripped me. Then anger.

"You were dancing, and you fell?" I asked.

She nodded.

Disgust filled me at the picture that shot through my mind. I took her to our bed and laid her down as gently as possible. I wanted to drop her, to make her hurt as badly as I was hurting. How many men had she danced with? In my mind's eye I saw them running their hands all over her, pressing against her. My wife. Her body was mine. Had she ever been unfaithful? She said not, but could I believe her?

My stomach rolled. I started to turn away, but she shivered, and I couldn't leave her.

I slipped her shoes off and maneuvered her practically lifeless body until I could pull the covers free and slide her underneath. She snuggled down.

"Thank you," she murmured.

"Go to sleep."

I was almost to the door when she spoke. "Hunt?"

I turned. She'd rallied and sat up somehow. "What, Nina?"

"I'm so sorry for this. All of this. I'd do things differently if I could."

She'd apologized more times than I could remember, so this one affected me about as much as the last hundred or so. "Everything will be okay. Just sleep."

"Will you lie down with me?"

I tensed. Usually she tried to seduce me when she was in this state, and I couldn't be further from aroused at the moment.

She lay back down. "I'm just so cold."

From the doorway, I could see she still shivered. My compassion stirred for her. I hated that I still loved her, but God help me, I did.

As I crawled in next to her, she turned. "I really am sorry. I love you. So much."

There was no seduction in her words. No crazy, hot gleam in her eye that excited me but ultimately left me emotionally cold.

"Do you want me to get you help, Nina?" I hadn't broached the topic in quite some time. She always grew so angry.

But this time her eyes filled with humble tears, and my heart melted as she nodded.

I gathered her close and let her cry. "I'll make some calls for you tomorrow."

And in those tender moments, something real happened between us that hadn't happened in a long time. We made love.

The next day she entered a rehab center, and when she came home thirty days later—dried out, her loving, fun, teasing self—she announced she was pregnant. My mind went back to that night. I knew, and so did she, that our baby had been conceived in the sweetest of moments. He was our new beginning, so it seemed fitting that we name him Adam.

If only he'd been enough happiness to rid her of the demons that came calling again.

Shaken and grimy from the bathroom floor, Nina sat up when the General knocked loudly on the door.

"You okay in there?" he hollered. "It's been an hour."

"I'm fine, General." She stood on trembling legs and opened the door.

The General looked her over, frowning. "It's about time we all get ready to go to the funeral."

Nina wanted to groan. The last thing she wanted to do right now was attend the funeral of a woman she hadn't seen since graduation night and who had never really been a friend, anyway. But Jill's point was valid. If she was going to rejoin the community, she needed to put forth an effort to show folks she cared.

"You look like something the cat dragged in," the General said.

The expression made her laugh. "I feel like it too."

"It occurred to me after all this that I should've known you meant rubbing alcohol." The General's expression seemed less gruff, somehow. "I'd like to apologize for putting temptation in your way."

Heat exploded in her cheeks. "What do you mean?"

"Are you going to deny it? After all these years?" He released a breath and walked across the barn to the new foal.

Nina watched him. "I'm not denying anything." Her defenses were in high gear. "I just don't know what you mean."

"Your drinking problem. You weren't just a weekender like those other teenagers. You took after your dad. And that's a fact."

Nina followed him to the stall. The foal had found her source of nourishment and nursed hungrily. "I guess you're right. I didn't know it back then though. I just thought I liked the way it made me feel. Drinking defined me as the rebel in our school." Nina smiled at the foal as it stumbled a little and righted itself. "I quit for several years while my daughter was little."

"That's good." His voice was soft, so unlike his typical rough exterior that Nina tilted her head to look at him. "Shows you had moxie."

She gave a short laugh. "Until I started again."

"It's always best to leave the past in the past."

"If only it were that easy." She didn't know how she'd resisted that brandy. If there were a bottle in front of her now, she highly doubted there'd be any way she could resist. "I wish I could forget I ever picked up a bottle of anything."

"Here's the thing, Nina." That was the first time Nina could ever remember the General calling her by her first name. "We all have sins or temptations that are harder to resist than others. Drinking wasn't my vice, but I smoked two packs of Lucky Strikes a day for forty years. Only quit when the doctor said emphysema would kill me if I didn't stop." He squinted. "It was the hardest thing I ever did, giving those things up. Tried the patch, the pills, the gum, and nothing worked. Until one day I just decided enough was enough. When I came to the end of my rope, God showed up. And when He showed up, I knew I wouldn't smoke again. No telling if I'd even be here now if God hadn't helped me do that."

Nina kept her gaze on the new foal as the General spoke. She wanted to tell him not to preach at her. That she had tried God and He wasn't interested in helping her with anything. Wasn't her whole life proof of that?

Nina's phone rang. Relief flooded her. She glanced at the screen and back to the General. "It's Jill. I need to take it."

He nodded.

She moved a few steps away and answered. "Hey, Jill."

"Nina! Where are you?"

"I'm about to leave the General's."

"Do you know what time it is?"

"Well, excuse me for saving a couple of animals."

A huff blew through the receiver. "All right. Sorry. But will you please hurry? We have to pick up Mom and Dad too."

"Why?"

"Mom won't ride to a funeral in his truck, and the car isn't running well. Besides, Meg decided she wants to go too."

"She did?" Nina couldn't keep the surprise from her tone. "Why does she want to go to the funeral of someone she didn't even know?"

"I don't know. Ask her when you get there. Just hurry."

She hung up and turned to the General. "Thanks for the pep talk, General. I'll be over sometime tomorrow to check on Tabby and the baby."

"I'm obliged to you." He patted her on the

shoulder like a grandfather. "I'm blessed to have you back in town."

"I'm sorry about what happened to your other horse."

He shook his head, his face clouding. "That's a mystery only God's going to unravel."

"Well, hopefully the crime lab and state patrol will give Him some help and solve it soon, before anything or anyone else dies."

"It's what I've been praying for. It's all we can do."

"Then I hope God shows up again for you."

His face broke into a smile. "You were listening."

Nina smiled back. "I was." She shoved her cell phone into her pocket. "Okay, I have to run. Jill is about to hyperventilate."

The General stood at the door of the barn while she jogged to the car, flanked on one side by Harvey who, thankfully, didn't seem in the mood to knock her over. She started the motor, waved at the General, and pulled out onto the highway.

It wasn't until she had pulled into Jill's driveway and shut off the ignition that she realized she'd passed every liquor store and convenience store in Abbey Hills on her way home and hadn't once thought about stopping.

A wave of stomach-fluttering relief washed over her. On the floor in that filthy bathroom, she'd been terrified to walk out of the barn.

She wasn't quite sure how she'd managed to get from there to here without stopping, but there was no way to articulate the relief flowing through her in that moment of realization.

Maybe God had somehow shown up.

CHAPTER FIFTEEN

I barely remember the months after I turned sixteen. I drank my way through most of it.

My dad waited up for me once. Staggering in, I planned to do what I always did—tiptoe as lightly as possible up the stairs to my room, fall onto my bed, and pass out. I walked in and stopped short when I saw him sitting in his recliner, stone-cold sober, looking at me as though I'd done something wrong.

I laughed. "You're kidding, right?"

His shoulders slumped, and he switched off the lamp and stood up. He walked into the kitchen, grabbed a beer, and headed upstairs.

Meagan could only stare at the back of the six pallbearers' heads and wonder which one was Stephan's.

They had gotten to the funeral home late, of course, so the only seats were way in the back, not even together. Grammy and Poppy had seats together. Meg ended up sitting next to a weeping old man who kept blowing his nose into a cloth handkerchief. He was grossing her out. Nina had found a seat next to Aunt Jill's neighbor. What was his name anyway? Markus, or something like that. Like she cared, but at least he wasn't blowing his nose and coughing all over Nina. Aunt Jill sat with a couple of cops.

Finally the minister stopped talking, and everyone who wanted to speak or sing had done so. Meg's stomach tightened as she walked up the aisle to pay respects to the body. She couldn't even look at the casket. Instead she scanned the row of pallbearers. Each one caught her eye as she passed. She walked out the side door.

Somehow she'd thought that with one look at her biological father, she would feel an instant connection. But as far as she could tell, Stephan could have been any one of those men.

Nina touched her shoulder. "Are you okay?"

Meg shrugged her hand away. "Yeah. I'm going to walk back to Aunt Jill's."

"The burial is next, and then everyone is going to Barney's."

"I'm not. I didn't even know her."

Nina scanned her face. Meg met the look without flinching, never wavering. Finally Nina nodded. "I'll see you back at Aunt Jill's this evening."

As she walked away, Meg pulled out her cell phone and pressed number one on speed dial.

Two rings later, he picked up. "Hello?"

"Hi, Daddy. It's Meg."

And she burst into tears.

Nina held a plate of untouched food and stood in a corner alone. Markus had made his apologies and left early. The General was seated with a group of men and women in his own peer group, and Jill was busy making the rounds, assuring folks there was no need to panic. Despite the fact that several animals and a woman had been killed in ritualistic, cult-style killings. Jill was good, but Nina doubted if anyone truly found much comfort in her attempt.

By the time Stephan approached her, Nina had stuffed her untouched plate into the garbage and was heading for the door.

"We should talk about Meg," he said.

"I'm just about to leave, Stephan."

"Can I give you a lift?"

She shook her head. "I have Jill's car. She's leaving with Barney later."

His expression soured. "I'll walk you out. We still need to talk about Meagan."

"Not really. She knows about you."

"I know. She called me."

Nina drew in a sharp breath at the news. "When?"

"Earlier. About an hour before the funeral."

He opened the door, and Nina slid through

ahead of him, not liking the forced closeness of the action.

Nina's frustration clogged her throat. She and Meg had driven to the funeral together, sat in silence the whole way. Meg hadn't said a word.

Nina's legs had gone rubbery. She swallowed down the lump in her throat and stood unmoving outside the door. "Well, I did tell her the choice to meet you or not was hers."

He frowned. "Isn't that a little heavy to put on a kid?"

Nina gave a shrug and raised an eyebrow, keeping her steady gaze fixed on him. "I was only a year older than she is when I got pregnant with her. That was pretty heavy too."

Stephan shoved his hands inside his pants pockets and averted his gaze. "I wish you hadn't gone through it alone." His voice held real regret. "I would have been there for you." A bitter laugh emanated from his chest. "Shoot, I'd have married you back then."

Nina shook her head and headed toward Jill's car. "We both know that never would have happened." She tossed the words over her shoulder and caught his expression as it darkened.

Stephan cast a furtive glance at a teary-eyed couple headed to their car. He lowered his voice. "Why did you leave the next day? You couldn't have known you were pregnant. I came to the hospital looking for you, and they said you'd snuck out."

His accusation grated on her. For seventeen years she had borne the brunt of that night while he went about his life. "You came to the hospital? Did you bring flowers?" She'd meant to be flippant, but he nodded.

She pressed the unlock button, and the car beeped.

Stephan reached around her and opened the door. "I brought roses. They seemed fitting after . . ." His face reddened. "I wanted to apologize. Do you remember everything that happened?"

"I remember someone handing me a glass of beer."

"Dane."

Nina slid beneath the wheel and tilted her head to look up at him. "Good memory. Almost as if you're hanging on to a guilty conscience."

"I am, but not for the reason you think." Stephan's hand clutched the top of the door. Clearly he had no intention of ending the conversation just yet.

Nina released a sigh. "I'm really trying to get my head around the idea that maybe you were as much a victim that night as I was."

His eyes widened. "Really?"

"Can you remember the rest of the night for me? Because I remember the beer, and I remember the woods, but nothing in between."

"You don't remember us . . . ?"

Her cheeks felt feverish, and she averted her gaze. "Only the way I felt afterward."

"Dane and the other guys from the team drugged your drink."

"I figured out the drug part, just not who did it." She gripped the steering wheel. "All I could think of was that you had drugged me and raped me. It was the only thing that made sense."

"Well, they wanted you to sleep with them. Dane said he was tired of you being a tease. Coming to all the parties, drinking the beer, and never putting out."

Anger flashed through her. She wanted to pound Stephan with her fists. "So I go back to my original conclusion. You took advantage of the situation." She shoved the keys into the ignition and cranked the motor.

"Wait a sec. That's not right. I had no idea what they'd done until later." He squatted down next to the car, making it impossible for her to close the door. He searched her face, his eyes pleading. "I honestly thought God had smiled on me when you started laughing and talking to me about old times. How we'd lie on your picnic table and stare at the stars and tell each other all about our dreams for the future."

Nina closed her eyes, remembering the only real friendship from her childhood. She took a long, slow breath, blew it out just as slowly, and turned to him. Trying to find answers was more exhausting than maintaining the belief she had held on to for the past seventeen years. "Didn't I slur my words or do anything to make you suspicious that maybe I wasn't in the best frame of mind for you to be putting the moves on me?" she asked.

"No. And that's what was so crazy. Someone blasted the music really loud, and we decided to go into the woods so we could actually hear each other talk. You didn't stagger like you were drunk. At least not until later. You had another drink in your hand, the second Dane had given you. We were walking. I took your hand, and suddenly we were kissing and one thing led to another. I had loved you my whole life, and I'd waited for you. It was my first time too, Nina."

Embarrassment flooded her at his raw admission. And even though there were still unanswered questions, in a way, she understood his feelings. If Hunt smiled on her right now, she'd be in his arms, thanking God for all she was worth. "When did you find out about the drug?"

"When I got back to the party, after our fight, the guys were asking about you and talking about a waste of drugs, and I realized what had happened. I went back to find you. I went back to the river, got into my car, and left before the raid. I found out later that the police had found you passed out and called the ambulance. I'm just so sorry, Nina. I'm sorry for everything."

"I'm sorry for the way things happened too." Nina leaned her head back, tears stinging her eyes. "But I wouldn't trade Meg for anything."

Markus waited for Nina to pull into the driveway and walk to the house. Her shoes were in her hand, swinging by the straps from her fingers. Her legs were not brown like Kimana's, but her feet were equally delicate. His lips curled into a smile. His princess. He ventured to the porch. Her eyes caught the movement as he had intended, and she stopped and waved.

He met her halfway between the two houses on the brick street.

"Hi." She smiled.

"Feet still blistered?" he asked. Band-Aids on her toes and heels covered the tender flesh.

She nodded. "My run this morning didn't help."

"I won't keep you on your feet." He glanced at the darkening sky. "Besides, it looks like our break from the rain is over."

"One whole day." She laughed. "I guess that's to be expected in the spring. The price of warm air sliding in and pushing back winter."

"That was quite poetic."

She shrugged, her blush sweet. "I guess it was corny."

"Not at all."

"You're being nice." Drops of rain began to fall. "I better go." She covered her head with the program from the funeral as the drops grew larger. "I'll talk to you soon."

Markus watched her walk away until she disappeared inside the house. She limped a little.

His heart sped up. Could he stand by and let Eden follow through on her promise to harm Meg or Nina—or both? He had two choices. Watch over Nina at all times or give in to Eden.

The thought of returning to Eden's coven sickened him, and his mind was suddenly overrun with rituals and blood. The kind of cruelty Eden inflicted was nothing short of evil. Markus had never enjoyed torturing his victims. They needed to die so he could live, but intentional cruelty left him cold. Eden enjoyed it. The thought of her torturing Nina filled him with rage. He couldn't let Eden take his second chance away.

He slipped inside and grabbed a clean towel, some Epsom salt, and a large pot. He knocked on Nina's door a minute later.

Her eyes clouded in confusion as she opened the door. "Markus? What's in the pot?"

"Nothing yet. Invite me in, and I'll tell you what I have in mind."

She opened the screen door for him. "Okay, don't keep me in suspense."

"I'm going to get a foot soak ready for you. It might help the blisters."

"You're going to . . ." Tilting her head, she searched his face. Markus wondered what she found. Desire? Hunger? Or had he veiled those emotions enough so that all she saw was the concern of a new friend? He knew he could play the game, but well enough? Her expression softened. "That's nice, Markus. Thanks. I could use the soak. My feet are killing me."

"Good. It'll just take a few minutes to get the water ready."

"In the meantime, I'll run up and change."

He freed his imagination. The hum of desire that rushed constantly around Nina grew to a roar in his head.

"Help yourself to a cup of coffee," she said, limping toward the stairs. "The pot is a little old, so the coffee always tastes burnt, but it's better than nothing."

He followed her through the foyer. "I'll pass. Not much of a coffee drinker."

Nina took one step and waved absently toward the kitchen. "Jill has more types of tea than I knew existed. Feel free to rummage around and find one you like."

"I'll do that. Is Meg here?"

She took another step up, shaking her head. "I haven't seen her. She might be with my folks. I thought she'd be here when I got back." Her tone betrayed concern. "She was pretty upset when she left the funeral home today."

"Upset?"

"Long story." She took a breath and smiled. "I'll be right back."

Markus carried the pot and Epsom salt into the kitchen. He filled the pot, set it on the stove to warm the water, and waited for Nina to return.

He had no idea how long she would allow him to remain, but he hoped long enough for the sheriff to get home. He wasn't sure the sheriff's presence would deter Eden, but for tonight it was his only option.

~

The beautiful thing about loving Nina was that she loved completely. Whoever she loved got the best parts of her. Me, Meggie, Adam. She laughed, teased, played, fed me with her passion. I stayed devoted to her during the difficult times because I hoped the good times would return. With the birth of Adam, I truly hoped she would remain the Nina we adored.

But the first time she brought home a bottle of wine for "us" to have at dinner, I knew it was the beginning of the end.

Nina is sober again. As much as I want to stay away, something in me responds to the memory of her teasing smile, her gentle passion, her fingers as she caresses Adam's curls. The way she lights up when Meggie laughs.

My Nina.

CHAPTER SIXTEEN

My mom came to visit me in Dallas a year after Meggie was born. She'd hired a private investigator, she said. Where had the money come from? I asked. She'd been saving money for three years, ever since she got the job at Price Cutter wrapping meat. Dad didn't know she had come, and she wasn't about to tell him.

I told her I was sorry she wasted her money. I wasn't coming back. And she had never paid attention to me when I was living at home, so why was she even here?

She wanted to make sure I was okay.

I was fine. More than fine.

Then Meg woke from her nap and cried. The shock on my mom's face was palpable.

"Yeah. I have a baby."

"May I?" she asked, and I knew she was afraid I'd say no.

She held Meg close and asked me to come home, to let her help me take care of Meg.

I couldn't help but laugh.

Depression hit me for weeks after my mother's visit. Why couldn't she have fought for me? Just once? I would never watch my daughter slip away without fighting for her.

Never.

Nina's eyelids swept shut. She sighed and forced them open to find Markus sitting at the other end of the couch, staring at her.

"I'm sorry. I must have dozed off." She wanted to ask him to leave but hoped he'd simply take a hint. The foot bath was a kind gesture, but she was ready to be alone, finally okay with being alone. "What time is it?"

Markus glanced at his watch. "Eight-thirty."

"Is that all?" It felt like midnight. "Meg isn't home yet?"

He shook his head. "Should you call her?"

Something in Nina warmed to him at his concern for her daughter.

She swung her legs over the side of the couch and stood, mentally trying to locate where she'd left her cell phone. She walked to the kitchen counter and found it buzzing. The caller ID said "Hunt." Her stomach tightened, and her heart rate rose.

She answered. "Hunt?"

"For crying out loud, Nina, I've been trying to reach you for hours."

"Sorry," she mumbled. "There was a funeral today."

"I know. Meg called me on her way home, crying her eyes out." He paused. "How could you let her walk home by herself after what she's been through?"

"What are you talking about?" *Tread carefully, Nina.* Maybe he didn't know about . . .

"Some Stephan? She says he's her biological father." The anger in Hunt's voice spoke a lot louder than his words.

"I wanted to talk to you about him in person. I'm so sorry, Hunt."

"I'll be there in three hours." His voice sounded dead, cold. "I have a hotel room reserved in Branson. I'll be at Jill's by nine in the morning. Then you can tell me all about this other father of Meg's. How does that sound?"

Did he really need to ask? The fact that he was coming a day early set the tone for the conversation they would have. Not that she blamed him.

After a curt good-bye, Hunt disconnected the call, leaving Nina standing alone in the kitchen, feeling foolish, afraid, and heartbroken.

"Everything okay?"

Nina swept around to find Markus standing directly behind her, almost too close for comfort. She slid along the counter, out of reach. "Yeah. Meg's dad is coming a day early."

"That bothers you, I take it?"

Nina bit her bottom lip in an effort to ward off the trembling. She nodded. "For more reasons than one."

"Want to talk about it?"

She just wanted to forget about Hunt's anger for the next few hours. She needed to call Meg, find out where she was. She dialed her daughter's number, but it went straight to voice mail.

Markus cleared his throat. "Perhaps I should go."

Nina met his eyes. Tenderness and something else behind his expression made her stop. Maybe she felt sorry for him. Maybe she knew a little too well how it felt for someone not to want your presence. For whatever reason, she shook her head. "I thought I'd make some grilled cheese. Would you like to stay for a light dinner?"

His eyes lit with surprise and relief. "That sounds great. What can I do to help?"

"Tell me more about Pierre Lafitte?" She smiled. "We never finished the story of his dad. Did he return?"

"I'd be honored to pick up where we left off."

A smile lit Markus's face, and Nina once again felt that rush to her head. What was it about this guy? He made her feel almost . . . well . . . she hated to think it, but he made her feel almost drunk sometimes.

To her relief, her phone rang. "Hang on a sec."

Meg's voice sounded breathy on the other end

of the line. "Hey, Mom. I just got a call from Daddy. He said he's going to be here tonight."

"Yeah, he called me too. Where are you?"

"Carrie saw me walking after the funeral and picked me up. We hung out at her house for a while, but she's going to a poetry reading at a friend's house. I thought I'd go with her. Is that okay?"

She was asking? Nina was caught off guard by Meg's warm tone, a please-can-I-go tone. "Um . . ."

"Carrie's dad said we have to clear it with you. So I'm clearing it."

Ah, that explained it. Meg knew Nina would get the picture in brilliant Technicolor.

"What about your dad?" Nina asked. "Shouldn't you pack?"

"He's not making me leave early. I think he's coming to see you, mainly." Meg didn't sound apologetic.

"I wonder why."

"I told him about Stephan."

"Yeah, he told me."

"So, the poetry reading?" Meg pressed.

Nina sighed. "I guess. Be back by eleven."

"Sure. Thanks."

"Meg, I gather," Markus said when Nina closed her phone, disconnecting the call.

"Yeah. She's hanging out with a friend."

"Are you okay with her spending most of her

time elsewhere? You'll miss her when she's gone."

Nina shrugged and headed to the fridge for the ingredients for grilled cheese sandwiches. "I guess I have to be. Sometimes I'm really tempted to force her to . . . like me, but I'm trying to take it slowly. One day at a time."

His deep-set brown eyes shone, and Nina looked away. She didn't deserve anyone's admiration, particularly where her daughter was concerned. And she definitely didn't want to get into a conversation that might end with Markus making all kinds of statements about her sobriety and how she had beat herself up enough.

She swallowed and forced a grin. "So, what about that vampire?"

Markus smiled. "Okay, next subject, I guess."

Returning his smile, Nina pulled the bread from the breadbox and went to work fixing their sandwiches.

"Pierre never saw his father again," Markus began.

"The end?"

"No." His eyes glittered. "Things would have been much better for Pierre if that were the end of the story, but unfortunately it wasn't."

"Now I'm curious."

"He was raised by the Osage tribe that rescued him, adopted by a great war chief. But he always knew he was different."

"Because he was white?"

"And because of what his father had done. Even though he never saw his father again, fear and rumor spread among the Indians in other tribes about a man possessed by evil who drank blood. The old ones said they knew the blood drinker to be cursed—a curse passed down from father to son. Many among my tribe scoffed at the rumors, but I knew them to be true."

"You?" Nina laughed. "When you tell a story, you really get into it, don't you?"

Markus lost some of the color in his cheeks. "Forgive me. Of course, I meant Pierre."

The skillet sizzled as the buttered bread touched the hot surface. "So what happened?"

"Pierre loved a young Osage maiden named Kimana."

"See?" Nina smiled. "I told you every vampire story has to have romance."

He nodded. "This one does. Stop me anytime, by the way. I don't want to force the story on you."

"You're not. I asked, remember? Besides, you've piqued my interest. Tell me about Pierre and his Indian girl." She flipped the sandwiches to reveal a perfect golden brown.

He laughed. "Pierre did everything to get her attention. He excelled in hunting and joined a few war parties, although by and large peace reigned in the area among the different tribes.

But when he fought, he received honor for his bravery." Markus's voice grew thicker, deeper.

"Sounds like quite the catch."

"After secretly loving her while they were children and pursuing her for two years, finally, when she turned sixteen summers, she smiled upon him."

Nina slid the sandwiches onto plates and pulled out a jar of dill pickle spears and a bag of plain potato chips, letting him pause while they prepared to eat. The two sat at the kitchen table, Markus at the end, Nina on his right.

He took a bite and smiled as he swallowed. "Delicious."

"Thank you." Nina poured them each a glass of iced tea. "Did he get her attention?"

"He did." His face darkened. "Unfortunately, her father had his own ideas for a suitable husband, and Pierre didn't fit into his schemes for his daughter."

"Because he was white?"

Markus shrugged. "Possibly. But Kimana's father was a powerful medicine man named Beshup. He sensed the evil inside Pierre."

"Evil? What evil?"

"His father's evil. His grandfather's. The generations before him who angered God and drank the blood of men."

"Was he bitten before his father ran off?"

"No, but remember I told you vampirism is

passed through the bloodline from parent to child. It isn't as the stories portray. If a human is bitten by a vampire, he will die, not return as an undead like those silly movies suggest."

Nina couldn't stifle a laugh. "Markus, I'm sorry, but you're telling this lore as though it's fact. Like you actually believe it."

His expression darkened, eyes narrowed. "Stranger things exist in this world. Much more than people like to believe."

Nina felt the urge to apologize. It was clear she'd offended him. "I'm sorry to laugh, Markus. I know weird things can happen. I believe in supernatural things, like ghosts and psychics and stuff like that. But vampires? Come on."

He tilted his head a little. The anger was gone from his eyes, but he remained solemn. "It's dangerous to close your eyes to something just because you've never experienced it."

Nina rolled her eyes. "There are a lot of things I've never experienced that I'd just as soon not. Skydiving, for instance." She laughed. "And vampires."

Markus shifted in his seat and sipped his tea.

"Sorry," Nina said, slightly chastened. "I'll stop interrupting."

Markus gave her an amused look before continuing. "Beshup refused to allow Kimana to marry Pierre. Pierre was distraught, angry. He felt the rejection turning to rage deep inside. The rage became something he'd never felt before —blood lust. He wanted Beshup dead. But not just dead—he wanted his blood."

A shudder ran up Nina's spine. "You're a vivid storyteller, Markus."

"Shall I stop?"

"No. It's taking my mind off my own issues." She'd have to deal with all of that soon enough. "So, Pierre wanted blood."

Markus took a bite of his sandwich and swallowed. "Literally. He waited until Beshup left the village alone to find healing herbs. When he was far enough away to escape detection, Pierre confronted him. Pierre's knife was hidden, but Beshup was powerful in the supernatural, and he knew Pierre wasn't there to talk.

" 'I have always known there was much evil in you,' Beshup said. 'Even if you kill me, you will not have Kimana.'

"His words only angered Pierre. 'Kimana loves me,' he argued back. 'She will marry me when there is no one to stand in our way.'

" 'She will not,' Beshup replied. 'I have told her the things I see. She is a true daughter. Her own healing powers are great. The evil in you is drawn to her power.'

" 'No. I truly love her,' Pierre said, though he could barely speak, so great was his anger.

"Beshup's eyes glittered darkly. Pierre became afraid under their intensity. 'I was among those who found you as a child,' Beshup said. 'I saw the blood of your mother spilled. I believed that day we should have burned you with the cabin, but the others would not hear of it. They didn't understand what you would grow to become.'

"Pierre's anger grew. He shook with rage and injustice. 'But I have become nothing but strong. I have killed the enemies of our people and protected our women and children. I have hunted and provided meat for my mother's fire and those of the widows of our village. I am a good man. I am not my father.'

"Beshup looked at Pierre, and his face changed from hard anger to pity. 'A man's worth is not judged by what he does with his hands but by what his heart commands him to do.'

" 'But my heart has commanded me to do those things,' Pierre insisted. 'To love your daughter and take her as my wife.'

"Beshup shook his head. 'Only your ambition to be loved commanded your actions. Love does not ask a young maiden to disobey her father. Love does not lie in wait with a knife to spill the blood of her father.'

"Pierre knew he could not allow Beshup to live. Doing so would mean his own death within the village. And even if somehow he received a pardon, the least he would receive would be banishment, not to mention losing Kimana for good. He couldn't allow that to happen."

Nina listened in silence, her sandwich almost untouched.

She jumped when the front door opened and Jill called out, "I'm home."

"We're in the kitchen," Nina called back.

"We?" Jill came into view and spotted Markus. "Oh, hey, Markus." Her eyes scanned the table. "Mmm. Grilled cheese."

Nina grinned and stood. "I'll make you one."

Jill plopped into a chair. "Thank you." She sighed. "This was a hard day."

"Are there any new clues about Amanda's murder?" Markus asked.

Jill shook her head. "No, except that her husband has verifiable alibis for the time of her murder and the animal killings. It has to be ritual. Satanic or something."

"Wiccan, maybe?" Markus asked.

Jill bent over to unlace her boots. "There's a coven in the area who swear up and down they don't condone black magic for anything. No blood sacrifices."

Nina poured a glass of tea and set it in front of Jill. "Do you believe them?"

"They've been around a long time, and nothing like this has ever happened before. I mean, I'm not crazy about having a group of witches around, but they've never done anything harmful that I'm aware of. They're Mother Earth types, more tree hugging than ritual performing. Certainly no killings. So yes, I'm inclined to believe them."

Markus stretched and stood. He took his plate to the counter, his sandwich half-eaten. "You've been a gracious audience for my ramblings," he said to Nina. "I'm afraid I let my food get cold."

"You want another sandwich while I'm fixing one for Jill?" she asked.

He shook his head. "I should go now. I've taken up enough of your time."

Nina stared into his eyes, reading something that confused her. She didn't know him well enough to sense his thoughts or moods. Sometimes he made her uncomfortable, yet he had been nothing but kind. "Were you keeping me company until Jill came home so I wouldn't be alone?"

His face darkened into a blush.

Nina reached out and touched his arm. "Thank you, Markus. Now I feel like I've taken up your time instead of the other way around."

He covered her fingers. "It was my pleasure. It's not often I have an audience for my boring stories."

"Boring? They're fascinating. I wish you'd tell me the rest."

"Another time." He turned and nodded to Jill. "Good night, Sheriff."

Jill's eyebrows sat high on her forehead, and

her eyes widened as she looked from Nina to Markus. "See ya, Markus. Come over anytime."

Nina started to follow him to the door, but Markus stopped her. "Finish what you're doing. I can see myself out." He smiled and turned.

When they heard the door shut, Jill stood. "What was that all about?"

"Nothing," Nina said, "so don't make something of it."

"Me? I leave for a few hours and come home to find you and my McDreamy neighbor sharing a moment."

"Oh, for Pete's sake." Nina slid the sandwich onto a plate and handed it to Jill. "He stayed because Meg's gone to a poetry reading or something and you were at work."

"Protector or seducer?"

"Storyteller."

"Oh?"

"He was telling me about the legend of a vampire here in the Ozarks. Ever here of it?"

"Vampire?" Jill chuckled and took her plate to the table. "I've heard a lot of old stories about ghosts and witches and paranormal stuff like that, but never vampires."

"Sounds like he's researched pretty extensively. He told it so well I left half my sandwich uneaten too." Nina raised an eyebrow. "Want to hear a vampire story?"

"Another time." Jill bit into her sandwich.

"Actually, I want to talk to you about the so-called poetry reading Meg's at. I'm concerned."

"She's with Carrie Grayson. You said she was okay."

Jill's brow furrowed. "Carrie's all right. It's the woman conducting the readings I'm worried about. The yoga instructor."

Nina sat across from Jill, frowning. "Really . . . the yoga instructor? Meggie said she's great. I was thinking about checking her out myself. Why?"

"I met her last night outside the video store. She was waiting while Carrie picked up food at Barney's." Jill took another bite.

"How is that strange? Carrie works there."

Jill sighed. "I know. It might be nothing, but I have a feeling something isn't quite right about her."

"Well, this'll be the last time Meg sees her anyway. Hunt's on his way."

"I thought not until Saturday."

"Meg told him about Stephan, and he's really upset."

Jill flinched. "Yikes."

"Tell me about it." Just when Nina was starting to feel less like a screwup, she'd caused another problem. She thought back to that bottle of brandy. Had that just been this morning? It seemed like days.

She held her hand close to her face and could have sworn the scent still clung to her fingertips.

• • •

After an hour of poetry, Meg was getting bored, and the incense clogging her nose and throat was beginning to make her head feel fuzzy. She felt a little silly, and the poetry was getting funnier and funnier. Only no one else was laughing.

> My love is like a vacuum,
> sucking all the impurities from my soul.
> And I am left, clean, white.
> Please take off your shoes
> before you walk all over me.

It was too much. A giggle bubbled up from deep down, though she tried to stifle it. Carrie nudged her.

"I'm sorry," Meg said between gulps of laughter. " 'Please take off your shoes before you . . . ' " She dissolved into laughter, unable to finish. The would-be poet stared daggers through her, his face red even in the dimly lit room.

Meg stumbled to her feet. Her head swam, and she staggered a little as she tried to remember where the porch was. She stopped outside the room and tried to get her bearings. A gentle hand touched her shoulder, and she turned.

Eden's beautiful smile greeted her. "Are you all right, Meagan?"

In her strange, different-colored eyes, Meg found concern and comfort. "I'm sorry, Eden. I don't know what's wrong with me. I think I must be allergic to incense or something."

"You just aren't used to its effects," the other woman soothed. "No one blames you."

"Tell that to vacuum boy in there."

Eden chuckled. "You have a quick wit. I enjoy that about you."

Even in her fuzzy state, Meg couldn't help but be pleased. To be singled out by Eden was an honor. She knew this instinctively. "I think you're fantastic, Eden," she gushed, then felt her cheeks warm. What was she saying? She couldn't stop. "I wish you were my mom."

"I would be honored to have a daughter like you. I'm just sorry your mother doesn't appreciate her gift."

"Gift?"

Eden brushed a strand of hair behind Meg's ear. "You, darling."

Meg's eyes stung with tears, but her face felt tender where Eden touched her, like an impression on her skin. "I hate her."

"Really?" Although it seemed to surprise Eden, she didn't seem bothered by it. Most adults would have scolded her or at the very least encouraged her to forgive and put her anger aside, to give her mom a break. After all, she was recovering. Trying.

"She's a drunk," Meg blurted. "Did you know that?"

"No, honey, I didn't. I'm sorry."

"She's been sober for three months."

"Isn't that a good thing?" Eden's voice seemed to come from even farther away.

Meg shook her head, hoping to clear it. "It is, but am I supposed to just forget about all the years she wasn't there for me, just because she's been sober for twenty minutes?"

"I certainly wouldn't."

"I need fresh air." Meg stumbled toward the front door and twisted the knob.

"I'll come with you."

Meg stepped onto the porch, and the night air surrounded her. She dropped to the top step and buried her face in her palms. "What is that stuff?"

Eden sat next to her. "I'm so sorry the incense affected you so strongly." She ran her hand over Meg's hair. The soft strokes felt soothing, gentle. Motherly. Tears began to flow and soon became deep, wrenching sobs.

"Shh," Eden soothed. "Meg, it's natural to feel this way about a mother who didn't care enough to be there for you. Mine was the same way."

Meg turned her head and looked at Eden. "Really?"

Eden wiped away Meg's tears with her long fingers. "Yes. It's why I'm so determined that you children have a place to come when life gets to be too much. It's why Carrie comes. She has felt so alone since her mother died when she was a little girl."

"I didn't even know that."

"Yes, and her father is so busy at the school, taking care of other kids, she feels completely abandoned. I don't know if he means to treat her like she's a second place priority, but Carrie feels it just the same."

Meg sighed. She felt so much better, more at peace than she'd felt in so long, all because of Eden's encouragement. She grabbed the woman's hand. "Thank you for understanding, Eden. I wish I didn't have to go home with my dad." Meg straightened. "Oh my gosh. What time is it?"

"Almost midnight."

A groan tugged at Meg's throat. "My mom is going to kill me! I was supposed to be home by eleven."

Meg jumped up, her eyes still trying to adjust to the dark and the fuzz in her head. She slammed through the front door and rushed back into the living room. The smoke nearly overwhelmed her. She grabbed Carrie by the hand and hauled her up from the rug, where she sat crossed-legged.

Carrie jerked her hand away. "What are you doing?"

"I was supposed to be home an hour ago."

Carrie's eyes grew wide. "What time is it?"

"Midnight!"

"Oh no." Carrie staggered out of the living room. "I am so grounded from the car."

"Wait, you can't drive," Meg said. "Give me the keys. At least I'm not as fuzzy."

Eden was still on the porch when they got there. "Girls, you mustn't go home in this condition."

It was nice to have someone who cared without yelling. Meg smiled. "We have to go. I think my head is clear enough." But as she turned, dizziness overwhelmed her. "Oh."

A smile tipped Eden's lips. "I can help." She stepped forward and cupped Meg's face in her hands, held her for a second, then took her hands away. "How's that?"

Meg's stomach quivered with the intensity of the moment. It was like stepping onto the stage when she was in the school play last year, powerful and terrifying at the same time. She turned her head back and forth. "Wow. Nothing. How'd you do that?"

"It's a gift. I think you have it too." Eden's eyes seemed to suck her in. Meg felt a flash of alarm. "I've felt it since the moment you walked into my home yesterday."

Eden turned to Carrie and did the same thing she'd done for Meg. Carrie smiled brightly. "Thank you so much, Eden. If I get grounded, I won't be here for a few days. So don't think I don't want to come. Okay?"

"Oh, I don't think you'll have to worry about that." Eden winked. "Trust me. Now off you go."

They'd reached the car by the time Meg's curiosity got the better of her. "Hang on, Carrie." She ran back to the porch and opened the door.

She found Eden in the living room, lounging on a flowered settee. The woman's eyebrows rose. "I thought you'd gone, Meg."

"What did you mean about me having the same gift?" Meg asked, strangely nervous.

Eden frowned. "Dreams, instincts, things like that."

Meg stared at her as the incense began to sweep over her once more. "I thought they were coincidences."

Eden stood and took her by the arm. When they reached the foyer, she leaned in. "People like us usually keep these things to ourselves so we don't appear strange. You're one of the special people. It would be a shame to waste your gifts. If you come back, I will help you bring out your gifts, but it's up to you to develop them."

Regret washed over Meg. Eden made her feel so special. Her parents certainly didn't think she had anything to offer. Let alone that she was "gifted," whatever that meant. But Meg wanted to find out. She hated that she had to turn down Eden's invitation. She could hardly keep from crying. "My dad is in town. I won't be able to come."

Sadness swept over Eden's face. "I'm sorry to hear that." She enfolded Meg in an embrace. "Maybe next visit. Now you'd better go."

Meg's thoughts spun in her head as she walked to the car. Maybe she could get away. Maybe her parents would be so engrossed in their conversations about Stephan, they wouldn't notice.

She gave a silent, bitter laugh as she opened the door to Carrie's car. It wouldn't be the first time they'd forgotten her presence, would it?

CHAPTER SEVENTEEN

Alcohol is the sort of addiction that brings a person to her knees, powerless against a pull. It takes distance, time, and the determination not to give in to this temptation again to beat it. That under no circumstances will she ever again touch a drink of anything.

Holidays? No.

What about an anniversary? A couple has to have a glass of champagne when they reach another milestone year, right? That's just an excuse to get loaded. Don't do it.

A person can be strong, sober, and perfect for years, but what her family doesn't understand is that while they sit back in relief, time moves forward for them, away from the addiction of the past, away from the memories of crazy nights of drunken episodes. But for the person who once staggered through life, addiction is just a day behind. Every time she makes it to bed without giving in, she survived that twenty-four hours. Recovery will forever be one day at a time.

You close your eyes, you smile, you sleep, knowing you haven't embarrassed, scared, or hurt anyone. And most of all, you can close your eyes knowing that somewhere in the house there isn't a little girl crying because of you.

Drops of warm liquid landed on Markus's neck, his chin, his mouth, pulling him from sleep. His tongue flickered across his bottom lip. He tasted ginger, honey, iron, and youth.

He reached into the dark. His thirst demanded more.

His hand encircled human flesh. An arm, soft and feminine, perfumed with a dizzying aroma, intensified his craving. He anticipated the heady rush of warmth even before he opened his mouth and bit down on the wrist.

He took, tasted, and became aware. Many times in the past few years he'd awakened, feeding, only to realize with relief that he'd been dreaming. But this soft, cool arm was no dream.

Disengaging, he flung himself back. He sat up against the headboard, and his eyes flew open. Candles flickered around the room, providing an eerie, ominous atmosphere. Markus didn't have to guess who was responsible.

Eden stood next to his bed, beautiful in a thin white dress, her long, dark arms contrasting with the fabric. His heart rate picked up, a response to her.

She sensed his reaction and smiled slowly. "Hello, my love."

"Eden. What are you doing?"

"I'm doing for you what you refuse to do for yourself. I had hoped to give you the girl next door, but Carrie came back instead of going home. Convenient, don't you think?"

Markus's gaze moved to the teenage girl who lay at the foot of the bed. A scarf was stretched between her lips and tied behind her head. Her wrist seeped blood onto the sheets. Carrie Grayson.

"You know you want more," Eden said. "Why do you resist? She doesn't know what's happening. I've made sure of that."

He looked at the girl again. Her eyes were open but dull; she was obviously drugged. Eden's show of mercy. She must have had a rare soft spot for the girl.

Anger flared inside Markus. "Why would you do this, Eden? Are you such a child that you can't accept when a man grows tired of you? I'm so tired of the cruelty. I want something beautiful for once."

"Be careful, Markus. Don't force me to punish you."

"You just did." He couldn't keep his eyes off the girl. The vein in her neck still pulsed, driving him crazy. Other than the occasional vagrant or criminal, he hadn't taken a human life in thirty-five years. He'd been tempted, but he'd always found the strength to resist innocent flesh.

He hated Eden in that moment. If he had the power, he'd have killed her. She would ruin him again and take everything he wanted.

She walked forward and lowered herself onto the bed. "Oh, Markus. I know you're angry. I don't like it when you're angry with me. Tell me you didn't enjoy the sweetness."

He had enjoyed it. Too much. He turned away from Carrie, and the battle inside him escalated to a full-fledged war. The sort of burning, fiery war that only those in the middle of such hell could ever understand. He had resisted for so many years, had truly believed he was ready to be with a woman like Nina again. Not any woman, only Nina. His princess. He wanted her to know him like he knew her. Nina would understand the draw to a substance that destroyed the soul. He wanted her to know who he was and love him anyway. Something Kimana couldn't do. Nina was his only chance for complete love.

But the sweetness of the girl drew him. He could finish her. She was as good as dead anyway. If he didn't take her, Eden would. Either way, Carrie Grayson wasn't going home. He inched toward the end of his bed, the slow drip of her blood driving him crazy.

"That's it, Markus," Eden purred. "Finish what you started, and then we can leave this place together."

Eden never knew when to shut up. At the image her words conjured, he found the strength to slide off the bed and put enough distance between himself and the girl to gain some control.

"You had your chance to save them, Markus." Her face twisted with anger, and for the first time, she was hideous to him. "If you truly don't wish to leave with me, then don't. But I assure you, I'm not going to let her have you either."

Markus sucked in a breath. "Stay away from her, Eden. I won't let you harm Kimana."

"Kimana?" Laughter burst from Eden.

"I see. The woman reminds you of your little Indian princess." She shook her head at him, disgust etched into the lines of her face. "Oh, Markus. It's sad to see what a fool you've become. It would serve you right if I left you to this woman."

Humiliated by his slip in front of Eden, he turned his back and stared out the window as Eden knelt over the girl and drank.

Nina's light was on. His heart sped up as he watched her silhouette move around her room. The taste of blood had left his mind weak, and his thoughts explored the memory of the pulse along Nina's slender neck. So much life—his second chance.

He didn't notice Eden had finished until she stood next to him, her hip pressed against his. She slid in front of him and pressed against the window, blocking his view.

She leaned in close, her lips centimeters from his. "You are what you are, darling, and it's time to stop fighting and wishing for dreams that can't be. I've been patient with these little defections because of my fondness for you." She turned and stared at Nina's window. "But my patience is wearing thin. Do not test me."

She turned and her mouth found his before he could react. For the first time, her lips failed to thrill him. He pulled away, disgusted to his core.

She tasted like death.

~

The day Nina told me about the events of her graduation night, she cried. Nina had never been a crier, except when drunk, and in that moment she was sober. I vowed to live my life making sure she was never hurt again. I sacrificed too much to mention during those terrible, sloppy, drunken years when I tried to love her unconditionally. I prayed for help and then picked up the pieces over and over.

I was a fool.

Shortly after the clock downstairs struck 4 a.m., Nina heard Jill's phone ring. The only middle-of-the-night calls Jill had received this week had been from her deputies.

Nina threw off her covers and slipped on her robe. She padded downstairs to the kitchen and started a pot of strong coffee. Two hours of sleep wasn't enough. It was bad enough that Meg had been out past curfew, which meant Nina was awake and fuming an hour after the girl finally got home. To top it off, Nina's mind wouldn't stop going over all the possible explanations she could muster to explain to Hunt why she'd never actually told him she knew who Meg's dad was.

She knew Hunt had to feel betrayed. How would he ever believe that she hadn't lied to him about being raped? Nina still had trouble believing it herself, but she knew Stephan was telling the truth. Too many of the pieces fit.

She was just sitting down to pour herself a cup when Jill entered the kitchen, carrying her boots.

"Early morning?" Nina asked, filling her mug. She held up the pot. "Want some?"

"No time."

The tension in Jill's voice sent an alert through Nina. "Why do you have to go in so early?"

Jill released a heavy breath. Her shoulders slumped as she sat, one boot on, one boot off. She looked up through troubled eyes, her face wiped of color.

"Good Lord, Jilly," Nina said, setting down the pot. "What's wrong?"

"There's been another murder in town."

"What?" Fear shot through Nina.

"A body was found at the river." Jill's voice quivered, and tears formed in her eyes.

"Who was it?" Nina whispered.

"Carrie Grayson. It's really bad. Trent got the call two hours ago. He went to the site alone to check it out because he thought it was just a prank. We've gotten some of those this week. He's pretty shaken up. As far as I could gather, it's like Amanda and the animals."

"Carrie." Nina had no idea what else to say. All she could think of was that Meg had been with Carrie until just past midnight. "It could just as easily have been Meg."

Jill nodded with sober agreement. "It's all I've been able to think about. Poor Principal Grayson lost his wife a few years ago and now his daughter. I can only thank God it wasn't Meg."

"She's going to take this hard." Nina sipped her coffee, shaking her head. "As if today wasn't going to be hard enough with Hunt showing up and demanding answers."

Jill bent over and put on her other boot. "The medical examiner has already taken Carrie to the morgue. They'll have to do an autopsy. The medical examiner will start DNA testing, and all the new evidence will be taken to the crime lab in Springfield to join the rest of the useless evidence."

"Are you going to the morgue or to Mr. Grayson's?"

"Grayson's." Jill's eyes clouded with dread. "I'm waiting for Reverend Bradley. He's picking me up, and we'll go over there together."

Reverend Bradley. The name rang a bell.

Nina must have been frowning, because Jill sighed. "He's the reverend who helped Dad."

The doorbell rang.

Curious about the man who had made such an impact on their father, Nina followed Jill to the door. Surprised to find a young man, probably no older than herself, standing on the porch, Nina was at a loss for words.

"Thanks for coming, Reverend," Jill said. Her voice sounded strained. Nina wondered if the preacher's presence was as much for Jill as it was for Mr. Grayson. "This is my sister, Nina."

His eyes observed her, kind but curious. "Your dad's mentioned you."

Nina's face heated, and she swallowed hard. "Two sides to every story, Reverend." She grinned, sheepish.

He smiled back. "Don't worry. It's all good."

"Well, the two of you better go." She hugged Jill. "Call me if you need me. I'm waiting up for Hunt." She turned to the reverend. "Nice to meet you, Reverend. And thanks for all you've done for my dad. He looks great."

His eyes smiled. "Your dad did all the hard work."

Nina held the door while Jill stepped out after him. Jill turned and said, "Lock up when I leave."

Nina didn't have to be told twice. She couldn't help a sense of loss as she twisted the flimsy lock. It wouldn't keep out a dedicated murderer. She imagined the locksmiths in Branson would be busy with the citizens of Abbey Hills over the next few weeks. Deadbolts and alarm systems would be in high demand.

Heading back into the kitchen, Nina's thoughts went to Carrie Grayson. Should she wake Meg and tell her? She considered the thought for a couple of minutes, then decided against it. Carrie's own dad was just getting the news. Morning was soon enough for Meg.

She sat at the table, staring into the empty room, her mind conjuring up Carrie's smiling face. It could have been Meg.

Her eyes locked on to her cell phone. She'd forgotten to take it upstairs earlier.

Without thinking, she picked it up and punched in Hunt's number. His sleepy voice answered.

"What's wrong?"

At the sound of his voice, Nina's fear and confusion—all the events of the past couple of days—converged, and tears poured from her eyes. She tried to speak, but the words wouldn't come.

"Dear God, Nina. Are you drinking?"

Hunt's question washed over her like ice

water. She stopped crying as quickly as she'd begun.

"No. How could you even ask?" His silence filled the space between their phones. "Okay, I know how you could have asked." She released a breath, wiping away tears. She sniffed and grabbed a tissue from the box on the counter.

"What's wrong then?" he repeated. "It's not even five o'clock."

"A girl was murdered tonight. Just like the lady whose funeral we attended yesterday." How could the people of Abbey Hills bear another funeral so soon?

"Is Meg okay?" Hunt sounded more awake.

"Yes. She's in bed, sleeping. But Meg was with this girl until after midnight tonight."

Hunt sucked in a breath. "I don't even know what to say. My whole body just went weak."

"I know exactly what you mean. The same thing happened to me when Jill told me the news. We're all thinking the same thing."

"Meg's sleeping, so I guess she doesn't know yet?"

Nina shook her head, even though he couldn't see her. "I debated whether to wake her up or not, but decided against it. Do you think I'm wrong?"

"No, I would let her sleep too."

He couldn't possibly know how much those words meant.

Silence fell between them until Hunt spoke. "You called to tell me about the girl?"

"I just couldn't stop thinking that it could have been Meggie. And I wanted to talk to you." She ran her finger around the top of her mug. "I guess it was stupid, considering everything."

"It wasn't stupid, Nina."

Relief shuffled through her at his words. His voice was still husky from sleep. She could imagine his sleep-tousled hair, his scruffy jaw line that always drove her crazy in a good way.

"It just doesn't change anything," Hunt continued. "We still need to talk about this guy claiming to be Meg's biological father."

"He's not just claiming to be. He is Meg's father. I'm sorry." Hunt didn't say anything for several seconds. "You still there?" Nina asked.

"Yeah. But I think I'd better go. We'll talk about this in the morning."

His voice had hardened. Her stomach sank.

This would be a difficult day. Not only for her, but for the entire town of Abbey Hills.

CHAPTER EIGHTEEN

If I'm not an alcoholic, then what am I? How do I go through life with my eyes open and my head clear? I want to run to someplace where no one knows me. Where I can start over as the new vet in town. Respectable. Divorced, but respectable just the same. Maybe I could get a dog and do volunteer work.

It would be so much easier to start over someplace new than reinvent myself in the place where I became who I am in the first place.

Memories, pain, struggle.

Am I who they think I am? Will I always be?

Sleep came and went, and with it came vivid, terrifying dreams. She saw herself dressed in black robes, standing in front of a stone altar. Candles burned, and she could smell incense. Eden was there, dressed in white.

Something wet and sticky flowed over Meg's hands. She looked down to find them slick with blood.

Horrified, she shoved them toward Eden, asking for help. But Eden smiled, nodded, and motioned toward the altar. Meagan turned her head to look. Carrie lay naked on the altar, her throat ripped open, blood staining the stone.

Meagan's own screams woke her. She sat up, bathed in sweat, her throat sore.

Her door flew open, and her light switched on. Nina stood in her doorway, a butcher knife clasped in her hand, raised and ready to strike. "Meggie, are you okay?"

At the sight of her mother ready to defend her, Meg snapped out of her dream fog. "Yeah. I just had a really bad dream."

"You scared me half to death."

"Obviously." Meg couldn't help the enjoyment she got from the moment. Maybe enjoyment wasn't the right word, but she was glad Nina would come running to protect her if she needed her. As long as she stayed off the booze.

"Nina," Meg said, "would you please put the knife down, or at least lower it? You're starting to freak me out."

Her mother lowered the knife without apology. "What kind of dream makes you scream like that? You've never gotten nightmares."

There was no way Meg could tell her about Carrie and Eden and the altar. She didn't even want to think about it, let alone voice it. "I dreamed I was on a roller coaster."

"That must have been one heck of a ride."

"Yeah. Can I go back to sleep now?"

Nina hesitated and walked over to the bed. "Your face is flushed. Are you feeling okay?"

"My head hurts."

She closed her eyes as her mother reached out and pressed a cool hand to her forehead. "You're pretty warm, Meggie. I think you have a fever."

Meg hated to admit how good it felt to have Nina hover. But then, she didn't feel good, so her defenses were down.

"I'm going to run to the kitchen and grab some Tylenol. That should get your fever down."

Meg laid her head on her pillow and had nearly dozed again by the time Nina came back with the pills and a glass of water.

"Sit up and take these."

Meg complied and lay back down.

"Keep the door open," Meg blurted as Nina turned to leave.

"Are you sure you want me to go?" Nina asked. "I could sit at the desk."

"And watch me sleep? That's just creepy."

Nina smiled. "I guess so." She hesitated. "I love you, Meg. So much."

An awkward chill spread over Meg. "You're getting mushy because I'm sick?"

"Just mushy because that's the way I am." Nina's smile seemed sad. "Go back to sleep. Your dad will be here in three hours. I'll wake you in two."

"What are you going to tell him about Stephan?" Meg asked, snuggling into the pillow-top mattress.

Nina shrugged. "The truth."

"Why didn't you tell him before?"

"I told him the only truth I knew." She met Meg's gaze. "I never lied about you." She switched off the light before Meg could respond. "Sleep tight, Meggie."

Meg heard Nina go into her own room and shut the door. A couple minutes later, she heard the shower.

She felt horrible and just wanted to go back to sleep, but when she closed her eyes, the nightmare came back. Meg's heart pumped faster, and fear gripped her stomach. Maybe she didn't want to go back to sleep. The dream was so real. It had to be because of that incense earlier. She couldn't bear the thought of closing her eyes.

Shoving aside the covers, she sat up and switched on the lamp next to her bed. She looked at her phone and noticed she had a message. A text from Carrie.

Wanna do early yoga b4 ur dad gets there?

Relief swelled in her. It had only been a dream then.

Ur not grounded for missing curfew?

LOL only from having the car. Eden will pick us up.

314

I have the flu or something. Fever, sore throat.

No worries. Eden can fix it. She has remedies for anything like that. Trust me.

Meg hesitated. She really wanted to see Eden again before she left. And she had heard about yoga people and their holistic medicines. Her head swam as she stared at the letters on her phone.

What time?
Ten minutes?
K cu

Meg crawled out of bed, opened her drawer, and pulled out a pair of yoga pants that she usually just wore for looks. Once dressed, she pulled her hair into a ponytail and paused at Nina's door to listen. The shower was still going, so she reached into her backpack and grabbed a notebook.

Nina,
    Feeling better. Gone to do yoga. You were in the shower. Be back in two hours or so.
    Meg

The kitchen light was on, and Meg noticed half a pot of coffee. With her lack of sleep, a little caffeine couldn't hurt. She snatched a mug, filled it halfway, and headed to the porch.

She didn't have to wait. A car sat in the

315

driveway, and the lights came on as soon as Meg stepped outside. A smile curved her lips as she slid into the front passenger seat.

Eden's face brightened at the sight of her. "I'm glad you decided to join me this morning. What are you drinking?"

"Coffee."

"No wonder you don't feel well. You don't take care of your body." Eden frowned. She handed Meg a to-go cup. "I picked us up hot green tea with a little chai mixed in. I'll trade you."

"Gladly. My mom makes coffee strong enough to choke a horse."

Eden opened her door and dumped the contents of the mug on the ground.

Meg sipped the spicy green tea. She looked around. "Where's Carrie?"

"She couldn't make it after all." Eden's long fingers brushed Meg's shoulder as she backed out of the driveway. "Is that okay?"

Something curled in Meg's stomach at the touch, but the feeling passed quickly and she relaxed. "Is she sick, or did her dad say she couldn't go?"

Eden shrugged. "I'm not really sure. Does it matter if she's here or not? You don't strike me as the type who needs someone with them to feel secure."

Meg felt the words deeply. As much as she wished they were true, she didn't like being alone. The buddy system had always been her method of comfort, and Carrie's absence bugged her more than she wanted to admit. "I'm cool. I just wondered."

The car smelled of new leather and spiced chai. The combination hit her head. It swam. Her fever and lack of sleep the night before, between getting home late and weird dreams, must have affected her more than she thought.

"You truly are ill, aren't you, Meg?" Eden's voice poured over her, warm and comfortable.

Meg nodded. "Maybe I shouldn't go."

"Shh. Don't worry. I'll take care of you." Eden reached across the seat and smoothed Meg's brow. Like something a mother would do. Meg closed her eyes, resting her head against the back of the seat.

"That's right. Just rest until we get home. All the tension leaving your body."

Meg's breathing shallowed, and she felt herself drifting.

The fact that Meg had left Nina a note instead of waiting for her to finish her shower, or at the very least knocking on the door to ask permission, annoyed her. Add to that the fact that the girl had a fever and knew very well Nina never would have agreed to her leaving the house and the fact that she was an hour late and had deliberately left her cell phone escalated Nina's frustration to angry pacing. Hunt was due any second, and Meg had been gone a full hour past the time she'd promised to be home.

So much for the three of them going to Barney's for breakfast. Meg could just fend for herself. She stopped the inward tirade and wondered how the girl was feeling. Was her fever down? Did her throat still hurt?

On a whim, Nina curled her fingers around the phone and carried it down the steps.

The doorbell rang when she was halfway down the steps. Nina's stomach tightened at the thought of facing Hunt. She needed him to believe her, to understand that she had truly thought the rape had occurred. That she hadn't intentionally lied to him about the night of Meg's conception.

He wasn't smiling when she opened the door, but he dropped the scowl from his face before he walked inside.

He hugged her. Nina took in the soft scent of his aftershave, wishing the hug could last a lot longer than the half second Hunt allowed. He looked so good. Her heart hurt again at the whole situation. How could she have let their marriage go?

"Have any trouble finding the house?" she asked.

That coaxed a smile from him. "No. You pretty much nailed it. Turn right and don't blink." He looked around. "Where's Meg? I've been trying to call her."

Nina held up Meg's cell phone. "Get in line. She left me a note while I was in the shower. Yoga."

"When is she due back?"

"An hour ago."

"I don't like that. Should we call Jill?"

"That's probably not a bad idea."

Nina's phone buzzed a text message. She glanced quickly at the text then at Hunt. "It's her. She must be using someone else's phone."

"What's the caller ID say?"

Nina shook her head. "Unknown caller."

Mom, it's Meg. Sorry I'm late!! the text read. Nice touch, calling her Mom instead of Nina.

I fell asleep during yoga. Still not feeling great. Eden didn't know I needed to be home and let me sleep. I'll be there asap.

Nina let out a frustrated breath. **Meet us at Barney's**

"Let's go," she said after she got Meg's cursory **K** in reply. "She'll meet us there in a little while."

An awkward silence filled the car while they drove, as though neither of them wanted to address the reason for the meeting.

Barney's was crowded, usual for a Friday morning. Nina and Hunt walked toward the General and his large table filled with old codgers who liked to drink free refills of decaf coffee and reminisce for a couple of hours. Barney griped about how much it cost him to keep the town's geriatric community in decaf, but according to Jill, he wouldn't have it any other way.

The General gave Nina a nod, and she stopped next to the table. "How's the foal?" she asked.

"Good." His expression remained solemn. "You coming by later to check on her?" He eyed Hunt with suspicion.

She smiled. "If I can't make it today, I'll be there tomorrow."

She turned to Hunt. "This is my ex-husband. He's here to pick up Meg."

The General stood and shook Hunt's hand. "Thought you wasn't coming till tomorrow."

Did everyone know her schedule? "That's Hunt for you," she said, forcing a smile. "Full of surprises. I'll try to get over there later today, General. Otherwise, I'll stop by tomorrow for sure."

After Hunt drove away with their daughter and ripped her heart out of her chest.

The restaurant's atmosphere seemed sedate. Though the place was full, the buzz was low-key. She heard none of the typical laughter. Nina looked at the solemn faces and teary eyes filling the dining room. Word about Carrie must have already spread. Still, Nina knew all eyes in the place followed her and Hunt as they found their way to a table in the center of the room.

Hunt frowned. "Isn't there anything a little more private?"

Giving an airy wave of her hand, Nina invited him to look around. "See a better place?"

He released a breath. "No."

"Well, then . . . we sit."

"How are we going to talk privately?"

"Keep your voice down, I guess, and it's private."

"Did you know this would happen?" He slid into his seat and pulled it forward. The chair scraped across the floor.

"It was a pretty good bet," Nina said. "You're the one who wanted to go out to breakfast."

"I thought it would help Meg feel better. You could have warned me about the crowd."

Nina smirked. "Maybe I wanted to show you off."

His face reddened, but he gave her a stern look. "Give me a break."

"Okay, look," she said, leaning forward. "Let's just talk about it. We'll keep our voices down, and if it looks like we aren't going to have enough privacy, we can finish breakfast and then go for a walk or something."

Suddenly the room grew quiet as the door opened and Stephan walked in. Nina felt the blood drain from her face. She stood.

"What's wrong?" Hunt asked, looking over his shoulder.

"Stephan," she said.

Hunt's whole body stiffened, and he stood as Stephan walked toward them. Nina knew every person in the room was staring. She didn't really blame them. Did they remember she and Stephan were once friends? What speculation was going on in their minds? She could only imagine the worst and suddenly felt small and sixteen years old again and could only imagine that in the back of their minds, her peers were thinking, "Oh, look. Puke is back in town, and she hasn't changed a bit. Still causing trouble wherever she goes."

The double doors from the kitchen swung open, and Barney emerged. His eyes were red, as though he'd been crying. He spotted Nina and moved toward her. "I didn't know you were here," he said. "Jill asked me to get a table in the back room ready for you so you could have some privacy."

"I'd like to be part of this conversation," Stephan said, arriving at their table as Barney finished speaking.

Hunt gave a curt nod of assent. Neither man offered a hand of friendship. Not that Nina had expected them to.

Barney sighed. "Follow me."

"Are you going to be okay, Barney?" Nina asked quietly as they wound their way through the tables toward the back of the restaurant.

"I just can't believe Carrie's dead," he said, shaking his head. "She was such a sweet, hardworking girl. Best waitress I ever had, even if she was just a kid."

Barney led them through a door and into the back room. He stopped beside a table with four chairs.

Stephan frowned. "What happened?"

"Carrie was murdered." Barney's voice broke. "Next to the river. They found her early this morning."

"Carrie Grayson?" Stephan asked, his eyes wide. "The little waitress?"

Nina nodded. "She and Meg hung out after the funeral yesterday until midnight, so the murder had to have occurred between midnight and four. That's when Jill got the call this morning."

Stephan took a seat across from Nina and Hunt. "Is Meg a suspect since she was the last person to see Carrie alive?"

That thought hadn't occurred to Nina. "I don't see how she could be. Meg was in bed."

"Just asking."

Hunt's eyes narrowed. He turned to Nina. "I want to get Meg out of here today."

"Hunt, please don't make her leave today," Nina said. "We're having dinner with my parents tonight. She'll be safe with all of us."

"Since when do you care about dinner with your parents?" Hunt asked.

"Since Meggie does."

They settled at the table. Nina couldn't help expecting to see Carrie sashaying toward them, her lovely smile beaming out at them like the sun through a cloud.

Barney set menus in front of each of them.

Nina caught his eye. "We'll miss her, Barney."

"This killing is making me mad," Barney said. "If the police can't figure it out soon, we might have to take matters into our own hands."

Nina's defenses rose. "Jill's doing her best." The man who claimed to love her should know that already.

"I'm talking about those yahoos in Springfield," Barney clarified. "What are they waiting for? Why are they taking so long with the evidence?"

Nina shrugged. "I don't know. Jill says it takes weeks in these cases."

He huffed. "What do you want to drink?"

After taking their drink orders, Barney shuffled off. Hunt cleared his throat, and Stephan shifted in his chair. The men sized each other up with unconcealed scrutiny, obviously ready to begin their conversation. Neither cared what the other thought. They had the same goal: Meg.

By the time Barney returned with iced tea for the guys and coffee for Nina, they'd finally gotten past the introductory small talk. She shook the contents of a couple of pink packets into her cup.

She clenched her back teeth and hoped what she was feeling wasn't a panic attack coming on.

Hunt and Stephan stared each other down while they discussed occupations. Stephan might be blue collar, but his roofing business was more impressive than Nina had realized. He owned two companies in two states—Missouri and Arkansas. She thought he might feel intimidated by Dr. Hunter, but Stephan could hold his own. He came from a professional family. He knew what he wanted and how to be successful in his own right.

Stephan laced his fingers on top of the table. "Look. I know Meagan is your daughter legally."

"And in every other way." Hunt drummed two fingers on the table.

"Not technically." Stephan's gaze never faltered.

Hunt's fingers kept drumming.

Nina reached over and grabbed his hand. "Cut it out."

He snatched her hand and held it as though he needed her on his side. Nina's heart sped up. Hunt needed her.

Leaning forward, Hunt squinted. "I don't care whose DNA she has. Meagan is my daughter. She's been my daughter since she was six years old. I've adopted her legally, and she's mine. End of story."

Stephan's jaw tensed. "All I want is a fair shot at knowing her. I'm not asking for the right to walk her down the aisle when the day comes, but I think we can all agree that I should have been informed of the pregnancy and given the choice to be Meg's father."

Nina held her breath, but the ensuing silence made it clear they were waiting for her to speak.

"Look," she said. "I believed something wrong all these years. And maybe it wasn't fair to you, Stephan, but at this point in Meg's life, there's not a lot to be done about it. I still think the choice should be Meagan's. She should get to decide how involved she is with you, Stephan."

Hunt released her hand, keeping his gaze fixed on Stephan. He flattened his palms against the table. The absence of his wedding ring saddened Nina, even though she knew he'd taken it off shortly after the divorce was final. She wished he'd fought for her with the same fierceness with which he clearly intended to fight for Meg. No, that wasn't fair. He'd fought through all those hazy years of alcohol abuse. He'd fought until he stopped fighting for her and started fighting against her.

Hunt eyed Stephan, the stern look she'd seen him use on patients when giving important follow-up instructions. It always thrilled her to see Hunt work, interacting with patients who looked up to him.

"First," Hunt said, "I think we should establish that you are her biological father."

"No," Nina interrupted. There was no reason to go that route. She knew there had been no one before Stephan that night and no one else for three more years.

"Nina, it's protocol," Hunt insisted.

"Only if it's court ordered," she said. "Let's try to do this amongst ourselves. I've never questioned who the father is, only how he managed it. I think Stephan has been very open in clearing all that up. And since nothing is going to happen in the court system here, let's just move on."

Hunt tilted his head, his blue eyes brilliant as a sun-glittered pool. "I'm still not convinced he's telling the truth. This could be nothing more than his way of making amends for a past wrong without actually admitting to anything."

"I believe him," she said. Stephan shot her a look of gratitude. Her phone chimed, and she checked the caller ID. "It's Jill." She answered.

"Nina." Jill's voice sounded hollow. "Are you with Hunt?"

"Yeah. He's right here." She looked at Hunt. He frowned, and she shrugged. "Did you need to talk to him?"

"No. I just don't want you alone."

A ball of fear formed in Nina's gut. "Is it Meg? What's happened?" Next to her, Hunt tensed.

"We're going to have to question her," Jill said.

Nina bristled. "What do you mean? Question her about what?"

"Relax," Jill soothed. "She's not a suspect, but she was with Carrie last night. We need to know if Carrie talked to anyone. If she seemed tense. If she shared any secrets. It's important, and Meg is our first real lead."

"Well, I'm sure Meg will be happy to come in and answer any questions that might help find the killer, but I haven't seen her since really early," Nina said. "She doesn't even know about Carrie yet, as far as I know."

"Where is she?" Jill asked.

"She left a note saying she was going to a yoga class, but she should have been back almost three hours ago."

"Hmm."

"What?"

"I don't know. I don't want to scare you, but isn't that a little strange?"

Nina's fear grew exponentially. "Yes. Now, it is. I wasn't worried in the beginning, just irritated."

"Have you tried calling her?"

"Repeatedly, until I realized she left her phone behind. But she texted me from someone else's phone. I assumed someone taking her class."

Nina's stomach tightened. She had been so irritated with Meg she hadn't even stopped to consider that she could be in trouble. "I have Meg's phone on me. Hang on." Nina slipped her purse off the back of her chair and grabbed Meg's phone, then opened her inbox. The last message she'd received had been from Carrie. Nina frowned.

Hunt nudged her. "What's wrong?"

"This is odd."

"What?" Jill, Hunt, and Stephan asked in unison.

"Jill," Nina said, feeling panic creep into her voice, "Meg got a message from Carrie at six this morning."

"She couldn't have. By then Carrie was already . . ."

"I know! That's my point. She got this message right after I talked to her, when I was in the shower."

Jill took a deep breath. "Okay, Nina. Stay calm and read the message."

"Okay, this is supposedly Carrie: 'Wanna do early yoga before your dad gets there?' " Nina's voice trembled. "This is Meg texting: 'You're not grounded for missing curfew?' Carrie said, 'Only from the car. Eden will pick us up.' Meg asked what time. Carrie texted, 'Ten minutes,' and Meg said okay."

Nina closed Meg's phone. She stared at Hunt, numb. Hunt's face had drained of color, and he took her hand, holding tightly, painfully, but Nina didn't mind.

She realized Jill was yelling in her ear. "Nina!"

"Jill, what do we do?" Her voice shook.

"Meet back at my house. I'll be right there."

Nina hung up and turned to Hunt. "She wants us to meet her at the house."

Stephan shoved his chair back and stood. "Did Meg hang out with anyone besides Carrie this week?"

Nina shook her head. "Not that I know of. After the funeral yesterday, she spent the afternoon and evening at Carrie's house before they went to a poetry reading at the yoga teacher's house together." She shook her head. "Jill knew something was off about that teacher. I should have listened to her. At the very least found out where the classes were held." The most she'd heard was "farm house outside of town."

Hunt squeezed her hand. "Okay, listen. One girl is dead, and the other is missing. As much as I hate to, I think we need to talk to Carrie's dad and find out if she ever said anything about this Eden and if he has any idea where the classes were held." He looked at Stephan. "Personal issues aside, I think Nina should drive my car back to the house while you and I have a talk with Carrie's dad."

Nina turned to Stephan. "You know Mr. Grayson. Will he talk to the two of you?"

Stephan nodded. "He'll understand, I think. It won't be easy for him, but I think he'd want to help any way he can before another girl is murdered like his daughter."

CHAPTER NINETEEN

In the grand scheme of things, I always believed I would end my life strong. Mostly because I was too stubborn to envision it any other way. But losing Hunt and the kids did something that alcoholism and other failures, even losing my practice, couldn't do: it left me hopeless.

Despair is an awful state in which to sink. It affects all other areas of your life. You question your ability to succeed at anything. Diets, managing a checking account, holding down a real job, being a mother again.

Mostly being a mother again. Will I ever reach that stage where I feel I've done the best I could and my children are better for having me as their mother?

I don't know . . .

Markus tried to forget the taste of blood, the way his body hummed and buzzed after feeding from a human. Animals gave him energy, but nothing like the rush he got from the life-blood of a human, especially a healthy one. And now that he'd taken again from an innocent, he craved more. He closed his eyes against it.

While he tried to control his thirst, he also tried to close his mind to the image of what must surely be taking place at Carrie's home. By all accounts, Mr. Grayson was too busy for his daughter, but Markus had no doubt that he loved her and was tormented with grief.

Markus sat alone in the silence of his living room. He hadn't turned on any lights. He needed the solitude to regain control before reemerging into society.

A frantic knock at his door followed by a rapid ringing of the doorbell brought a deep growl to his throat. He sat, unmoving, waiting for whoever it was to go away.

"Markus!" Nina's voice. She pounded on the door.

Panic erupted inside Markus. Nina was the main reason he needed to control these cravings. She was the person he fought the hardest to resist. He didn't want her to die the way Kimana had died. Not if he still had a chance to make her his.

"Markus!" she shouted. "I know you're home. I see your cars in the drive. Open up, please. It's important."

He gathered as much fragile control as he could muster and went to the door. Nina nearly fell into his house when he opened the door, she was pounding against it so hard. "Nina. I'm sorry it took so long to answer."

She frowned. "You look terrible."

"I'm not feeling well." Her scent—blood, flesh, and sunshine—pounded into him. "I'm sorry. I can't ask you in."

"It's important. I'll risk illness."

Reluctantly, he stepped aside, and she entered his home. "What can I do for you?"

"Have you heard about Carrie Grayson?"

His gut tightened. "Carrie. The waitress at Barney's? What about her?"

"She was murdered last night."

"Another one?" He hoped he sounded convincing. "Found the same way as Amanda?" Markus fought the sudden rush of memory.

Nina nodded.

He could almost hear her heartbeat. "Nina, I'm truly sorry, but I have to go lie down. I think I have the flu." He opened the door for her, but she didn't move.

"Markus, listen to me! My daughter was the last person to see Carrie alive."

Not exactly. He shuddered with regret.

"Do the police think Meg had anything to do with it?" he asked.

"Not seriously. But Meg's missing."

Alarm struck him like a spear to the chest. "Missing? Since what time?"

"Sometime around 6 a.m., we think. We're looking for someone who might know the yoga instructor, but so far no one does. Or if they do, they're not coming clean about it. I thought you might have seen something. I-I've seen you through your window, and I know you're up all hours like I am."

He nodded slowly. "Now that you mention it, I saw a car pick her up at that time." He'd been watching out the window and had seen Eden's car. He'd assumed she was simply muscling him, trying to prove she could get to Nina if he didn't cooperate.

She'd certainly made good on her threat to go after Meg. Markus had no doubt the girl was dead. Whether he swooped in and tried to rescue her or not, Meg was gone. And he would lose Nina with her.

He didn't have much time to make his decision, but it wasn't a difficult choice. "I think I know where Meg is. We don't have a lot of time."

Nina grabbed his arm, her eyes wild. "You do? Where is she? Jill will be back any second."

"I'm not positive, but if she's where I think she is, we'd better go in quietly, just the two of us. We don't want Eden to feel cornered."

"Eden? So you do think it's the yoga instructor?"

"I know it was. I had no idea when I saw her

in your driveway. If I had, I might have been able to do something. I would have stopped her, Nina." He reached out to her. "Will you trust me?"

Meagan opened her eyes. Her head nearly exploded, and she was thankful for the dimness of the room. She sat up as her eyes adjusted to the dark and surveyed her surroundings. Fear struck at her heart, which beat loudly in her ears. Her head felt fuzzy, the way it did when she'd first woken up after having her appendix removed. Everything felt unreal and weird, even worse than the way the incense had affected her. She pressed her hand to her head. Even to her own touch she felt hot. At least her mom and dad had been there when she woke up in the hospital. Now she was alone, disoriented and afraid.

She lay on a small bed. Now that she was more awake, she realized the room wasn't all that spooky except that the lights weren't on. Meg turned on the lamp next to the bed and looked around. It looked like a regular bedroom. Neat, with a dresser, bed, nightstand, and bookcase.

She must have passed out, and Eden had brought her in here. She wondered what time it was. Like an idiot, she'd left her cell phone at home, and she never wore a watch. Nina was going to freak out, and her dad—she needed to get back to Aunt Jill's to meet her dad.

Meg went to the closed door and turned the knob, but it was locked. She couldn't find a way to release the lock. Eden would think she was a world-class moron, not able to figure out a door, but there was nothing to do but knock and try to get someone's attention. Surely one of the yoga students would hear and let her out. She raised her fist and knocked a couple times.

She finally heard a key being inserted into the lock from the outside. Frowning, Meg stepped back and waited. Why had they locked her in? Eden opened the door.

Meagan's eyes scanned the other woman. She was dressed in white, and the contrast between the thin white gown—more of a toga—and her dark skin was stark. The image struck a familiar chord. Eden looked exactly like she had in Meg's dream.

"Meg," Eden said. "I'm glad you're up. How are you feeling?" She pressed a cool hand to her head. Instinctively, Meg pulled back. She needed answers, not mothering.

"Eden, what's going on?" Meg asked.

"You, my dear, fell asleep in the car. We let you sleep because you're still running a fever. Paul from class carried you in. Do you feel up to drinking some juice? We have a good blend that will replace those nutrients you sweated out."

"Eden, I need to get home. My dad is here, and we're having breakfast. What time is it?"

"Around ten. But that's not what's important right now."

"Ten! Eden, my mom is going to kill me."

Eden smiled and slipped her arm around Meg's shoulders. "Come into the kitchen and have some juice. You'll feel better. I've already contacted your mother, and everything is fine."

Meg's legs felt trembly. She allowed herself to be led out of the room, down a hallway, and into the kitchen.

"You sit right down, and I'll get you some of that juice," Eden said.

"You said you called Nina?" Meg asked. "What did she say about me being late?" As if she couldn't imagine what *that* conversation was like.

"Just that you could stay as long as you needed. Between you and me, I think she was relieved that she could have some time alone with your dad."

Meg tried to shove away the hand that clutched her heart, squeezing painfully, trying to make her cry. That was just like Nina. Always thinking about herself.

Eden set a glass of juice in front of her. "Now as soon as you finish that, come into the other room. I'm about to start a new class."

"Maybe I'll grab a ride home with someone from the last class." She glanced at the clock. It was almost ten-thirty. "Is anyone still here? I'd

337

like to get back and see my dad. He's a doctor. He might have some antibiotics or something on him."

"No. They're all gone. You can go after this class is over."

Meg frowned. Who did this woman think she was? Meg was perfectly free to go anytime she pleased. "I guess I could walk."

"With the flu?" Eden's lips twitched with amusement. "Honey, don't be difficult. You wouldn't get half a mile before you keeled over. As soon as we're finished, we'll take care of you, okay? Be a good girl and drink your juice, and I'll see you in a few minutes." She bent and pressed a kiss to Meg's forehead.

Meg watched her go. She reached up and wiped the kiss away like a five-year-old.

Meg sat back in the chair and sipped the juice. She glanced around at the earthy kitchen, painted in shades of beige and tan. Just what she would have expected of Eden.

She jammed her chin into her palm as her elbow rested on the table. Eden was being sort of nervy, forcing her to stay until she decided Meg could leave.

Meg stood. No one was going to tell her what to do. She walked the glass of sour juice to the sink and dumped it. A buzzing sound caught her attention. She glanced around the kitchen, following the sound as it buzzed again. Eden's bag sat on the counter, slouched over, its contents threatening to spill onto the floor, including the buzzing phone.

She waffled. Normally, she'd never go through someone's purse, but this phone was buzzing in plain view and about to vibrate right onto the ground. The next buzz settled it. She snatched it up.

The phone was only vibrating to let Eden know she had messages.

Meg turned the phone over in her hand. Eden had the same phone as Carrie. *Actually . . .*

She noticed a heart sticker on the back of the phone. This *was* Carrie's phone. But Carrie had texted her. How was that possible if she didn't have her phone?

Meg wrapped her fingers around the phone and walked into the smoky, incense-filled room, where a dozen men and women held their bodies contorted in such a way that they looked like Cirque du Soleil performers. In the corner, a small man wearing tights and a tank top sat on a mat, accompanying the class with a bamboo flute.

"Keep your core tight," Eden said, her voice a hum. "Hips up, Brandy. Beautiful. Now breathe."

Meg walked up to Eden and opened her mouth, but only a squeak came out as she started to demand an explanation. Eden held a finger to her own lips and shook her head.

Meg coughed as the incense caught the back of her already raw throat. She walked to the far end of the room and slid down the wall until she sat, legs crossed. Her head swam. She closed her eyes, listening to the hum of Eden's soft instructions to the class and the light trill of the flute. Next to her, a stack of rolled-up mats seemed to beckon. She took one, lay down, and used it as a pillow.

As blackness welcomed her, Meg thought about how, as soon as Eden's class ended, she planned to give the teacher a piece of her mind.

Something wasn't right. Often over the past three months, Nina had dreamed that she was drinking wine and awakened to find with relief that it had been nothing more than a nightmare. But this wasn't like that.

In fear and heartbreak, she searched her foggy brain for the moment when she'd succumbed to that first drink, but she couldn't locate the memory. So why this intoxication?

She lay on a damp surface. She shivered and tried to answer the dozen questions rolling around her brain, tried to remember anything that might give her a clue as to what had brought her to this moment.

It took great effort to pry her eyes open the merest slit.

"Don't be afraid." A voice soothed her.

"Hunt?"

"No." The voice turned frigid.

"Markus?"

Now she remembered. They were on their way to find Meg. She tried to sit up, but pain pounded in her head as though she were being beaten by a thousand clubs. She surrendered to the pain and laid her head back down. "Where are we? Where's Meg?"

"I'm sorry I had to deceive you, Nina. I didn't mean for this to happen. I wanted . . . well, it doesn't matter what I wanted. Eden forced me to this."

"Markus," Nina groaned, "make sense, please. My head is bursting. What are you doing? Where's Meg?"

"Meg is with Eden. There's nothing you can do for her. More than likely, she's dead already. If not, it's only because Eden has other plans for her. Either way, you've lost her."

"What are you talking about?" Nina tried to wrap her head around the realization that he had lied, that they weren't going to find Meg. He had kidnapped her. "What do you mean there's nothing I can do for Meg?"

How could she have been so stupid? She'd known this man for less than a week, and she'd thrown her trust over to him, allowed him to lure her from the safety of Jill and Hunt to . . . here. Wherever she was.

"What did you give me?" she asked. "It wasn't alcohol, was it?"

"No. But I have some brandy here if you'd like a glass."

She'd give anything for a glass of brandy right now. So much so that she could actually taste it on her tongue, feel the burn at the back of her throat. She tightened her fists, fighting the desire until her nails bit into her palms and gave her the tiniest bit of control.

"What's going on? Why have you brought me here?" she demanded, both to distract him and to distract herself.

"Don't you recognize it?" Markus asked. "We've been here before."

"Recognize it? I can't see anything."

"I'm sorry about that."

She heard a crack, and a strange green glow filled the area. Nina looked at the stone wall rising up next to her and the leaf-strewn floor on which she lay. Markus sat a few feet away from her.

"I have some glow sticks," he said, lifting the glowing rod in his hand. "I can't build a fire in the cave. It isn't ventilated well enough."

Nina forced herself to sit up. "Listen. I don't know what you're thinking, but please, I need to go look for my daughter. Let me go, Markus."

He smiled, which looked odd in the dim glow of the synthetic light. "I would if it could possibly make any difference, Nina. Trust me."

"Trust you?" Anger flared inside her. "Did you say that to me earlier? Right before you drugged and kidnapped me? What are we doing in a cave anyway?" She gasped. "Oh no. You're the murderer?"

She saw herself lying on the ground like the deer on the General's reserve. Blood drained, cross-shaped markings on her chest and throat. Dead.

"No," Markus said, shaking his head. "I'm not. I swear I had nothing to do with Amanda or the animals around here. Not the ones found in the open."

"You left out Carrie. What did you have to do with her death?"

He moved so quickly, her heart didn't have time to move to the next beat before he was in front of her, almost nose to nose. She could feel the cool of his breath on her face, her neck.

"I didn't mean to," he said fiercely. "She was forced upon me."

Nina listened as he explained, horrified, trying to wrap her half-fuzzy brain around the images his words conjured. Fear nearly exploded inside her. He was too close.

"What are you saying, Markus?" Her voice trembled. "You're a Satanist? You drink blood?" Oh, Lord. Meg. Where was Meg?

He sat back on the cave floor. She remained

tense. "I'm not a Satanist," he said. "I don't have any religion. Although I wish . . . If I could believe something, maybe I wouldn't need you."

"Markus, please. Let's go—"

He heaved a sigh. "You know the story I told you about Pierre Lafitte?"

Nina closed her eyes, her heart nearly erupting in panic. Her daughter was God-knew-where, and Markus wanted to talk about a legend.

"I'm Pierre Lafitte," he said.

She rested her head against the cave wall, her eyes still closed. "Well, that sounds about right."

"You believe me? Just like that?"

"Charles Manson thought he was Jesus Christ, so I guess someone thinking he's a reincarnated vampire isn't too far-fetched."

"You're mocking me."

Nina opened her eyes and met his angry gaze. "I don't mean to mock, but my daughter is in danger, and you think you're a vampire. I don't know what else to say. I honestly thought you were a good guy."

"Nina, the story I told you is true. I'm a vampire. A 250-year-old vampire who was lured into feeding on Carrie. But I didn't kill her. Eden did. I stopped myself before draining the life from her."

"I admire the restraint." Nina was terrified that her baby girl might have already become the next victim and that she was soon to follow. She determined that the first chance she saw, she would run for it. She didn't seem to have anything to lose.

"I killed Kimana's father in the woods that day because I knew he would go back and tell the village about my father and the evil inside him. He would have told my people that I followed him into the woods to kill him and that I too lusted after blood. Although at that time, I had yet to give in."

Nina stared. "You truly believe everything you're saying to me."

"It's the truth."

"No, it isn't. Markus, listen to me. You're sick. You need help. Let me go so I can find Meg, and I'll vouch for you with the police."

He gave her a sad look. "I know you don't believe me now, but you will."

"Is that a threat?"

"No. Let me tell the rest of my story, Nina. I need you to hear it."

Nina scanned the cave for anything that might deliver a knockout blow. It was impossible not to imagine Meg, imagine the worst. Her heart nearly beat its way out of her chest in panic. She had to get out of here. Meg was still alive. Nina could feel it. Wouldn't a mother know if her child were dead?

"Beshup was the first human I fed upon,"

Markus continued. "It was like being born. Afterward, I disposed of the body, cleaned up in the river, and returned to the village. Beshup's disappearance fostered a lot of fear and excitement. We searched for him but of course never found him. After an appropriate mourning period, I redoubled my efforts to win Kimana's heart, but Beshup had not been lying when he revealed he had spoken with his daughter about the evil that resided in me. She would not even consider allowing my attentions. Each day I grew more frustrated, until finally I knew what must be done."

"Let me guess," Nina said. "You drugged her and carried her off to a cave."

"I didn't drug her. But otherwise, yes. I had no intention of harming her, but she would not see reason. Finally, I could resist no more. I wanted her for my wife. To love her, father her children, raise a family in our village. But she wouldn't consider it."

"So you killed her."

He nodded, sorrowfully it seemed. "In my effort to woo her, I became amorous. She would not respond. I couldn't have her, and in my frustration, instinct took over. The next thing I knew, she was dead."

Nina didn't know what she found most disturbing—that he believed so firmly in his story, or that he truly seemed devastated by telling it.

"I wandered for years alone, feeding when I needed to, but loathing my existence every moment. And then not long after the Civil War, I met Eden."

"Eden. So she's an old vampire as well?"

"She isn't as old as I am. Her mother was a slave and her father—"

"Was the master."

"Yes. Please, Nina, just listen." He paused a moment to make sure she would obey, then continued. "Eden fascinated me from the moment I met her in St. Louis. I had lived a terrible existence for nearly a century. I had tried to commit suicide many times, to no avail. When I met Eden, everything changed. She was like me. Her vampirism had come down through her father's side, but she was something more. Her mother practiced the black arts. Voodoo, demon worship. She was truly someone to fear and admire. And she wanted me."

"Lucky you."

"Yes," he said, as though the sarcasm swept over him without entering his consciousness. "And for a time, it was enough. I never participated in her rituals. When I fed, it was because I could no longer resist. I need blood to sustain me. When she fed, it was done for more power."

"More power?"

"Eden's vampirism combined with her mother's voodoo makes her very powerful. She is magical in a way most humans who crave darkness only dream of."

The caustic humor drained out of Nina. His words were beginning to ring too much like the terrifying truth.

"If Eden was such a fascination, why aren't the two of you together?" she asked. "Or is this the way you lure new prey? You move into a town and scope it out before inviting her?"

Markus looked toward the cave entrance, his eyes far away. "The first time I left her, we had been lovers for over forty years."

"Why did you leave?"

"I was tired of the sport. Tired of Eden. Tired of the wild blood lust she adored."

"Says the vampire," Nina scoffed.

He turned toward her. "Not vampire by choice. I was born to it."

"You can't tell the alcoholic daughter of an alcoholic that you had no choice. Especially one who has been sober for several months."

He let out a slow breath. "If only it were that simple."

Nina shook her head. "Simple," he'd said.

"I was born in this part of the Ozarks," he continued. He hardly seemed to be talking to her anymore. "Raised here with the Osage, until I fled. Years later, when I returned, there were only white settlers where my home had once been. My people had been driven out. The buffalo were largely gone. I settled into the life of a normal man, feeding on animals and the occasional outlaw or abusive husband. Never the innocent."

"And you're qualified to judge guilt or innocence because . . . ?"

He shrugged. "Inherent right and wrong, perhaps. I justified it because I wasn't consumed by evil the way Eden was. I only wanted to be alone." He paused. "Eden found me again after a few years, and I gave in to her persuasion once again until I couldn't bear it. I have been free of her for thirty-five years, living in this cave for half that time, knowing she was looking for me."

Nina registered the impact of his words. "You moved into this cave around the time I was born. You lived here all those years? How were you not discovered at some point?"

"I'm good at hiding. Patient."

Nina struggled to absorb everything he'd told her. "So Eden has found you yet again. She killed Amanda and Carrie, and now she has my daughter. Does that sum things up?"

"Precisely."

His short answer elicited a dark fear in Nina. So dark that panic erupted. She had to get out of there. Hunt had no idea what was going on. With both of them missing, he'd be frantic. She had to get to the bottom of Markus's plans even if his plans meant disaster for her. Better to know what she was up against. "All right. Then what are your plans for me? Because I need to go after the crazy vampire witch who has my daughter." She turned and began crawling toward the cave entrance.

"My plan is to keep you safe."

His words stopped Nina midcrawl. "Safe from what?"

"Eden. If I don't go back to her, she'll kill you."

"That's seems a little unfair, considering I'm no one to either of you."

Markus seemed to hesitate for a second. "You're someone to me. And she knows it."

"How could I be a threat to her? You don't even know me."

"I do. I brought you here once before. I've known you for lifetimes."

He was crazy. "You brought me here?"

"Yes. Seventeen years ago. You and Stephan were fighting."

"That night?" A gasp tore at her throat. "That was real?"

"I've been waiting for you for seventeen years, Nina. Eden sensed it when I first encountered her here in Abbey Hills."

"So you've been waiting to kidnap me?"

He shook his head. "My preference has always been to win your heart, for you to love me just as I am and stay with me out of choice."

Nina didn't think her heart could beat any faster, but it did. "Markus, you don't have any idea what love is."

"But I need you, Nina. You are my chance to have something beautiful in this cursed life. My second chance—my Kimana."

Considering what had happened to his Kimana, Nina wasn't comforted.

She crawled across the cave until she reached him. "Listen to me, Markus. I have to save my daughter."

He reached forward and tenderly cupped her cheek as though soothing a child. "I'm sorry."

She forced herself to cover his hand with hers. "You want me to come with you of my own free will? I will. I swear I will. If you help me save my daughter's life, I will go wherever you want me to go. I'll be your Kimana. And I'll never try to run away. You won't have to force me with tricks or worry about me telling anyone what you are. You can have me."

He didn't respond.

"At least let me contact Hunt," she pleaded, unable to keep the desperation out of her voice. "Let me tell him where our daughter is. He'll go after her. He'll save her, and I'll come with you. You won't have to keep me drugged or anything. We'll have a good life for as long as I live. As long as you save my daughter. Otherwise you'll have to kill me. I will not be yours. You can beat me, bite me, or kill me, but I will never give up trying to run."

He stared at her in the dim light of the glow stick as though trying to weigh her words. "If I allow you to walk into Eden's home, you will be killed," he said.

"Maybe," she replied. "But at least I will have tried to save my daughter. I'll die trying."

~

After our talk with Mr. Grayson garnered no leads, Stephan and I headed back to Jill's house. Nina's car was in the driveway, but Nina was nowhere to be found. According to Jill, Nina had never met her at the house as planned. I suspect the pressure drove her back to her old ways. I hate the thought. I don't want her to fail. She's doing so well. Or she was.

Stephan and Jill begin to search the outskirts of town. They've gotten a few leads of strange activity. Not sure it will pan out, but they're going to look for Meg while I search for Nina. I can't help it. I need to find her.

I drive through the streets of Abbey Hills and along the rural roads, scouring every bar and liquor store. Everywhere an alcoholic might go to numb the pain and escape the fearsome reality of her missing daughter. Nina's father sits in the passenger seat, pointing the way, a veteran at locating these sorts of places, though he stays in the Durango at each stop.

"Even after all these years," he says. "I'm one mistake away from starting all over again."

I understand, I assure him. And he assures me he will do whatever it takes to find his daughter.

"I led her down this road." The regret in his voice stabs at my heart, but I'm concerned about my own daughter. And Nina. I don't have much in the way of comfort for him, and I don't believe he expects it.

As I pull into each site, I pray I won't find Nina. Not in the places I'm searching.

I search the last bar Nina's father can think of, thankful she's not here. As I slide back into the Durango, I close my eyes and pray. I pray for Meg. For Nina.

I remember Nina's declaration of a few months ago. "If God would show up, just once, I'd be His." In my heart, I remind God that she spoke those words, and I ask Him to use this awful situation as an opportunity to show up for Nina.

Please help us find our Meggie, Lord.

And Nina. Where is she?

CHAPTER TWENTY

Epiphany: appearance of a god; the manifestation of a divine being.

At the end of every lesson, there should be an epiphany. That moment when you finally understand and everything falls into place. Unfortunately, I've never been a very good test taker.

Life tests go without saying. They are what they are, and there's no escaping. Not if you really want to fulfill a purpose, a destiny. For too long, the meaning of life for me came in a bottle filled with 750 milliliters of wine. And when that was gone, life stopped.

I want life again, but not the kind found in a buzz. Something real. The kind only a divine being, only that higher power, can deliver.

If only He shows up.

That's my epiphany.

When Meg awakened, the guy was still playing the flute in the corner. She opened her eyes and slowly sat up; she felt dizzy. Light from the candles flickered on the wall, making animal shapes. Wait. The guy was gone. It was a girl this time. Meg looked at the yoga class. Different students. She stood on shaky legs. Her body felt leaden, and she struggled to walk forward.

Enough was enough. She wanted to find her dad and give Carrie back her phone. Where was that phone, anyway? She had it a little while ago. Meg blinked, trying to focus, and stared at the floor where she'd been lying. No sign of the phone.

She turned to Eden, whose soft voice carried through the room with that soothing hum that had lulled her to sleep earlier. Meg wasn't going to be sucked in by it anymore.

She was leaving. But first she was getting Carrie's phone back. She stood up and moved to the front of the room, but the instructor hadn't acknowledged her.

"Eden!"

"Shh. Meg we're in the middle of a class." Her eyes held Meg, transfixed. She shook her head. "Don't be rude."

"Where is Carrie's phone?"

"Well, I don't know. You'll have to ask Carrie." She motioned toward the wall. "Now, go sit down. You're not well."

Meg planted her feet despite her spinning head. She was getting that phone and leaving whether Eden liked it or not. Even if she had to beg one of the yoga students to help her. "I saw Carrie's phone. How could she have texted me this morning right before you picked me up from my aunt's house if her phone was with you?"

"Carrie and I have the same model. We are constantly mixing them up. I assure you, the one you retrieved from my purse," she said pointedly, making Meg squirm a little, "was and is mine. Not Carrie's."

Doubt crept in at Eden's confident tone. "Well, then you can keep it," Meg said, "but I'm going back to Aunt Jill's to see my dad and mom."

She backed out of the room and headed toward the front door.

Eden followed. The older woman grabbed Meg's arm. "Don't you think you should wait until I can drive you home?" she asked.

"I don't think you ever will. I think you've kidnapped me."

The woman's laugh didn't come close to her eyes and barely touched her lips. "To what end, darling?"

Meg sprang for the door, but Eden stepped in front of her.

"Don't waste your time, Meg. It's locked and needs a key."

Meg's mouth dropped open. "So I'm kidnapped for real?"

"Kidnapped is such an ugly word."

"*Kidnapped* is me not getting to leave and go home to my mom and dad."

Eden reached forward and smoothed Meg's hair. "Shh. Don't get excited. You're still running a fever. You're confused."

Meg jerked away and stumbled on shaky legs to the other room. Her mind felt fuzzy. All she could think of was getting away from Eden.

The yoga class had stopped, and everyone stared. Meg rushed to the first person she saw, a pretty fortyish woman with graying blond hair and mismatched workout clothes. "I need help," she said. "Please. Will you drive me home?" Tears warbled her words. "My mom and dad are probably scared."

The woman gave her a sympathetic smile. "I'm sorry, hon." Everyone else averted their gaze from her.

"Are you people kidding me?"

Eden stepped forward. "They know I'm your true mother."

Meg sucked in a breath. "Are you crazy? I have a mom."

"One who neglected you; she hurts you. One who didn't want you around today."

"I don't believe that." Meg scowled. "Nina would have insisted I be home to have breakfast with her and my dad. She brought me Tylenol and water and tucked me in." Meg's voice trembled. She wished more than anything that she had asked Nina to stay until she fell asleep. Her smoke-fuzzed, fever-ravaged brain fought to understand the implications. She shook her head. "It doesn't matter. I have to go home."

"You don't even call her mom," Eden said. "She's Nina to you. You know I understand you. I know how badly you need a real mother. Come with me, Meg. You'll be happier than you've ever dreamed."

Meg backed up. "You're crazy." She looked around at the catatonic group. "You're all crazy, mindless idiots. This woman is holding me against my will, and no one is helping me. All of you are going to be in big trouble when my aunt, *Sheriff* Parker, hears about this." She backed up another step, and Eden advanced.

"Don't you dare come any closer." Meg backed one more step, and her elbow caught the edge of a candle. It tipped and dropped to the ground before she could grab it and landed on the bottom of a curtain. The flames spread almost instantly, crawling up the old fabric. Two men raced forward and tried to pull the curtain down, but it was too late. A rug on the wood floor had caught, and the fire was spreading.

Eden's eyes widened in rage. She made a grab for Meg, but Meg ducked, evading her. "You idiot!" Eden shouted. "I should have killed you instead of trying to make your life better!"

Meagan twisted past Eden and ran deeper into the heart of the house. She had no idea where she was going. She just knew she had to get away from Eden.

Sweat dampened Nina's palms as Markus drove down the gravel road, presumably toward Eden's hideout.

Hang on, Meggie. Hang on.

Markus had stopped and filled up several gas cans before they left town. The only way to stop Eden, he'd said, was to cut off her head or burn her, and he doubted they'd get close enough to her to cut off her head.

True to her word, Nina had kept quiet. She hadn't done anything to draw attention to herself.

"Geez, you planning on burning down your house for the insurance?" the twenty-year-old kid behind the counter asked with a laugh.

"Well, it wouldn't be very smart to buy all this gasoline in broad daylight if that were the case, would it?" Markus replied.

"Naw. I was just kiddin'."

Markus smiled. "For our generator. The weatherman called for storms tonight, and we want to be prepared in case of a power outage."

"Good thinking."

A few miles from town, Markus parked his Lexus in a grove of trees. "The house is about an eighth of a mile straight ahead through the woods. It's doubtful we'll have the element of surprise. In the short amount of time Eden has lived in Abbey Hills, she's already gained followers. Enough that we'll be lucky to make it out alive."

Nina kicked open her door.

"Wait."

Nina stopped. "What?"

He pointed toward the house. "There's already a fire. Let's go."

With her heart lodged firmly in her throat, Nina ran behind Markus. The house's front door flew open just as they reached the porch, and a group of people dressed in athletic clothing streamed out.

Nina grabbed a young woman whose eyes were wide with fright. "I'm looking for my daughter. She has dark curly hair. Her name's Meagan." The woman stared and tried to pull away, but Nina held her fast. "Listen to me. Is she in there? That's my daughter!"

"I didn't have anything to do with it. I was only here for yoga."

Nina grabbed her by the shoulders and shook. "What do you mean? You didn't have anything to do with what?"

"There was a girl in there trying to get out, but Eden wouldn't let her go."

"And no one tried to help?"

"I'm sorry. Let me go." The petite woman pulled away and ran off.

Nina turned, expecting to find Markus waiting, but he was gone. She slammed through the door. Smoke filled the foyer, and flames engulfed a room off to the right. "Meg!" she called, burying her face in the crook of her elbow.

Someone grabbed her arm. Nina jerked her head around and found Markus's stormy gaze. "Nina," he said, "get outside before you're killed."

"Not until I find Meg."

"Markus," a soft voice spoke.

Nina turned, and her eyes found a woman who could only be Eden.

Shoving Markus aside, Nina stepped up to the other vampire. She raised her chin in order to meet the woman's gaze, but she wasn't going to be intimidated when her daughter's life was at stake. "Where is she?"

Eden sneered and laughed. "Who—Meg? She started the fire and ran off."

"Ran off where? Outside or inside?" Panic filled Nina as the smoke grew thicker.

"That way." Eden waved toward a room clogged with black smoke, then turned to Markus. "Let's leave these weak humans to their fire and go. Come with me. Please, Markus."

"No." His short answer brought a flash of

fury to Eden's face. "Come on, Nina. Let's go find your daughter."

Nina started to turn, but caught a glimpse of movement from the corner of her eye as Eden pulled something from her waistband. Nina tensed but didn't have time to call out a warning.

With a screech, Eden flung herself at Markus, and they tumbled to the ground. Nina saw the flash of a blade as Eden raised it high and plunged it toward Markus. He moved, but Nina had no idea whether the knife found its target.

Nina had to let him fend for himself. Meg needed her. She took her opportunity and fled into the heavy smoke and flames. She could hardly see as she made her way through the room to a door on the other side.

"Meg! Where are you?"

Frantically, Nina searched each room. The fire was beginning to spread, and she could hear the wood beginning to crackle. She rushed into a lushly decorated office near the back stairs. The room contained a bay window with a window seat. The pillows were flung on the floor.

And suddenly, Nina knew she'd found her daughter.

The moment felt surreal and unbidden, as a memory slid across her mind's eye. It was the first night she and Meg spent in their apartment in an old boarding house before Hunt came into their lives. Meg was only four at the time. She had gone missing, and Nina searched everywhere until she finally found her, curled up inside the window seat, sound asleep.

"Meg!" she called and lifted the seat.

Relief nearly left her faint at the sight of her daughter's tear-stained cheeks. Meg looked up with enormous brown eyes, and once again, she was Nina's little girl. Nina reached in and took her by the hand. "Come on, Meggie. We have to get out of here. The fire is spreading fast."

"She kidnapped me. I-I think she did something to Carrie. She has her phone."

Nina's breath stilled. "Listen, the first thing we have to do is get you to a safe place. We'll let Aunt Jill deal with Eden."

"What if she's waiting for me? Everyone was scared to help me."

"Markus is taking care of Eden." Nina tugged on her hand until Meg sat up. "That's my girl. Let's go."

They reached the doorway. Thick smoke curled around them. Nina took Meg in her arms and covered the girl's face, leading her from the room.

"I saw the back door when I came in this room," Nina said. "We can make it. I need you to drop down and crawl before the smoke gets to us." Meg did as she was told, and Nina dropped down beside her. "Stay next to me, keep your legs against mine so I can make sure you're with me, and crawl. The hall is wide enough. We're almost there."

They crawled and felt their way down the hallway. Nina's lungs were so thick and heavy she wasn't sure she could make it. She just wanted to lie down and rest her head on her arms.

"Mom! Keep going," Meg cried, shaking Nina's shoulder.

Nina hadn't known she'd stopped.

Ahead the door opened. Nina realized Meg was pulling her from the house. She gathered enough strength to crawl onto the back porch and down the steps. They stumbled to the yard and collapsed on the grass.

They sat together, staring at the engulfed house, holding each other tight.

They wouldn't make it out of there. He wouldn't anyway. The flames were too hot. Fire could kill them. Plus, Eden's dagger had sliced deep enough that there would be no healing. She might as well have beheaded him. This was just a slower, more agonizing way to die.

Markus closed his eyes, ready for the end.

Eden sat on her knees next to him. The smoke was so heavy he could barely see her.

"Markus, the dagger . . ."

"I know. It's deep."

"Too deep. I-I didn't mean to stab you there. But you moved."

"I know, Eden. It's over. You did me a favor. I'm ready to find something different. Something beautiful."

"No. I can't let you die." Eden's voice choked with tears. The smoke couldn't hurt her, but the fire could. Markus knew instinctively what her plan was.

If he replenished the blood pouring out of his throat, he would live. Eden knew that. Markus steeled himself.

"Get up, Markus." Eden yanked him to a sitting position. Her strength was twice his at the moment. "We're going outside to find you a human, and you will drink."

Markus pushed her away and fell back to the floor. "No, I won't. You can try, but I'll never hurt another human being."

She screeched in frustration. "It's because of her! If you die, I will kill her. I won't rest until she dies. You have no choice. Either you get up and live, or she dies."

Markus knew his blood was almost gone. He would soon be free. Free from this life, anyway. He had no idea what lay beyond for him. He only hoped whatever it was would bring peace.

The ceiling and walls around them were engulfed with flames. He reached over and took Eden by the hand. "Come here," he said, barely above a whisper. "I need to tell you something."

"What is it, Markus? I don't have a lot of time. I must take you outside." She bent closer to him and tilted her head so that she could hear.

She was so intent on saving him, she didn't even notice how close she was to death. Eden had always thought herself invincible. Her pride would be her fall.

The ceiling began to give way. Eden turned. Her scream tore through the inferno.

"Markus!"

Markus summoned all of his strength, grabbed her, and held fast.

The ceiling collapsed, raining fire on their heads.

Nina and Meg walked around to the front of the burning house just as the roof began to collapse. Nina didn't look back into the flames, afraid to see Markus burning, but she felt a tremendous weight on her heart. He had saved them. He had sacrificed himself for her daughter.

The fire department arrived. Jill followed close behind, and as the squad car came to a halt, Hunt jumped out of the passenger side.

Meg ran to him and fell into his arms, sobbing against his chest.

Jill caught Nina in tight a hug. "Thank God you're both safe. What happened?"

"You won't believe me," Nina said, "but I'll tell you after things settle down. Eden killed

Carrie. You should know that. And neither she nor Markus Chisom made it out of the house alive."

Jill's eyes grew wide. "You'll fill me in later?"

"Give me a little while. Then I will." She coughed and felt the thick tears in her eyes.

Hunt looked at Nina over Meg's head. "An ambulance is on its way."

Meg pulled out of Hunt's arms and came to stand next to Nina. "Mom saved me." Her calm, confident words spread like salve over Nina's heart.

"I'm fine," Nina said. "Meg should get checked out for sure though."

Hunt stepped forward. He took Nina tenderly by her shoulders and looked down into her eyes. "I think you should get checked out too."

"Mom saved my life, Daddy," Meg said excitedly. "You should have seen her."

Nina smiled. "We saved each other's lives, I think."

"She was a hero," Meg insisted. "You know you were, Mom, so don't deny it."

Hunt pulled Nina close. Tears came, and like Meg, in Hunt's arms she sobbed out her fear and frustration of the last few hours. She felt his hand cup her head and stroke her hair. "Shh. You did it, Nina. Everything is okay. Meg's safe." She pulled back and wiped at her eyes. He reached forward and kissed her forehead. "Let's go."

Hunt slipped his arm around her as they walked, nestling her into his side.

Peace enveloped Nina. She leaned in and spoke close to his ear. "God showed up."

EPILOGUE

As far as weddings went in Abbey Hills, Jill's to Barney was pretty status quo. The community church was filled to capacity, and the reverend officiated. Flowers filled the front of the church, and bubbles were blown over the couple as they walked out together into the blustery autumn day. Barney's buddies and half the town's teenagers had participated in decorating Barney's Jeep Cherokee with cans, shaving cream, and a Just Married sign.

Nina stood next to Hunt and watched the Jeep drive away. Everyone would meet at Barney's for a quick reception, and then the happy couple was off to Florida so Barney could see Disney World. All in all, a perfect day for a wedding. Of course, when you were in love, almost every day was perfect.

Adam had grown five inches, it seemed, since spring. Though Nina had seen him a few times, each meeting seemed to follow a growth spurt. The boy was growing up in snatches of time.

Reverend Bradley shook Hunt's hand.

"Good ceremony, Landon," Nina said.

"Well, they made it easy." He chuckled. Nina

loved that about her pastor. His easygoing smile and ability to look past . . . well, the past. His eyes found her. "We're without a singer for Sunday morning since your sister's gone. You going to fill in for her?"

Hunt chortled, and Nina smacked him. "Don't be insulting." To Landon she said, "Trust me. You don't want me to sing. But I'll be there."

Landon beamed. "We'll see you then."

Nina had made the decision to remain in Abbey Hills. With relative ease, she'd obtained a Missouri veterinary license and opened a small business in the extra cabin at the reserve. It had taken her a month to get it cleaned out. The General was no help at all.

His gentle goading, however, had finally convinced Nina to try out a Sunday service, and she hadn't missed one since. That was four months ago. She was slowly beginning to find the God she had been looking for since she was ten years old. The reverend encouraged her to keep seeking, keep asking, keep knocking, and he assured her that, eventually, some sort of clarity would come. And he'd been right. Like living sober, knowing God was a process.

As for Stephan and Meg, they had fallen into an easy camaraderie, but each acknowledged a friendship was all there could ever be between them. Their relationship consisted of e-mails, phone calls, and lunch when Meg visited Nina.

Everyone seemed okay with it, so Nina had stopped fretting.

"You ready?" Hunt asked her. "I can't believe Barney is catering his own reception."

Nina laughed. "I'd have been surprised if he'd left it up to anyone else."

"Are your parents riding over with us?"

Nina nodded.

Healing wasn't something that happened overnight, but Nina's relationship with her parents was proof that it could eventually happen. One day at a time. Between Sunday dinners together and constant updates about Meg or Adam's most recent e-mail, Nina and her parents managed to communicate every couple of days.

It was okay. For Nina, life was rolling along at an even pace. She found comfort in the day to day.

"Hey." Hunt tugged on her hand.

"Yeah?" She grinned.

"Come back. You seem like you're a million miles away."

"Just thinking." She angled her gaze and looked up at him. "Did you know that today is my nine-month anniversary of sobriety?"

"Well, then . . ." He bent and touched a soft kiss to her lips.

The action sent a thrill through her. She lifted her brow. "What's up with that?"

He grinned. "Nine months is a big accomplishment. I thought it deserved a kiss."

"A kiss? I'm honored."

"You're doing great."

Nina felt tall with the praise. She rested her head against his shoulder and relaxed. She was willing to wait for however long it took to regain his trust. She knew he loved her, but they were taking things slow. She needed this time to discover herself again, to build into the woman she was growing to be. But that didn't mean she didn't enjoy a well-placed kiss every now and then.

As if he heard her thoughts, Hunt pulled her close. "It occurs to me how much I miss having my arms around you."

She tilted her head and looked up at him, a smile tipping her lips. "Interesting. The same thing occurs to me."

He dipped his head. "It also occurs to me how much I miss this." He lowered his head until his lips touched hers again. Only this time, there was nothing light to his kiss. He pressed her close, and Nina's arms slipped up over his shoulders.

One thing she'd learned—she could stand alone. She battled her demons daily, and so far, every day she was winning. It wasn't easy to make good choices when she'd been making poor ones for so long, but with each right decision, she gained the strength to forge ahead to the next right decision. And even though sometimes the path twisted and she took a step or two in the wrong direction, getting back on track was becoming easier and easier.

She'd made the decision to be strong and confident and to find serenity. And in this moment, in Hunt's arms, watching her children laughing and smiling, she suddenly realized it felt like Christmas.

DISCUSSION QUESTIONS

1. Nina's struggle with alcoholism taints everything in her life. It destroyed her career and her relationship with her family. Trying to rebuild her life is the hardest thing she's ever done, especially with temptation lurking behind every confrontation and choice. Do you relate to Nina's struggle? Is there something in your own life that you've fought the way Nina fights her addiction to alcohol? How did you feel when she nearly succumbs? when she triumphs?

2. At the beginning of each chapter, Nina relates a piece of her childhood. How do you think these events led to the woman Nina is today? Did seeing these glimpses into her past affect your perception of her?

3. Much of the book centers on Nina's discomfort with returning to her childhood home and confronting her past. What would returning to the scene of your childhood be like for you? What things do you hope would have changed, and what things do you hope would be the same?

4. Markus's obsession with Nina grows out of her resemblance to the wife he loved—and killed. He is drawn to her and wants to possess her, but in the end, he gives his own life to save hers. Do you think he truly loved her? Does his sacrifice bring him redemption in your eyes?

5. Markus tells Nina his history by presenting it as a local legend. How does his origin affect your perception of vampires? of Markus's choices in life? What can we determine about our role in our personal choices—how much is determined by nature versus our free will?

6. In contrast to Markus, Hunt is depicted as having a steadfast love for Nina. Yet he divorces her when her alcoholism takes over. Do you think he made the right choice? Should he have stood by her no matter what? What would you have done in his situation?

7. Meg's relationship with Nina is strained, and she seems to want nothing to do with her mother. How did you feel toward Meg while reading the book? Do you think her anger toward Nina is justified? What could Nina have done differently to repair their relationship? What could Meg have done differently?

8. Do you think Nina could have handled the situation with Stephan in a better manner? How would you have responded if you believed what she did? Did you sympathize with his desire to be in Meg's life?

9. After the night of the graduation party, Nina left home without telling her parents where she was going. She felt unloved throughout her childhood and still feels bitterness toward her parents. She has little desire to see them again when she returns to Abbey Hills. In what ways do Nina and her parents misunderstand each other? How much of Nina's pain and anger is warranted?

10. As the other vampire in the novel, how does Eden differ from Markus? Why has she pursued Markus all these years? With her charismatic personality, Eden collects followers wherever she goes. What parallels can we draw between her and dangers in our own world?

11.   Nina's belief in God hinges on him "show- ing up." At the beginning of the novel, she doesn't believe because God has never shown up for her, but by the end of the novel, she tells Hunt that He has. In what ways did God "show up" for Nina? Can you trace His

hand through her journey? What role did the General, Hunt, Markus, and Nina's family play in her path to faith?

12. In what ways does Markus's vampirism parallel Nina's alcoholism? How does he fight temptation, and what happens when he gives in? What similarities do Nina's and Markus's shared thirst give them?

Dear Readers,

When the idea of writing this book presented itself, my first thought was, "How am I ever going to write a vampire novel that glorifies God?" To be honest, I struggled with the idea, wrote and rewrote possible plots, and ultimately ended up dismissing every scenario my wild imagination (and a few overly vivid dreams) conjured up. I was about to give up on the idea when I remembered something my editor said as we kicked around the possibilities: "Vampires are metaphors." Traditionally, they've represented good versus evil, for example, a young girl's horrible experience as a high school student *(Buffy the Vampire Slayer),* and the inward struggle of mankind—sin versus righteousness (the character of Louis in *Interview with the Vampire*).

As I thought about the possibility of writing this novel in the light of a metaphor, I began to pray. I truly asked God to show me if this was just a random idea or if it was his idea. And my characters began to take shape in my mind.

Coming from a family with addictions and struggling with my own addictive personality, I saw my vampire as a relentless lover, promising safety and serenity when the opposite was actually true. Destruction, death, captivity—those were the things he represented to anyone who fell under his spell. Alcoholism seemed the logical parallel.

With so many inside and outside the four church walls addicted to prescription medicines, street drugs, and alcohol, I knew I would find a readership that understood what I was trying to accomplish. To show that we have power inside of us to overcome. To rise up and say, "Greater is he that is in you, than he that is in the world" (1 John 4:4, KJV).

Addiction is awful and hard to overcome. But there is a truth that in my own clumsy, imperfect, human way I tried to show.

Perhaps the *Veggie Tales* characters sing it best: "God is bigger than the Boogeyman."

What is your "I can't"?

Whatever it is, I hope you, like Nina, will dive deep, all the way to the real you—perhaps even to depths you didn't know existed—and pull out a strength you didn't know you possessed.

Until next time . . .
May God bless you as you live, move, and have your being in Him,

Tracey Bateman

ACKNOWLEDGMENTS

WaterBrook team, each step in the process from acquisition to production exceeded every hope I held in my heart when we began this project. I gave the best I had to offer, and each of you played your part and made Thirsty so much better.

Shannon, words can't express my gratitude for your insights and ability. I'm very blessed for the opportunity to work with you.

Cover designers . . . I wish I knew you by name . . . THANK YOU for this beautiful, perfect cover.

Steve Laube, no one believes in me like you do . . . well, except for Mom and all of my brothers and sisters and the ton of friends I have, and oh, then there's the guy that owns the video store where I rent my DVDs and that one lady with the mole I said "hi" to yesterday. . . . ☺ Okay, but there's only one YOU. Thank you so much for everything. You are a gift.

Chris and Angie. Two BFFs who waited "anxiously" for each next chapter. Your finger-prints are all over this book.

Jesus, I struggled with how to write a vampire novel that would bring you honor. I pray I accomplished that goal. For your glory.

Center Point Publishing

600 Brooks Road ● PO Box 1
Thorndike ME 04986-0001 USA

(207) 568-3717

US & Canada:
1 800 929-9108
www.centerpointlargeprint.com